MRS. GREENTHUMBS

How I Turned a Boring Yard into a Glorious Garden and How You Can, Too

CASSANDRA DANZ

Drawings by Merle Nacht

CROWN TRADE PAPERBACKS
New York

Copyright © 1993 by Cassandra Danz

Illustrations copyright © 1993 by Merle Nacht

Published by Crown Publishers, Inc., 201 East 50th Street, New York, New York 10022. Member of the Crown Publishing Group. Random House, Inc. New York, Toronto, London, Sydney, Auckland

Crown Trade Paperbacks™ and colophon are trademarks of Crown Publishers, Inc.

Manufactured in the United States of America

Library of Congress Cataloging-in-Publication Data

Danz, Cassandra.
Mrs. Greenthumbs : how I turned a boring yard into a glorious garden and how you can, too / Cassandra Danz.—1st ed.
p. cm.
Includes index.
1. Gardening. I. Title.
SB455.3.D36 1993
635.9—dc20
92-17969
CIP

ISBN 0-517-88010-5

10 9 8 7 6 5 4 3 2 1

First Edition

Contents

Acknowledgments

Many thanks to Charlotte Sheedy, my agent, and Jane Meara, my editor. Thank you, New York Horticultural Society.

Deepest gratitude to Walter and Sam—my loves, and my life. The same to my dear friends, Ron Lackmann and Bobbie Gelman. Thanks to George McCue.

A tip of the hat and much love to Mom, Bob and Lydia, Gertrude B., Jim M., Pam DuBois, Mary and Jimmy, Paul W., Richard F., and all the other dear friends and relatives who populate the pages of this book.

"Magnificent Seven" poem by Mary Fulham.

A Note on the Book

I have arranged the chapters by month, beginning in January and ending in December. It seems logical that a gardening book should follow the calendar. Perhaps it is not as logical for a gardening book to follow the calendar as it is for a book on astrology, but it still makes sense. This book has nothing to do with astrology, thank God, but this was the simplest way for me to arrange it. Most of the chapters were based on my weekly radio program, ''Mrs. Greenthumbs' Gardening Show,'' broadcast in upstate New York; the programs follow the seasons and are naturally done in chronological order. Each chapter deals with a specific gardening topic and contains factual information, personal observations, and a great many interesting digressions.

JANUARY

Not only did the bamboo half-cover the side yard,
it grew to an average height of twelve feet.

Gertrude Jekyll and the Invasion of the Bamboo

A lot of people think that to make a garden, all you have to do is put a few seeds in the ground. These are the same people who think that conceiving a baby makes you a good parent. But the real secret of gardening is the same as the real secret of parenting—a lot of patience, a lot of love, and devotion.

There aren't many people who have the good fortune to make their hobby into their profession. I am one of that fortunate few. I have lived many hours of my life in a garden, and that's about as close to Eden as I am ever going to get.

I'd like to tell you that it wasn't easy to become Mrs. Greenthumbs, Gardening Expert and Horticultural Raconteur. I'd like to tell you that it took years of struggle, personal sacrifice, and physical pain. I'd like to tell you all of that, but it would be a lie. Learning my craft has been the greatest pleasure to me. Attending classes at the New York Botanical Garden School of Horticulture was not frightening, especially if you discount the train ride through the Bronx. Going to seminars at the New York Horticultural Society was not painful; it was positively glamorous.

I got to hang out with a nice crowd at the Horticultural Society. Garden people tend to be much less boisterous than motorcycle gangs, even though they're just as dedicated.

Gardening keeps me busy all year long. I have a weekly radio gardening show in upstate New York. I teach gardening. I design other people's gardens professionally. I even tour in a one-woman show entitled "An Evening with Mrs. Greenthumbs." Horticulturally speaking, I've been very lucky.

Since I was twelve years old, I've wanted to be a gardener. Unfortunately, I didn't have a garden because I lived in New York City. I lived in Brooklyn. So the only way I could learn to garden was by reading.

I read the great garden writers: Russell Page, Vita Sackville-West, Christopher Lloyd, and Gertrude Jekyll. Gertrude Jekyll was my idol. She was an English gardener of the Edwardian period known for flowers and a deep sensitivity to color. And the best part was that everything she did was done with great art, and like all great art, looked completely natural, full, and abundant. Somewhat like Miss Jekyll herself.

She was four feet ten inches tall and must have weighed in at 175 pounds. She could have rolled around her garden if she didn't want to walk and she lived to be eighty-nine years old. Since longevity seems to be one of the happy by-products of gardening, if you're just starting out, you have plenty of time to develop.

She was also legally blind for the last forty years of her life. She wore thick Coke-bottle glasses that didn't do her much good. They didn't do her appearance much good, either.

It may seem strange for a gardener to be blind, but it's no stranger than Beethoven, a composer, who was deaf. Beethoven's symphonies were magnificent gardens of sound. Gertrude Jekyll's gardens were magnificent symphonies of color.

She had pink roses cascading over walls, garlands of clematis draped around windows, woodland gardens filled with daffodils, ferns, and enormous white, fragrant lilies. She had a 120-foot-long, 20-foot-deep perennial border that went from pale, cool blues, to pinks, to apricots, to yellows, to reds, and back to cool colors again as you went down the path. She had an old well surrounded by early spring bulbs. She even had a special border of asters and gray-leaved plants that bloomed only in September. Really gorgeous stuff.

She never had just one of anything. She had at least a dozen and probably eighty-five. She had a great eye, a real talent, and a staff of expert gardeners. She was rich. Her family had money. But I knew I could have a garden just as nice, without having a lot of money. At least I was going to try. And this is how I did it.

About eight years ago, my husband Walter and I bought a house in the town of Hudson in upstate New York. The house was 135 years old. It needed some work, such as foundations, walls, a roof, and, of course, windows. But it was ours. And it had a yard! It had a front yard, a backyard, a side yard off the porch. It had a yard!

The yard was in worse shape than the house. First, there were the ailanthus trees—hundreds of big and little ailanthus trees. You are all familiar with the ailanthus tree, otherwise known as the tree that grew in Brooklyn. It's a tree that could grow on Mars. Each year, one ailanthus tree can put out thousands of seeds, all of which will germinate almost anywhere. It is the rodent of the arboreal world. And when you cut down an ailanthus tree, twenty more will sprout from the roots, like unwanted facial hair.

There were also lots of maple tree saplings. Gardening under a maple tree is like trying to garden in a wine cellar. I wanted flowers, not mushrooms. I left a couple of big maples near the driveway, but that was it. Getting rid of the maple and ailanthus trees wasn't too bad. After all, trees don't have feet and I do. They can't run away from me when I come after them with the loppers and chain saw. You've heard of the *Texas Chainsaw Massacre*? This was the "Hudson Chainsaw Massacre"! So much for the saplings.

The Japanese bamboo was another story. The side of the house, where I dreamed of having a flower garden à la Gertrude Jekyll, was half-covered with Japanese bamboo (*Polygonum cuspidatum*). Like the kudzu vine, this weed was exported from Japan in the 1950s as a miracle plant; it was a miracle ground cover; it would grow anywhere; it could totally cover a steep bank—like the Grand Canyon. What is more, it competed well with native plants. It competed with native plants the way the white man competed with the Native Americans—it killed them.

The previous owner must have planted the bamboo in the 1950s because not only did it cover half the side yard, but it grew to an average height of twelve feet. It was so thick, we had no idea there was a gazebo in the middle of it—a small building in which you could have fit a six-piece chamber orchestra—until after we chopped the vegetation down.

The truth is, my husband chopped the bamboo down using a machete he had bought mail order through *Soldier of Fortune* magazine. I remember the sweat glistening on his torso. I felt like Ava Gardner in *Mogambo*. In a tropical frame of mind, I put on my muumuu and quickly mixed some Mai Tai cocktails. We sat on the porch, looking at the bamboo stumps, and waited for the elephants to stampede. Gardening is more fun than you think.

The elephants never came, but a week later, the bamboo was five feet tall again. We started to dig up the roots. Each clump was connected to a huge pod, about four feet wide. It looked like the invasion of the pod people. We dug under the pod. The roots were so deep, it seemed as though the bamboo was trying to get back to Japan the hard way. We couldn't dig it up. Well, we could dig it up—with a steam shovel. Too expensive. We thought of using an herbicide, just drenching the yard with Roundup, which is sort of an Agent Orange for home use. I wanted to make a garden, however, not win the war in Vietnam. And anyway, we all remember how well that went.

After drinks and intercourse, we decided to do it the natural way, the organic way, the cheap way. We would mow the area and keep the leaves from emerging. No leaves, no photosynthesis, no food—herbal death. Well, that's what we did, and it's worked pretty well. I put my flower borders on the other side and mowed the bamboo area. It's been six years now, and it's mostly grass, with just a little bit of bamboo coming up here and there, which I pull.

I would never have had the nerve to wage war against the bamboo or to strive to have a garden like Miss Jekyll's had I not been encouraged by two previous attempts in gardens belonging to other people.

The first garden I ever made was in upstate New York, not too far from where my house is now. My brother Bob and his wife (now ex-wife) had bought a small country property from their psychiatrist. The story of this purchase is very interesting, but it is more a subject for a roman à clef than for a gardening book, so I won't go into it here. Suffice it to say that the country house, like most such properties, had a good deal of land surrounding it.

My brother and his ex-wife had bought the property in the early 1970s, when the drug, sex, and Back to Earth movement was in full swing. My brother's ex-wife was nothing if not in the swing of things. She was the Queen of the Hippies. She and my brother grew and canned all their own vegetables, made clothing, and generally handcrafted a lot of things that can be done better and more cheaply by machines.

I was never a member of the Back to Earth movement. While I have always subscribed to its fundamental principles—empathy with nature, revolt against the stresses and materialism of an industrial society, and the use of organic gardening methods—there was something about the movement that turned me off. It's irritating to be around newly converted devotees of any creed, but militant vegetarians are the most repulsive, especially at meal times. Especially after meal times. If you have ever tried to digest a bean, cheese, and broccoli casserole, you know what I'm talking about.

Walter and I visited my brother often. Every weekend that we could, Walter and I made the trip from Brooklyn to the Catskills, a path worn deep by generations of nature-loving New Yorkers, immigrant Jews, Italians, the Irish, and borscht belt comics. They went to the large hotels for which the area is so famous. But to me, my brother's place was far more delightful than any hotel, because I could garden there.

I had no interest in growing vegetables. I was bored by the potato field, the tomato plants, and the zucchinis that were so prodigious they could have fed China. I hated the practical, but hideously ugly, black plastic mulch they used on the truck garden, as well. I didn't want a garden that had the word *truck* in it. I wanted a garden that had the word *flower* in it.

With my brother's blessing, I chose a small triangle of land immediately adjacent to the house for my first attempt at gardening. I turned over the weeds and added manure and compost. My ex-sister-in-law had plenty of it. Manure and compost were the wine and the wafer of her new religion. My brother Bob did the digging and the shoveling. While my ex-sister-in-law believed fervently in having an organic garden, she didn't believe in actually digging one, so it was always my brother who did the labor on their little farm. I had to get that in, and I hope my ex-sister-in-law reads this book.

I went to the local nursery and bought all the plants I could for about twenty bucks. You could buy a lot of plants for twenty dollars then. Potted-up plants were about a dollar twenty-five a piece, and you could buy a six-pack of perennials for three dollars. So I bought quite a few plants. From my reading, I knew enough to put the tall ones in the back, the medium-size ones in the middle, and the short ones in the front. I also knew all the proper botanical names of the plants and exactly what they'd look like when they bloomed.

The summer passed. Nothing happened.

One or two of the perennials bloomed in a halfhearted way, but the rest just grew a lot of leaves and sat there taking up space. This was not my first disappointment with the difference between books and real life (my first was sex), but it was one of the most heartbreaking. What I did not know, because Gertrude Jekyll had failed to mention it, was that perennials don't do all that much the first year after you plant them. They are mainly establishing themselves, setting down roots and putting out leaves. This is especially true of cheap seedlings, which is what I had bought. But, as we say in Brooklyn, "Go know."

I doggedly planted some tulips and daffodils between the perennials and called it a season. At least I was sure the bulbs would bloom.

The following spring I got a call from my ex-sister-in-law. "My garden is blooming! My flower garden looks lovely!" Her flower garden! Typical.

Walter and I started going up to the Catskills again on fine summer weekends and it was worth it. My ex-sister-in-law was right. Her flower garden was lovely. I staked the blue delphiniums when they grew to seven-foot spires, I weeded, I mulched, I watered, I dug a little trench around the bed to keep the grass out. I removed the dead flowers from the lupines, the coreopsis, and the black-eyed susans and made sure the columbines and the sweet williams reseeded themselves. I cut back the poppy, iris, peony, and daylily stems. I loved the work. It brought me peace and happiness.

When guests came and admired my ex-sister-in-law's garden, she graciously told them that I had helped her. I couldn't very well argue that it was my garden just because I had made it. Besides, it would have caused a fight, and I didn't believe in fighting in those days. Good hippies never got angry; it wasn't mellow. I merely contented myself with the beauty of the flowers, and, like the Lord in the Old Testament, I looked upon my garden and saw that it was good.

This story has a happy denouement. The garden was beautiful for a number of years after, and best of all, my brother is now remarried to a lovely person who digs her own garden, both literally and figuratively. So there.

The second garden I worked on belonged to two friends who jointly own a farm in northeastern Pennsylvania. This second gardening experience was, and is, an unadulterated joy. Walter and I were, and still are, frequent guests there, along with our son Sam. Our host Ron had been my high-school drama coach and is a man of culture and refinement; our hostess Barbara is a real gardener. Their 1840s farmhouse is full of books and antiques and lovely things. The food is great. They eat meat.

Barbara, whom we call Bobbie, is also a voracious reader of gardening books, so when she and Ron got the farm, she was eager to try out her theories, and I was eager to help her. Just for starters, she put in a seventy-five-foot-long, ten-foot-deep perennial border along the front of an old stone wall. Lucky for her, there was no bamboo on the site. Ground was broken with a rototiller and amended with a truckload of cow manure from a nearby dairy farm. Needless to say, it cost her a fortune for the plants, but her motto was: "Give all you have for beauty and never count the cost." And she did give, and she didn't count. I gave freely of my labor and even more freely of my opinions. We had a great time.

A strange thing happened in that garden, which I've never seen happen quite so perfectly in another garden before or since. Unlike me, Bobbie didn't believe in choosing plants by color to make a specific color scheme.

I argued with her, but she simply chose those plants that she liked, which was about every other one in the catalog.

In the second year of the garden, after it got going, the strange thing happened. In June, the border was all pastel. There were pink lupines, powder blue delphiniums, white Siberian irises, salmon-pink poppies, lavender-blue bearded irises, dark pink cranesbill, pale yellow columbines, et cetera. I don't have to tell you, it was stunning. As the summer progressed, the paler colors finished and the golden black-eyed susans, red bee balm, purple aconitum, golden daylilies, et cetera took over. Stunning again. At least I was stunned. The colors in the garden were perfect.

Now Bobbie swears that she didn't plan the garden this way on purpose, and I believe her because I was right there planting with her. I'm not sure she or I could deliberately repeat it, but never mind. The chief thing I learned from working on Bobbie's garden is that nature often surprises you. Accidental beauty is one of the delights of gardening. Since then, I have learned not to be so surprised by nature's accidents, but I have never stopped being delighted.

As you can see, gardening is never a perfect art. I wonder what Gertrude Jekyll would have done without her staff of gardeners if she had encountered my hit-or-miss gardening friend, Bobbie, a forest of bamboo, or my ex-sister-in-law, the Queen of the Hippies.

WALKING THE YARD

Somehow it seems incongruous to be talking about making a cottage garden in January. After all, a cottage garden, by definition, is a sunny, colorful, flower-filled spot, just outside the door. A cottage garden suggests early spring or high summer, and maybe even late fall, any season but the middle of winter. Not even a lunatic would give the word *winter* when asked by a psychiatrist to free associate on the words *cottage garden*. At least none of the lunatics I know. The middle of winter is best described by using Edgar Allan Poe words: bleak, drear, sere, and that old standby, nevermore. My garden is dead now. Dead as Marley's ghost, dead as Anna Karenina, dead as Gunga Din. Gone with the winter wind.

I feel like the Birdwoman of Alcatraz. Lousy winter weather has made me a prisoner in my own house. There might as well be bars on the window as I gaze longingly out at the garden and contemplate the meaning of death.

But even convicts get to go outside for an hour a day to exercise. In Alcatraz, they called it "walking the yard." So that is what I'm going to do today. I would like to take you for an imaginary walk around my yard. As we go along, I will describe everything to you as accurately as I can. After reading this chapter, you'll have a pretty good idea of what my garden looks like, so you can refer back to it later. Feel free to consult the map on page eleven.

Before we go out, let me tell you a little bit about the history of my house and garden.

When we bought the place in 1984, it had been neglected by the previous owner since the 1960s, when his eyesight, health, and joie de vivre failed him. He was a retired New York City policeman and practicing eccentric, who left the house only to attend to his pigeons and chickens, which he kept cooped in the backyard. He was known as the nice old man in the haunted house by the local kids and as a kook by everybody else. In a way, I'm grateful to him for not taking care of the yard or the house. If he had been more conscientious about the house, he might have modernized it and torn out all the Gothic detail; and if he had been more conscientious about the garden, he might have mowed everything down so it would look "neat." So I say, bless his lazy heart. He's dead now. When he died, it is rumored that he left an estate of a quarter million

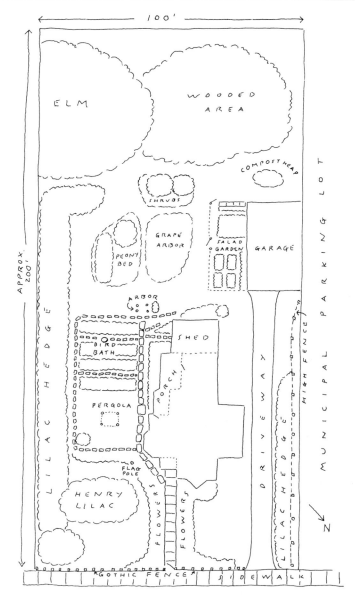

Feel free to consult the map.

dollars. My guess is that New York City policemen were paid a lot of money in the thirties, but not necessarily by the city.

Horticulturally speaking, Walter and I are very fortunate to have an old house. There were lots of mature shrubs and long-lived perennials, like peonies, hostas, and old-fashioned lemon lilies, already growing in large clumps around the yard. There were also lots of weed trees and over-growth, but once they were removed, the bones of the old garden were revealed.

The presence of the peonies and shrubs suggested, even imposed, a garden design. I suppose I could have pulled everything out and started all over again, but why should I have? People wait years for peonies to get to be four feet around, and the shrubs—deutzias, old roses, mock orange bushes (*Philadelphus*), and an enormous old lilac that obscured the view of the side yard from the street, to name only a few—were just the sort of flowering bushes I would have put there myself a hundred years ago, if I had been there. Come to think of it, if I had been there a hundred years ago, I'd be dead now.

I also found scraps of other plants that emerged after the weeds were cleared away. Struggling tiger lilies (*Lilium tigrinum*) poked their wands up in front of the old rose. There was a very interesting shrub clematis, some snowdrops (*Galanthus*), and old tulips that normally would have been played out years ago.

Somehow, the tulips had survived, and they even bloomed the follow-ing spring. Their existence seemed even more improbable when I noticed that they were striped like the tulips in old Dutch paintings, the sort of tulips that inspired the "tulipomania" of the seventeenth century. The stripes indicated that these tulips had a virus considered fatal by many horticultural experts. Fatal to whom? Obviously, these tulips didn't know from experts.

Since Walter and I wanted to restore the house and garden, not abolish it, we did some research to try and find out exactly what the property had looked like when it was first built. This is not so easy to do, but we were lucky. A mutual acquaintance put us in touch with the grandniece of the man who built the house in 1851. The grandniece was in her eighties, no spring chicken herself. She told us all about her family and the fact that she had been married in our house. She even let us reproduce some old photos of the house and garden taken in 1923, when she and her husband were courting.

Miraculously, she also had an oil painting that had been done by an itinerant painter, shortly after the house was built. We took a color photograph of her painting and so had a terrific reference point for most of the restoration we had to do. Walter was most interested in the paint colors, the architectural details, and so forth, but I was interested in the garden.

The old painting showed that the yard in front of the house originally had a fence—a dark-colored Gothic-style picket with a gate. By the time we got there, the fence was long gone, probably a victim of demolition when the town paved and widened the street in the twentieth century. Behind the fence, there were lots of flowers and shrubs, planted in an informal, cottage garden style, and no lawn.

The painting also showed a number of evergreen trees, like pines and spruces, growing in the yard. If the evergreen trees really had been planted there, they were removed years ago, because there is no sign of them now. I doubt that they ever existed, however, because the trees would have cast too much shade for all those flowers in the painting. Between you and me, I suspect that the itinerant painter added some of those flowers and trees to his picture to doll up that front yard for the benefit of the client.

I must confess that I never had the intention of reproducing the garden exactly as it appeared in the painting. No sooner did the idea of a historically accurate plant collection cross my mind than I dismissed it. That would have meant using only those plants that were available in 1851 or before. I had other ideas for that garden, and they included modern cultivars like hybrid clematis, floribunda roses, and perennials like *Achillea* 'Moonshine'. It would have been torture to leave out a plant I loved just because it wasn't historic enough to suit a museum curator.

Yes, I had another idea for my garden, an idea that was suggested by the architecture of the house itself. Although the house is now in town, it was originally intended as a country or suburban cottage, along the lines of the gothicized cottages of Andrew Jackson Downing. Andrew Jackson Downing had a mentor whose name, unfortunately, was Alexander Jackson Davis, a confusing and monotonous coincidence of nomenclature. They're both dead now.

Downing and Davis were architects and landscape designers who popularized the Picturesque style of house and landscape design in the early part of the nineteenth century. I use the word *popularize* loosely here, because the truth is, the Gothic style was never very popular in America. Most Americans of that period preferred other styles, like the Italianate or the earlier Greek Revival, and even gave their towns names like Athens, Corinth, Rome, and Utica.

The Gothic Revival style was very popular in England, however. We are all familiar with the House of Parliament and those adorable "gothick" cottages that are used in illustrations for children's books such as *The Wind in the Willows* or Beatrix Potter's stories. My cottage—actually a large house by modern standards that seems even larger when I have to clean it—looks like the cottages in those children's books.

The children's book illustrations also show gardens around the house, with flowers taller than the heads of the characters. Of course, the flowers appear to be large because the protagonists are often field mice or frogs. We are somewhat larger than rodents. Walter is six feet four inches, our boy Sam is five feet three and growing, and I am five-feet-five. Even a fantasy-ridden woman like me realized that a garden with storyland proportions was out of the question, since there is no such thing as a twenty-foot daffodil or a six-foot forget-me-not. But I decided to plant as many tall and large-flowered specimens as possible and to use arbors and vine-covered uprights to achieve the miracle of having flowers overhead.

Okay, let's go out. Since this is only to be an imaginary walk, we can pretend that it is not January, but a beautiful day in May! Who's going to stop us? I open the front door and behold! The sun is warm, the air is gentle, the earth is fragrant, the plants are sprouting, the animals are pregnant, and everything is new again. Don't forget your sun hat and you can bring your Mai Tai with you. It will be warm out there.

We'll begin our tour on the sidewalk in front of the house, looking back at the house and yard.

I have a double town lot. Each lot is fifty feet across by two hundred feet deep, so the entire property is one hundred feet across by two hundred feet deep. That's about half an acre, more or less.

The house stands on the right side of the property, about twenty-five feet back from the sidewalk. It is dark brown, with a lighter brown trim and sand-colored shutters. The front door is painted a deep ochre yellow, with a raised Gothic trefoil design picked out in dark brown. The windows, which in front have diamond-shaped panes of glass, are painted a very dark green—almost black. These colors were typical of the way a Gothic cottage would have been painted in 1851, and we know they're accurate, because we copied them from the oil painting.

As we look at the house and yard from the sidewalk, we see the Gothic fence, which is made of wood and painted the same dark black-green as the windows. Walter and my brother put up the fence two years ago, and now it serves as a frame for the picturesque house and garden. It's amazing what a fence will do for the appearance of a house. The fence railings are about four feet high, so we can still see the front garden very well.

The path leading from the gate to the front door is made of large, square bluestone blocks, with six-foot-wide flower borders on either side of the path. Next to the left border is the enormous lilac that takes up most of the lawn on that side and completely obscures the rest of the yard behind it. To the right of the path and flower border is a small (eight feet by ten feet) patch of grass, surrounded by a stand of bridal-wreath (*Spiraea Vanhouttei*), a small lilac, and hostas planted in front of the bay window of the house. There are tall plants behind the fence and short ones peeking out from under it.

To the right of the small lawn is a driveway that leads to a separate garage located behind and to the right of the house. The garage is so far back it cannot be seen from the street. To the right of the driveway is a lilac hedge and a tall fence that defines the end of our yard on that side.

We were very lucky to have the lilac hedge already in place. It must have been planted at least fifty years ago and runs the length of the property line from the street to the backyard. Fortunately, there is a matching white lilac hedge on the other side, between our yard and the house next door on the left. Both hedges are about fifteen feet tall and about ten feet wide. In addition to being quite beautiful, they serve to screen the yard from our neighbors on the left and partially obscure the municipal parking lot on the right. To really cut off the view of the parking lot, we have erected a tall, solid wooden fence just behind the lilac hedge.

Well, don't just stand there looking, open the gate and come in! Welcome to my garden. It's May and the lilacs are in bloom! The white lilac hedges are covered with flowers, as is the huge lilac on the left side of the front yard. This lilac is clothed to the ground with true lilac-pink panicles that are much larger and of a different shape than the white ones. I've never seen a lilac like this anywhere before. Like the white lilacs, it was already well established when we bought the house, and I was dying to find out the name of this unusual variety. After a lot of searching through plant encyclopedias to no avail, I found it by chance listed in the Winterthur catalog, which sells plants from the collection of the famous H. F.

du Pont estate in Delaware, along with expensive reproductions of garden furniture and ornaments. It turns out that my lilac is called Henry. Really. Its botanical name is *Syringa* x *Henryi* and, according to the catalog, it's no longer "in commerce." In other words, it's almost impossible to find it for sale anymore. Winterthur states that the lilac grows to ten feet high and eight feet across, but this one must like it here because it's spectacular, about twenty feet across and fifteen feet high and looks like Scarlett O'Hara's hoop skirt, if Scarlett were as tall as a two-story building.

The soft May air is laden with the perfume of the lilacs and bathes us with sweetness as we linger in ecstasy just inside the gate. There are more flowers in the borders flanking the front path, chosen to complement the color of the Henry lilac.

At lilac time, there are white, pink, and "black" (actually dark maroon) tulips, apricot dwarf irises (*Iris pumila*), pale yellow lemon lilies (*Hemerocallis flava*), dark purple violas, and blue and yellow pansies. Blue forget-me-nots (*Myosotis*) have seeded themselves (with my help) along the front of the border and in the cracks of the stone path. The sight of such floral excess, the scent, the warm breeze, not to mention the Mai Tais, have made us slightly giddy. But with admirable self-discipline, we pick ourselves up from the path and observe some of the other plants that are growing in the borders but are not yet in flower.

As the season progresses, these borders will change color as the other plants come into bloom, and warm colors will replace the soft pastels of May.

By the end of the month, when the lilacs have become a green backdrop, there will be tall bearded irises (*Iris* x *germanica*) in red, yellow, and deep purple, along with bright orange Oriental poppies (*Papaver orientale*). In early June, the old-fashioned white Festiva Maxima peonies (*Paeonia*) will bloom, along with blood red and orange Asiatic lilies (*Lilium*), dark red sweet williams (*Dianthus barbatus*), lipstick red maltese-crosses (*Lychnis chalcedonica*), maroon drumstick alliums (*Allium sphaerocephalum*), and pure yellow sundrops (*Oenothera fruticosa* var. *Youngii*).

From July on, red, orange, and yellow climbing nasturtiums (*Tropaeolum*) will tumble over the fence. The borders will be filled with russet-red heleniums (*Helenium autumnale*), purple aconitum (*Aconitum napellus*), lots of taxicab yellow black-eyed susans (*Rudbeckia fulgida* 'Goldsturm'), three large stands of white phlox (*Phlox paniculata*), Black Dragon lilies (*Lilium auratum*), red and coral dahlias, purple spider flowers (*Cleome Hasslerana*), gray-leaved rue (*Ruta graveolens*) and lamb's-ears (*Stachys lanata*), clumps of brick red and oxblood daylilies (*Hemerocallis* vars.), hollyhocks (*Althaea rosea*) in pale yellow and "black," red astilbes (*Astilbe* x *Arendsii*), cinnamon, pale yellow, and Tuscan red chrysanthemums, very tall canna lilies with purple leaves, airy white boltonias (*Boltonia asteroides*), and a large stand of eight-foot golden glow (*Helianthus*) growing over the fence, about as inconspicuously as a school bus.

The pleasure of watching the garden change day by day as the season progresses is indescribable, at least by me. It's like watching a painting change right in front of my eyes, and best of all, I am the artist! Truly, gardening is a sight for sore eyes and a balm for sore egos.

Let's walk up the path to the front door, but instead of going inside, we'll follow it around the corner of the house to the left. The flower border continues to flank the path, with an old flagpole on one side, planted with a climbing red rose called Blaze and a very vigorous sweet autumn clematis (*Clematis paniculata*) that unpatriotically engulfs the flag by the Fourth of July.

To our right is the house. Tall red canna lilies have been planted in the area between the house and the path. I bed out annuals like coleus and bachelor's buttons at their feet as my salute to Victoriana.

Straight in front of us is my secret garden, the garden of my delight. Framed by the house on one side and the white lilacs on the other, the enclosure is about forty feet wide, and it runs the length of the side of the house, which is about seventy-five feet long. I have planted a shrub and flower border on this side of the Henry lilac, to further obscure the view from the street at the front end.

At the back end of the enclosure is a large highbush honeysuckle (*Lonicera tatarica*) and a vine-covered arbor that defines the end of the garden and leads into the backyard. We stand here under an enchantment; it is a magical place.

The birds are singing their heads off, luxuriating amid the white blossoms of the stately lilacs. One of the shrubs in the border to our left as we enter is a Chinese tree peony (*Paeonia suffruticosa*) with a dozen huge pink blossoms that look as if they were made of silk crepe. In front of the tree peony are light blue intermediate irises (*Iris intermedia*) and rose-colored tulips with a green stripe on the edges (*Tulipa viridiflora* var. "Greenland"). Next to them is a large stand of columbines (*Aquilegia* var. "McKana Giant Hybrids") in soft pastel shades of yellow, pink, red, purple, and white.

Friends tell me that when they come around the corner of the house and enter the side garden, they can't believe that they are in town. It is as if they have entered another world entirely. I take that sort of remark as a great compliment, and, of course, I only repeat it here for reasons of strict accuracy. To me, coming around that corner is like entering heaven.

In the middle of the yard stands a rusticated eight-by-eight-foot free-standing pergola made of unfinished cedar logs with grape vines trained along its beams, surrounded by a six-foot strip of grass. The arbor leading to the backyard is also rusticated, and it is planted with clematis vines, the earliest of which are just beginning to open.

There is an old-fashioned birdbath among the flowers and some metal garden chairs from the 1950s that were there when we bought the house. We painted these historical lawn chairs the same very dark black-green as the porch, fence, and windows. They don't look half bad. The chairs are under the grape pergola, so we can sit out there in the evening.

There are stone paths made of crazy paving throughout the garden. The main one is four feet wide and runs from the front of the house to the rusticated arbor at the back. There are four stone paths at right angles to the main one and another smaller one parallel to the main path that runs along the lilac hedge. Except for the six-foot strip of grass around the pergola, the areas between the paths are planted with flowers.

In early May, the flower beds are filling up with the fresh green leaves of the plants that will bloom later. Right now, there are columbines, lemon lilies, and tulips—a hundred of the white lily-flowering tulip cultivar called White Triumphator, and a hundred Rembrandt tulips, planted in long drifts among the emerging perennials. They give me hope. The blue, blue forget-me-nots, which have seeded themselves in every spare nook and cranny of the flower beds, are just beginning to open, and we get a hint of the undulating sea of tiny flowers they will become in a couple of weeks. Several of the blue irises have opened, as well. They are just the first of many large clumps of twelve different varieties of blue bearded iris that absolutely floor me in late May and early June. Only one of the peonies is out now, an early red double that is a bright spot among the soft pastels. The others show a lot of potential. There are five or six different varieties, in shades of pink and white, some single, some double.

All of the other plants that flower later are still babies now: pink and white ten-inch hibiscus (*Hibiscus moscheutos*), sweet pastel hollyhocks (*Althaea rosea*), pink and white phlox (*Phlox paniculata*), tall lavender-blue asters (*Aster novae-angliae*), white Shasta daisies (*Chrysanthemum maximum*), pale yellow daylilies (*Hemerocallis flava*), lavender-blue bell-flowers (*Campanula persicifolia*), white lilies (*Lilium regale*), soft red bee balm (*Monarda didyma* 'Cambridge Scarlet'), hot pink obedient plants (*Physostegia virginiana*), pinks (*Dianthus* vars.), sweet williams (*Dianthus barbatus*), white Japanese anemones (*Anemone* x *hybrida*), blue balloon flowers (*Platycodon*), silvery blue globe thistles (*Echinops ritro*), blue del-phiniums (*Delphinium elatum* vars.), blue veronicas (*Veronica spicata*), lemon yellow sundrops (*Oenothera fruticosa* var. *Youngii*), silvery-leaved mulleins (*Verbascum Thapsus*), tall yellow thermopsis (*Thermopsis caroliniana*), white feverfew (*Matricaria*), and the rest of the flowers that will surprise me with their beauty because I've forgotten what else I planted. The roses, three of which are located in the flower bed between the house and the main path, are just starting to bud. The largest one, an old-fashioned pink cultivar called Mme. Pierre Oger (more about her in the chapter on roses) is trained against the side porch, which runs about half the length of the house.

Although the house has no front porch (front porches didn't come into vogue until late in the nineteenth century), there is a kitchen porch. What a great invention! When Walter and I first bought the house, the kitchen porch had been screened in, probably in the 1940s or '50s. Those were the days when Americans went to war on "bugs" with the same vigor that had spelled curtains for the Axis. We could imagine the old man and his wife (she's dead now) sitting behind their screening, Flit gun in hand, zapping the mosquitoes with DDT, and never worrying if the spray got into the lemonade.

After removing the screening, which was in tatters anyway, we found that the porch still looked the same as it had in the 1923 photos. Luckily, none of the original railings and Gothic-style architectural ornaments had been demolished.

After some painting and minor repair, the porch now has dark black-green latticework railings and fleur-de-lis pattern gingerbread around the roof. I have put chairs out there and a table that serves as a desk or a dining area, depending on the time of day. The porch looks out on the secret garden. That's not just a coincidence, though. I located the garden there in the first place because that is the area of the yard that I see most of the time, and it's closest to the kitchen.

A wooden shed is attached to the porch at the back of the house. We suspect that this shed was used as a summer kitchen 100 years ago, when the heat of a wood-burning stove would have made cooking indoors unbearable. It still contains a standing pipe that looks as if it had originally been used for a pump, and there is a circular hole in the wall that must have been made to accommodate a stovepipe. My kitchen is now blessed with a modern gas stove, so I use the outside room as a garden shed. It works very well. The door to the shed is wider than normal, so it's easy to get the wheelbarrow in and out. Don't laugh. Little things like that can drive you crazy.

The backyard can only be glimpsed through the rusticated arbor at the far end of the secret garden, because there are shrubs planted on both sides of it. To the left of the arbor is the highbush honeysuckle (*Lonicera tatarica*). On the other side is a double-flowered kerria (*Kerria japonica*) and a Japanese flowering quince (*Chaenomeles*). Luckily, the quince blooms a couple of weeks before the kerria, because the flowers of the kerria are yellow-orange and the flowers of the quince are coral red. If they bloomed together, they'd look like a couple of clowns. Next year, I'm sure they will.

Well, let's walk under the arbor and take a look at the backyard. According to the surveyor's maps, the yard extends for another hundred feet. In reality, the ground is flat for about fifty feet and then slopes down sharply. I have allowed the weedy saplings to remain on the slope, and they have done their best to establish a small wooded area consisting of ash, black locust, silver maple, sumac, and ailanthus trees, which is fine with me. Let them battle it out back there.

On the left side of the slope is an ancient elm tree, miraculously spared by Dutch elm disease. It grows near the bottom of the slope, but it is so large, it arches high over all the younger trees and provides a wonderful backdrop to the whole yard. I was concerned about the tree's future health, and I called the county agricultural agent about saving it. His answer was extremely irritating. In a funeral director's oily tone, he said that the elm tree's death was "just a matter of time."

"So's yours!" I retorted, and hung up. The elm is still alive, but I haven't heard from him since.

Now we are standing in the middle of the backyard looking toward the slope. Behind us is the rear wall of the garden shed, the arbor, and the kerria bush. To our left is a small grape arbor in a state of disrepair. To the left of that are the remnants of a peony bed, and to the left of the peony bed is the white lilac hedge.

Looking right, we see the driveway and the side wall of the garage. Alongside the wall of the garage is a salad and cutting garden, which is enclosed on the three other sides by a rusticated fence made of cedar posts and cheap lathe slats (five dollars for a bundle of fifty) that Walter nailed in place in a couple of afternoons, without complaint. There are several shrub roses trained along the outside of the fence, and they doll it up nicely, especially in June. The fence has been made woodchuck-proof by tacking chicken wire around the inside and burying it about a foot and a half deep beneath the fence, because the only thing woodchucks do better than eating is digging.

The compost heap is located out of sight behind the garage, on the side facing the slope.

The garage looked like Hitler's bunker when I first saw it. It must have been built by the old man in the 1970s as a pigeon palace. Boy, he must have loved those pigeons. It's solid. It's made entirely of cinderblock and steel supports. It's big enough to hold three cars. The side wall is thirty feet long from front to back. Tearing it down was out of the question due to a lack of either TNT or professional demolition equipment, so one of the first things we did was to paint the cinderblocks dark brown. Walter attached guide wires to the wall, so I could use them for training a wisteria vine (*Wisteria floribunda* 'Alba') and climbing roses, New Dawn and White Dawn. After several years, the wisteria and the roses have done their job; the whole thing looks a lot better—you can hardly see the cinderblocks at all. Now it looks like Hitler's wisteria and rose-covered brown bunker.

Let's follow the path between the vegetable garden fence and the back of the house. At the corner is a common but well-maintained purple lilac (*Syringa vulgaris*), to which I have added a purple-leaved sand cherry (*Prunus* x *cistena*) and several Russian sage bushes (*Perovskia atriplicifolia*), just to fill in.

Now we are standing in the driveway. It had once been blacktopped but is now in a becoming state of disrepair, with bits of grass coming up between the cracks and no trace of blacktopped driveway b.o., that *eau de tar* you always smell on warm days. It's nice and shady here, too, because we are standing between the shadow of the house and the one large maple tree I left alone when we cleared the yard. The strips of land between the driveway and the house on one side and the fence on the other is more or less filled with various shrubs and hostas. It's pretty messy here because, frankly, I mostly ignore it. Let's walk around to the front of the house and go in.

21

We loiter in the doorway for a moment, enjoying a few last lungfuls of divine lilac-laden spring air, before reluctantly going inside.

What a lovely hour we have spent, visualizing the garden on a gorgeous day in May. But here we are, back in January, sitting by the window, looking out at the Edgar Allan Poe landscape. I hope you've enjoyed walking the yard. I must say, it's done me a lot of good. Our walk has reminded me that spring will come again, the flowers will bloom once more, and the garden will grow and flourish, even though it seems to be dead now.

PLANNING THE GARDEN

The only cure for winter blues is working on the garden. We can't very well go out and start puttering around the posies in the middle of January, but there is one project we can tackle—making plans for next year. Ironically, a plan will, in the long run, be more valuable to our ultimate enjoyment of the garden than many hours of hard digging. The overall garden scheme will determine whether or not we use and enjoy the land we are blessed with or merely visit it on Saturdays to do chores.

There are an infinite number of ways to design and plant any area of land, but after research, observation, and personal horticultural disasters, I have discovered a few tips about garden planning that will be helpful in deciding where and how to plant almost any kind of garden.

The first thing to do when planning any garden is to decide its purpose. What is it to be used for? Growing food? Entertaining? Enclosing children or pets? Or just sitting around doing nothing? (That's a good one.) My flower garden has a purpose, although it may not be as obvious as the purpose of a staple gun. It is restful and peaceful. It is beautiful, lovely, and . . . beautiful. It's just beautiful. Taking care of it has put me in touch with nature and has made me feel at one with the universe. You might say that the purpose of my garden has been to save a fortune in psychiatrist's bills.

Let's start with the topic of landscaping in general. There are two basic reasons to landscape a yard, aside from showing off for the neighbors. One is to improve a view, the other is to hide one. Since I live in a small town, most of the shrub and tree planting I do is to block off views of uninteresting or ugly objects, like the parking lot next door.

There was no parking lot 140 years ago when my house was new; it was built about 20 years ago. It's located on the side of the house that overlooks the driveway and the garage. Fortunately, my kitchen porch and garden is on the opposite side of the house, so I can enjoy my garden without being at all aware of the parking lot. Nevertheless, with a little help from my friends, I put up as tall a fence as the law allowed, so no one in my house would have to see the parking lot from the driveway or from indoors. I even put the fence four feet from the edge of my property line and this enabled me to keep some overgrown maple and ailanthus trees between the fence and the parking lot to further obscure the view.

Some people are luckier than I am. They can plan to enhance beautiful views.

One such lucky stiff is a friend of mine named Jim Miles. Jim is a professional horticulturalist with a degree from the New York Botanical Garden School of Horticulture. He is in his middle thirties, an excellent age for a man, and he is handsome and witty. Best of all, he is that rarest of all creatures, a happy human being. He also has well-proportioned, tanned muscles that he developed by many years of lifting beautiful but heavy objects, like earth and trees. He looks like a forest god, or even like a tree itself, with strong, thick muscular branches and hard, erect trunk . . . I don't want to go any further with this description. I'm a married woman. My fantasy life is my own. When I want to talk about my fantasy life, I'll write another book and call it *A Petunia Named Desire*. Until then, I'll stick to gardening.

Now where was I? Oh, yes. Jim Miles has a home out in the country. It's a nineteenth-century cottage set well back from the road, with at least half an acre of mature woodland and wild overgrowth between his house and any traffic. When Jim first bought the house about five years ago, no one had gardened in that place for years. In fact, there were trees and wild overgrowth all over his three acres, right up to the porch.

In addition to old pines and maples, hickories and weedy ailanthus trees, there grew an abundance of wild blackberry thickets, woodbine, and large stands of sumac—all plants common in an old garden that has once been cultivated, seduced, and abandoned. Even the remnants of the original garden had gone wild. Wisteria strangled the house like a boa constrictor and an ancient red trumpet vine had insinuated itself into the parlor. Most people would have slashed away all the vegetation around the house, put in a lawn, and called it landscaping, but Jim is a great gardener with the eye of an artist. He knew exactly what to do. He did nothing.

He stomped around that three-acre weed patch cum primeval forest for a year. He walked the boundary lines to see what was on the other side of his woods in spring, summer, fall, and winter, the exercise bringing a glow to his already radiant cheeks. With clear, far-seeing eyes, he noted the direction and quality of the sunlight at all times of the year. He took the time to see what was already growing there—like old roses, peonies, and ostrich ferns. Thousands of daffodils and Siberian squill struggled through the overgrowth in springtime. He got to know his land with a degree of intimacy shared only by lovers and bartenders.

Let's face it, this was a job for Superlandscaper, and Jim was more than equal to the task. Because of the density of the vegetation, the area beyond Jim's own property was not visible from the house. This was an advantage in the front, because the trees gave him excellent privacy from the road. The backdoor, however, faced a very attractive open meadow, which would have made a lovely view from his kitchen door, if he could have seen it. Unfortunately, there was a thick stand of weed trees in the way. Jim removed the weed trees in the center of his line of vision and left a few trees on both sides of the view. In landscaping, this is called "framing a view."

A pretty meadow is attractive, but a pretty meadow framed by trees is a picture. I think we've all noticed that some landscapes look better than others, and not just because of the presence or absence of a nuclear power plant in the middle distance. Sometimes it's difficult to see why one view works and another doesn't. Among the other things I've learned from Jim is that the real trick to making a great landscape is not so much the subject of the view—that can be anything: water, mountains, meadows, buildings, or the Grand Canyon—but rather the presence of a "frame," or a frame of reference.

If you don't believe me, look at some old photographs you might have taken on vacation. I have plenty of those. My husband Walter, an avid vacation landscape photographer, has taken literally hundreds of depressingly boring photos of landscapes from here to Canada. But Walter's pictures have improved enormously ever since he learned to put a tree or even a telephone pole in the foreground of the picture. Not only does the near object frame the distant one, but it immediately gives a sense of proportion to the view. Even the Grand Canyon looks bigger with a tourist standing next to the rail, especially a short, thin tourist.

Jim used the "tourist and the Grand Canyon" method to make a view off the old-fashioned porch that wraps around the front and side of his house, and this view is really spectacular. Part of Jim's success was pure luck, but the rest was thanks to the simplicity of genius.

Since there was no view off the side porch because of the leafy overgrowth, there was nothing to do but to chop away the jungle and open up the area under the trees, which he did. Now he had a view of some very stately oaks and spruces, but here's where genius and luck combined to make this view one of my favorite places.

Jim's nearest neighbor, on the porch side, happens to be an old stone church with a churchyard next to it, about half the length of a football field away. Were it not for the weeds, the trees, and the general disorder, the church would have been directly in the line of vision from the porch. Jim removed the center trees and pruned some of the lower branches of the trees on both sides of the line of vision to form sort of a natural Gothic arch. He widened the area near the porch and progressively narrowed it as it got closer to the church. By the time Jim was finished, the whole impression was of looking at a Gothic church through a Gothic arch. And because the arch narrowed as it went along, the church seemed farther away than it actually was.

By cutting out a few trees and pruning a few branches, Jim had made a view, a leafy grove, and best of all, a place of peace and quiet away from "civilization" (I use the word loosely) but very close to nature. It is not the sort of scene I could have made in town, but that grove is a garden, even though he never planted a single flower.

Most yards that I see around me don't have such a private place, and it's a shame. Flowers, trees, and shrubs are used only as decoration for the outside of the house. Most suburban yards are open to each other, so that boundaries are undefined and plantings are plunked down here and there like random thoughts.

I think that places, like people, ought to have boundaries. Who ever said that gardening was a public activity, anyway? Gardening, like making love, feels a lot better than it looks. Nobody buys tickets to gardening competitions. There's no such thing as the Gardening Olympics. There is no gold medal in Speed Weeding or Double Digging. Maybe there should be, but I wouldn't compete in a gardening Olympiad for all the compost in China. I go through ungainly contortions when I garden. I squat. I crawl around on my hands and knees. Most of the time I bend over, upended. That angle may be flattering to a Dallas Cowboy cheerleader, but it is not flattering to me.

When I planned the side garden off the porch of my house, I intended it, as much as possible, to be a secret garden—not secret from my friends and family, but at least secret from the eyes of casual passersby on the street. As I have mentioned, there was an enormous lilac bush on the street side of the garden when I got the house, so I didn't have to put up a fence or a hedge on that side. If there had been no lilac bush, I would have immediately planted a row of evergreens there and put up a fence, as well. The more dense the local population of your neighborhood, the more you need enclosure.

After privacy, the next most important tip to remember when planning a garden is that familiarity breeds flowers. In other words, if you see a flower bed every day, you will take care of it. If you don't, you won't, that's all there is to it. And you won't if you put it out of sight behind the garage, or worse, lined up in front of your house so that the neighbors can see it, but you can't. Place your plantings so that you can see them from *inside* the house. It's hard to avoid weeding a patch that you see out the window all the time, and you'll know right away if a plant is dying or needs water, because it's lying there, gasping pathetically, right in front of you. Proximity is especially important if you own a weekend home, because there is even less time to give it attention. If you haven't gotten around to tending to the flowers by Sunday afternoon, the opportunity is gone, and you have to kiss them all good-bye for another week.

The second thing I've noticed is that the best tended home gardens are the ones that are right near the kitchen door. There's a good reason for this. Food. We all like to spend time in a place where food is accessible. It's comfy, and when your garden is near where you eat, you'll have to look at it at least three times a day, and so you'll keep it well tended. I don't know why gardens aren't put right outside the kitchen more often. Most houses have the kitchen in the back, anyway, and that is usually the most private area of the yard, as far as possible from traffic smells and street noises. The flower garden off the kitchen porch entices me to come out on a summer morning and putter around, even if I'm still in my nightgown. (That's another reason privacy is so important.)

I realize that I have been referring to urban gardens and suburban lots of a half acre or even an eighth of an acre (or less). But no matter how large your property is, even if it consists of hundreds of acres, I would still suggest putting the garden near the house, and if possible, near the kitchen. Unless you have the gardening staff of the Arnold Arboretum, you'll never get out to the back forty and start tending the rose garden, and it will always look like a meeting of Weeds Anonymous.

My third tip is tedious but true. Start small. Be realistic. Don't plant more than you think you can take care of. Even better, don't plant more than you *really* can take care of. Only after you have one flower bed under control should you start another one. Two flower beds may be enough. If they're two hundred feet long and seventeen feet deep, they'll be plenty, believe me.

When I began my garden, I thought I could cultivate my entire half acre to perfection right away. In addition to the front and side-yard flower gardens, I wanted to have a gourmet vegetable garden, a woodland garden, and roof garden on top of the garage. After seven years, the gourmet vegetable garden is just a fence surrounding some asparagus, the woodland garden is still a wood (with a few daffodils in the spring, tra-la), and the roof garden is still a roof. (The roof garden was a stupid idea, anyway.) The flower gardens look terrific, though.

Here are a few tricks to use when planning a flower garden, once you have determined where to put it:

1. *Place the borders so that they are perpendicular to your line of sight.* According to Gertrude Jekyll, a flower border looks best when seen with its length stretching away from you, rather than flat across your line of vision. To get the idea, imagine you are standing at one end of a long border and are looking down toward the other end. When you're looking down the spine of a border, that is to say perpendicularly, all you see is the tops of the plants that are blooming. This is good. You can't see all the places where the tulips are browning off and looking rotten, or the spaces where the poppies have finished, or the weeds that are growing up between the peonies. Like a meadow, all that can be seen is the plants that are currently in flower. I suppose this occurs in nature to make it easier for insects to find the flowers, but if Mother Nature can do this, so can we.

So, following Miss Jekyll's advice, I placed my flower borders perpendicular to the porch. That allowed me to get a lot more borders in. Instead of one border going all around the perimeter of the yard with a lawn in the middle, I have several, connected by intersecting paths. One intersection of the paths was a perfect place to put a stone birdbath. A birdbath is not the most elaborate bit of statuary to put in a garden, but simplicity is a virtue. Simplicity is also cheaper. Visually, the birdbath serves as a focal point among the flowers, and it really does attract birds! My cat loves me for it.

Instead of placing the tall plants along the back of each border, the medium ones in the middle, and the short ones in front, as all the books tell you to do, I put the tall delphiniums and the New England asters at the far end of the garden as seen from the porch. Just for variety, and to increase the feeling of being in a storybook garden, I've tucked some tall plants among their shorter companions, as well. After all, as I tell myself whenever I look into a mirror, perfection is monotonous.

When I plan other people's gardens, I try to set the flower borders perpendicular to the line of sight wherever possible. At first a lot of clients object, but they generally fall into line, especially after I offer a ten-percent discount.

2. *Assume that everything you plant will be bigger than you think.* This can be confusing, because when the plant arrives, it always looks a lot smaller than you expect. A lot. I ordered a *Magnolia stellata* from Wayside Gardens about four years ago. In the catalog, the *Magnolia stellata* was a glorious flower-bedecked shrubby tree about fifteen feet tall. What they sent me was a skinny stick with roots at one end. It was like ordering an oak and getting an acorn. I was extremely disappointed, but I should have known better. Because it was so small, I planted that stick much too close to a wild cherry tree, and every spring I have to hack away at that cherry tree, like George Washington in a Presidents' Day commercial.

To avoid this common mistake (at least common with me), I mark out an area equal to the eventual size of the plant (as described in catalogs and on plant labels with varying accuracy), especially if it promises to be a large one. I place a stake in the spot where the plant is to grow and I use string to make a large circle around the plant describing its ultimate width. Then all I have to do is dig the hole in the middle of the area I have marked out.

If it turns out that the plant will be too big, I either have to put it elsewhere or eventually remove whatever else is growing in the way. I usually opt to locate the new plant somewhere else, because when I have to take a plant out to fit another one in, I get into a crazy situation.

I start out with one shrub to plant, say, an oak-leaf hydrangea. I decide that it would prosper in a semishady area that is presently occupied by a tall astilbe, so I dig up the astilbe. Now I have a hydrangea and an astilbe to plant.

I run around the garden with the astilbe, hunting madly for a place to plant it before the roots dry out. I look for another shady spot. Ah, here's a spot with some weeds and nothing else! I dig there and sink my spade into a large clump of rare pink daffodil bulbs, murdering several. I dig up as many as I can to salvage them.

Now I have a hydrangea, a tall astilbe, and twenty-five daffodils to plant. Okay, okay . . . plant the astilbe. I run to the compost heap to get a spadeful of compost. Astilbes are heavy feeders. I come back with the compost, losing half of it along the way. That's all right. I throw it in the hole. The hole is too small. I enlarge it, digging up some more daffodil bulbs, a few crocuses, and some grape hyacinths along the way, and plant the astilbe. I run to get the bucket of water, which has the oak-leaf hydrangea soaking in it. In my frenzy, I pour the oak-leaf hydrangea onto the astilbe along with the water. Now I can't find the hydrangea! The ground around the astilbe is covered with twigs; which one is it? I step on a few more pink daffodils, crushing them, while looking for the twig with a label on it. I finally find it and run for some more water to plant the damned thing. At last, the oak-leaf hydrangea is in place, and I have achieved my original aim.

Now I only have thirty-five bulbs to plant! That should take another hour.

Sometimes you must move one plant to put another one in. Adding new specimens is one of the most satisfying aspects of gardening, and we all do it. But frantic hysteria is not the emotion we want to elicit in horticulture. Let me remind you that in gardening we want to call forth contentment, refreshment, not to mention the peace that passeth understanding. That's why it's better to plan ahead. Now I try to do any moving that's necessary before the new arrival comes. No more painting the nursery while the labor pains are starting.

3. *Use upright objects, such as poles or branches, to see what a tree or shrub will look like before you plant it.* Get a long broomstick, pole, or branch and stick it in the appropriate spot. Let me rephrase that. Insert a stick in the ground in the same place that you intend to plant your tree or shrub. That's better. The upright stick will at least give you an idea of the placement of the tree or shrub in relation to the house or other plants.

There is an even better way to figure out where to place a plant. If you have a large friend, have him stand in the spot that the shrub will occupy, and if you can get him to raise and extend his arms and think like a bush, you will not only be giving him a valuable class in Method acting, which can be quite expensive, but you will benefit by getting a sense of width as well as height. I had Walter acting the part of a witch hazel one afternoon, and he was very good, too.

To sum up, the first thing to do when planning a garden is to ascertain its purpose. Its purpose may be either to obscure or to enhance the surrounding environment, or you may simply want to make a beautiful place in which to abide, protected from what is laughingly called "civilization."

There are hundreds of other landscaping and garden-design techniques, which you will discover as you go along. I have given you a few, based on personal experience. I would have given you more, but I'm not being paid by the word. For further information, such as the best flowers, shrubs, and trees for your own part of the country, I would like to refer you to the many excellent gardening reference books that are available, hopefully, in the same section in which you found this one. Books like *Taylor's Encyclopedia of Gardening* and *Hortus Third* are as invaluable to the gardener as a dictionary is to the Scrabble player. They contain lists of plants for every situation and instructions on cultivation and planting. I must warn you that most gardening instruction books are not funny. But purchase a copy anyway; it would tickle me silly to think that my book was sitting on the same shelf as they are.

Cartography (Gardening on Paper)

When planning a garden or just a new flower border, nothing is more helpful than making garden maps. It's much easier to move plants around on paper than it is in the garden, and there is absolutely no chance of root damage. The variety of plants in the catalogs can be overwhelming, especially if you're gardening on a budget, so having a map to follow is as useful as having a shopping list when you go to the supermarket.

The first thing you have to do is determine whether you want the map to include the whole yard or whether you only need a planting chart of one particular flower border. Sometime in January, go out and measure the area you want to map as accurately as you can. Pick a relatively warm day, if possible. Now you are ready for the fun part.

How to Draw a Garden Map

You need:

Graph paper	Ruler
Pencil	Tape

You probably already have most of this stuff in the kitchen drawer. If the area you want to map is a large one, you may have to tape several pieces of graph paper together to make one big sheet. The amount of paper you need will depend on the scale of the map.

When I first began my garden, I wanted to make my maps as complete as possible. My idol, Gertrude Jekyll, drew incredible maps of her flower borders. Each plant variety was meticulously included, every square foot of that border was accounted for, there were no spaces between the drifts, and she had handwritten the name of every plant, in Latin, inside each drift. The detail was remarkable. Remarkable and completely illegible.

Unfortunately, the map of her two-hundred-foot-long border had been reproduced in a book that was only ten inches wide. That's quite a reduction in scale—one inch equaled twenty feet. Finding an individual plant on that map was like trying to find your cousin Larry in a photograph of Yankee Stadium during a World Series game.

I decided to make my own maps somewhat larger. I used the more legible scale of one inch equals one foot. Not only did that scale allow enough room to put the name of the plant inside the circle or drift, but I was also able to include the color, height, and month of bloom, using a little code I made up. *M* was for May, *J* for June, *JL* for July, and so forth. To be fair to Miss Jekyll, if her maps had been reproduced on that scale, they would have made a very nice dining-room mural.

Once you have determined the scale, draw the dimensions of the area on the map using a pencil and a ruler.

As we have seen, it's usually better to make several maps of different areas than to make one map of a very large area in microscopic scale.

Draw a circle to indicate the eventual size of each plant, or a long oval to show drifts of several plants of the same variety. Label everything as you go along, with the name, color, height, and time of bloom.

Draw any permanent structures and existing plantings first. For example, if there is already a four-foot rose bush in the area, indicate it by drawing a four-inch circle in its proper spot. If there is a tree, use a circle for the trunk and broken lines to show the extent of the top and to allow for the shade it casts. You can still site plants around the trunk, but at least you'll be aware that they are in shade. After the existing plants have been accounted for, go ahead and draw the ones you intend to add. Feel free to use the eraser as much as necessary.

Drawing my own maps to scale was a sobering experience. It takes far fewer plants than you think to fill a twenty-by-six-foot border. If I had actually planted all the flowers I wanted to, I figured out that my perennial border would have been three football fields long and would have cost $180,000.

I had to modify my plans somewhat. I was forced to choose only those plants that I couldn't live without, and then I had to go through the list and choose only those plants I *really* couldn't live without, and then actually buy only half of those. I consoled myself with the thought that I could buy more plants in subsequent years as I increased the area under cultivation, but the decisions were painful, nonetheless.

Map making serves other purposes as well. All the best garden designers suggest that you should plant in groups of three, six, or even twelve of one variety to avoid "spottiness." In other words, if designing a flower border is like painting a canvas, you want a landscape by Claude Monet, not Jackson Pollock.

In gardening, more is more. To take a familiar example, we've all seen forsythias planted in front yards all across the country. One forsythia in full yellow bloom is a pleasant, if hackneyed, reminder of spring. Now, imagine what fifty forsythias planted in front of a small evergreen woodland would look like, all golden, with 1,200 purple and white crocuses planted around the base. It wouldn't look hackneyed anymore. On the contrary, such a scene is the stuff that winter dreams are made of.

I don't have room in my garden for fifty forsythias or any plantation that large. But the principle of planting in mass still applies.

The main difference I can see between gardens that look anemic and ones that look smashing is not the color scheme or even the choice of plant material, but the generous way in which the specimens are planted. Six petunias do not a garden make. When I find myself with six petunias, I put them in a ten-inch pot and stick them next to the doorway. That way it doesn't seem as though they're trying to do a bad impression of a flower garden.

Make a separate list of the plants somewhere on the map or on another piece of paper.

The list should look something like this:

> 3 Siberian iris 'Caesar's
> Brother'
> 3 Astilbe 'Superba'
> 6 Lavender 'Hidcote'
> 6 Phlox 'White Admiral'
> 6 Coneflowers, white
> & etc.

That's your shopping list. You can check off the ones you already have. Making a map ensures that you have enough of each plant to make a good showing, and the map tells you exactly how many of each variety you'll need to cover the ground. If, like me, you find it is financially impossible to buy more than one of a variety right away, a map will help you remember what the garden is supposed to look like when the plants have grown large enough to be divided into drifts in a couple of years. With a map I found it was easy to be sure that I put the short plants in front and the tall plants in back (even if I should decide to ignore that rule later on) and that there would always be something in bloom each month of the season. That first winter I planned intelligently, carefully, madly. I couldn't have been more excited if I were planning the seating arrangements for my wedding.

Use the map as a guide, but not a dictator. In truth, you won't be able to stick to it exactly, especially as the garden matures. Anyway, too much control is antithetical to the idea of a cottage garden.

My own plans all came out fine, except where they went wrong. The best laid plans of gardeners, or anybody else, can be sabotaged by nature, but in gardening, you don't know that they've been ruined until a year later, when the plants have reached their full potential. This happened to me with some meadowsweet (*Filipendula rubra* 'Venusta') that my friend Bobbie had given to me out of her garden. It has hairy, but attractive, olive green leaves and tall panicles of pink flowers that look like elegant dust mops. I had planted them in the back of the border because they had grown to about six feet tall in Bobbie's border.

In my garden a year later, they grew to only two feet tall. That fall, I moved them to the front, and the next year, they were seven feet tall and devoured the pansies. Patiently, I moved them to the back of the border again, and they dropped dead. Perhaps the soil was too dry, or something ate them back there, who knows? The irony of it all is that some of the meadowsweet's roots in the front of the border survived, and I now have a seven-foot jolly green giant of a meadowsweet thriving in the front of the border. I gave up and called it an "accent plant."

I was looking at my original maps recently, in preparation for writing this chapter. Boy, has everything changed! Some plants have made huge clumps, sometimes several huge clumps. Others have gone . . . God knows where . . . dead, moved to the Sun Belt, address unknown. The present garden looks substantially different from the one I had planned, but it looks good, even if I do say so myself. The plants that have thrived have given the garden its own character, unique appearance, and sense of place. It's as if the garden is saying, "These plants do well here, because this is a place with its own individual soil and climate and air. This is not exactly like any other garden in the world."

This is literally true. Nowhere else on earth is the soil exactly the same, or the amount of air pollution or lack of it, or the sunlight or the rainfall. Like a child, each place on earth has its own individual soul. Sometimes I feel as if I'm as tied to this one as a mother is to her child.

I still make changes from year to year. I rearrange things and add some new candidates for inclusion. I don't bother to make maps anymore, although I should. After eight years, the garden is not yet as over-populated as the slums of Brazil, although there are now seven borders as large as the first. There is still more grass than I want, as well as an uncultivated area in the back, so if a plant gets too lusty and threatens to take over, I can stick it in the wild area and let it fight it out with the weeds. I now have *Filipendula rubra* 'Venusta' all over the place, and I've given it a nickname. I call it "Phil."

FEBRUARY

Americans are suspicious of fences in general.

A Brief History of Gardens

While we are still in the depths of winter, a time of the year known to bored gardeners all over the Northern Hemisphere as "the planning stage," there is still plenty of time (unfortunately) to think about the garden in general terms. We have more time than we want to contemplate questions such as: "What is a garden? What are the elements that separate it from a wilderness, or a farm, or a plant collection, or a suburban front lawn for that matter? What the heck is a *garden*, anyway?" I decided to find out. I set out to learn about the history of gardens and discovered that the essential thread that runs through all gardening styles is the idea of the garden as a separate place, an enclosure, controlled nature, somewhere between the wild world and the house.

Planting and cultivation go together like the chicken and the egg, and they have a similar relationship. You might say that cultivation of the land is the mother of civilization, because without agriculture, cities, and later, states could not have come into existence. So, gardening is the chicken, but it is also the egg. Private pleasure gardens have always come into being as a result of civilization. In order for citizens to have gardens, they needed enough personal safety, prosperity, and spare time to till the earth for purposes other than mere subsistence. Pleasure gardens have always been a reflection of a culture's sense of beauty and of its attitude toward nature and the larger world around it. Historically, pleasure gardens have always been a great place to make out.

There is a good reason for this. According to tradition (and I don't mean just Western tradition, but world tradition), private gardens, up until the eighteenth century, have been enclosed by walls, and not just for aesthetic or erotic reasons but to keep animals and barbarians out. This tradition goes back to the beginnings of recorded history and probably beyond that. In fact, the Bible describes the Garden of Eden as having walls, although there was presumably nothing yet outside them. This evidence leads us to the assumption that the very concept of a garden included the existence of walls. It also leads us to the assumption that logic was not a high priority in the Old Testament.

Walled gardens were common in ancient Egypt by the time of Ramses III, who lived from 1198 to 1166 B.C. (Like most people in those days, he lived backward.) The Persians had hunting parks and walled gardens by the time of Cyrus the Great (sixth century B.C.). The word *paradise* meant garden in the ancient Persian language.

In warm climates, walls were usually built around an area that contained a well or a natural spring. Not only was the well used for practical purposes, such as watering the plants, but it was often the source of an ornamental pool or a fountain, what we now call a "water feature" in gardenspeak. It is not known if the Persians, the Egyptians, or the ancient Hebrews used the water for bathing. Soap wasn't invented until the Romans, who also invented interesting sex. (Since my editor informs me that a gardening book is not a proper venue for discussions of interesting sex, I will go into this topic in more detail when I write my private memoirs, *A Petunia Named Desire.*)

In ancient China, the houses of the rich were enclosed by a concentric series of walls, which were so complex and circuitous they resembled a jigsaw puzzle. There are records of these enclosures dating from the Han dynasty (c. 206 B.C.–A.D. 220), but like most things Chinese, this style of garden goes back much, much further than the records show. The upper classes in China made complicated rock gardens within the enclosures, and like rock gardeners of today, would collect many rare, unusual, and teeny-tiny plants from as far away as possible, just to show off.

Walled gardens were à la mode in pre-Columbian America, as well. The private houses of the Aztecs had courtyard gardens, filled with flowers, vegetables, and fruits, as well as herbs useful as medicines, dyes, and even poisons for political purposes. How good-old-days! How Aztec!

The Aztecs also gardened on the roofs of their houses, but even the roofs had walls. William Hickling Prescott wrote in his *History of the Conquest of Mexico* (1843): "The flat roofs were protected with stone parapets, so that every house was a fortress. Sometimes these roofs resembled parterres of flowers, so thickly were they covered with them. . . ."* According to Prescott, the roofs reminded the Spanish conquistadors of the Hanging Gardens of Babylon, and they admired them greatly, just before they lobbed their cannon balls onto them and killed everybody in the house for the glory of God. How conquistador!

We have only to visit a museum and look at old paintings to see that most private gardens in Europe were enclosed by walls, hedges, or fences,

---

*Quoted in Anthony Huxley, *An Illustrated History of Gardening* (Paddington Press, New York and London, 1978).

40

right up until the eighteenth century, when the "natural," or "picturesque," landscape first came into vogue. As we shall see in a later chapter, this "natural" style has had a profound effect on American landscaping in the twentieth century.

We've all seen pictures of medieval tapestries that show a lady sitting by an old well in a walled garden with a unicorn resting his head in her lap. What the tapestry doesn't show, tapestry space being limited to what a group of women could weave in a lifetime between babies, wars, plagues, and tournaments, is what was going on behind the wall: the miserable, brutal world of the Middle Ages. There were bears, Huns, lions, angry villagers, wolves, and even lustful barons. In Europe, as everywhere else, the garden enclosure was the place where the outside world stopped. There was nothing in that medieval garden but flowers and fruit trees, sunshine and soft air, and the lady and the unicorn.

In North America, prior to World War II, we had a long tradition of fenced-in gardens, from the wooden palisades of the early settlers, to the neat white pickets of the formal gardens of Colonial Williamsburg, to the brick-walled garden "rooms" behind nineteenth-century brownstone town houses.

Through books and some fascinating lectures at the New York Botanical Garden and the New York Horticultural Society, I learned that the idea of a secluded area, separate from the rest of the world, has been essential to the definition of a garden, and I decided that I, too, wanted to have such a traditional earthperson's garden. I figured that if an enclosed garden was good enough for Cleopatra, it was good enough for me.

I couldn't very well build a twelve-foot wall around my yard, but I could get the same feeling of privacy and enclosure by using shrubs and fences and arbors and paths. Luckily, the enormous lilacs were already growing around the perimeter of the garden, so all I had to do was to make the arbors and paths.

Well, okay, it's the twentieth century and we are no longer threatened by lions or, for that matter, by an overabundance of lustful barons. (I miss them.) But in the modern world, we need privacy more than ever.

The truth is, the twentieth century with its world wars, threat of total nuclear destruction, and ecological disorder is as terrifying as the ancient world ever was. It makes even the horrific fourteenth century with its Black Death and Hundred Years' War look like a walk in the park. Not to put too fine a point on it, I'm scared stiff by the mechanized horror that industrialization has created, and I don't think I am alone in feeling this way. It invades every moment of our lives. How many of us can spend a day or an hour without hearing the roaring, buzzing, belching, groaning, hissing, banging, squeaking, shrieking, and whining of machines? Oh, it's not so bad, is it? Close your eyes and listen. What do you hear? An automobile? An airplane? The refrigerator? A lawn mower? A snow blower? The telephone? The squawking of the television or the radio, frequently the neighbor's? All right, I know you're reading a book, but try it. Close your eyes and listen.

You heard a machine, right? I'm sure you did. Unless you are on a mountaintop or in a cave, there is practically nowhere in what we are pleased to call the "civilized world" where you can get away from it.

It seems to me as if there is a war going on against life itself. For the past two hundred years, humans have been conquering nature and snuffing out species with more thoroughness than the conquistadors ever dreamed of. As Francis Bacon said in 1620 (in Latin), "Nature to be commanded, must be obeyed." Nobody listened to him then, and as a result, we have gotten ourselves into a pretty pickle. The natural world, the community of life on the planet, erroneously referred to by press and politicos as "The Environment," has been trashed by us humans, in some places beyond redemption. This is no revelation. We all know it.

I don't know whether the damage has been done through carelessness, ignorance, or greed, and I don't care. The simple truth is that humankind will have to learn to live within the natural world, or else . . . or else we'll destroy the very life which supports us, and of which we are a noisy part. You want to make a lot of money in the chemical industry so you can go live in Palm Beach? Go ahead, but even Palm Beach won't be so pleasant if there's no ozone in the upper atmosphere and the temperature is 180 degrees in the shade. I think what we all need is a little humility, a little sense of exactly where we stand in the nature of things.

Humility hit me on the head last summer. I was in the vegetable garden one evening, eating tomatoes that I had grown by the scientific, French, organic-intensive method and feeling very virtuous and smug about it, when a swarm of mosquitoes attacked me, and not for the first time, either. But at that moment, I had been feeling so proud, so ahead of the game, I was shocked. While I had been eating the tomato, the mosquitoes had been eating *me*. The mosquitoes hadn't said to themselves, "Oh, she's a writer, raconteur, and organic gardener, let's not suck her blood." They couldn't have cared less about me and my pretensions. At that moment I saw myself as I really was, just another part of nature, just another living creature, a meal. Even writers die. And so do industrial civilizations. Only life itself goes on, even when it's as stupid as a mosquito.

Nature to be commanded, must be obeyed.

Like many a civilized person since time began who lives in a wild and frightening world beyond his control, I have made a private garden to live in, a lovely, divine Eden to which I can retreat, sort of a local temperate-zone Tahiti right in my own yard.

Since my garden is in the middle of a small town, not out in the country, I hear the drones and screeches of civilization most of the day. But there is one hour each day when I can beat the system, when I can be truly alone and at peace, and that is at five A.M. In spring, summer, and fall, I go downstairs at dawn and work in my garden, that separate place of controlled nature somewhere between the wild world and the house. No one else is awake yet. No one else is mowing the lawn or revving a motorcycle, or getting and spending and laying waste their powers. I have one precious, beautiful, measly hour. I move slowly up and down the wet stone paths, pulling weeds, staking flowers, smelling the good earth, and listening to the rustling of leaves, the singing of birds, and even the drone of the mosquitoes.

By six o'clock, the moment has passed. Already, the overachievers are whooshing by in their cars, in order to arrive early to work at the power plant. Soon the hordes of barbarians (the ones without the mufflers) will invade my space with their noise. But I have had my hour in my private garden. No one there but flowers and birds, sunshine and soft air, and the lady and the unicorn.

My hour in the garden teaches me something more than even that quotation from Francis Bacon, the other eternal verity that I would like to hang over my garden gate:

Nature always has the last laugh.

Anyone who visits my garden knows that this is true.

GOOD FENCES MAKE GOOD NEIGHBORS

It would be cruel to glorify the importance of enclosure in a garden, to praise the benefits of privacy, to hype the joys of having a secret garden and then leave my dear readers in a state of irritated frustration, wondering what to do about it in their own gardens. So I feel that it is incumbent upon me to discuss some ways to provide that feeling of seclusion.

"Good fences make good neighbors."

I've heard this quoted by a couple of friends of mine, who shall remain nameless, while they were in the process of putting up a fence. They were quoting Robert Frost in his poem "Mending Walls." The quotation was correct, but I think they had the context all wrong. According to my ninth-grade English teacher, Mrs. Freud, Robert Frost was being sarcastic when he used the old expression. He was using the stone wall as a metaphor for the emotional walls that people put up against each other. He wasn't praising fences, quite the reverse!

I know you're thinking that my reference to "Mending Walls" is just another one of my interesting digressions, a cheap literary device to lead you into this chapter on hedges and fences. That's true, but I mention it for another reason. Robert Frost was expressing a common American attitude toward fences—narrow-eyed distrust. Americans are suspicious of fences in general, and fences around private yards in particular. Putting up a fence in a suburban neighborhood is considered an unfriendly act. The neighbors' attitude is usually "What's the matter, don't you like me? You think I've got cooties?" Or, "A fence, huh? What are you hiding? Are you some kind of weirdo or something?" This is a very strange point of view in a country whose Supreme Court defines privacy as a basic human right. Or at least it used to.

As you know by now, I love fences and hedges and walls around my garden. And it's not because I want to keep my neighbors from talking to me, either. I like my neighbors, at least the ones on the left side of the house. On the right, however, is the municipal parking lot, not a good neighbor at all. I don't have to tell you how much I hate that parking lot, and I've put up the solid fence along that side as high as the zoning regulations will allow, and I don't care if it's unfriendly.

Actually, it was my friend Ron, of Bobbie and Ron's farm in Pennsylvania, who put up the fence, or at least paid to have it put up. Shortly after I moved in, he came to visit and stayed in the downstairs guest room, which unfortunately overlooks the parking lot. That Saturday night there was a stag party in the Benevolent Society of Buffalos' Club, which adjoins the parking lot on the other side. The party broke up around two in the morning, and for the next hour, there were people shouting good night to each other, revving up their automobiles, shining their headlights through the window, and generally ignoring the laws against DWI. Ron is not a particularly light sleeper, but he'd have to have been comatose not to be awakened by such a racket.

The next morning, he appeared with circles under his eyes and presented us with a large check to cover the cost of putting up a tall fence. Good fences make good neighbors, and good friends make good fences.

Fences are wonderful for keeping unwanted animals out, like woodchucks, rabbits, gophers, deer, and buffaloes. As I've mentioned, the way to make sure that rabbits and other small mammals don't burrow under the fence is to bury six to twelve inches of chicken wire along its length. One way to keep deer and other large mammals, like besotted buffalos, from jumping your fence is to make sure that it is at least eight feet tall. Another effective method is to shoot them. I wish I had the nerve.

If, like me, you love the feeling of a private garden away from the world, but you're afraid that your neighbors, like most Americans, will misunderstand you, I suggest that you have a talk with them first. Explain that you want to make a garden, and that a garden implies enclosure. They'll probably misunderstand, anyway—it's an amazingly touchy subject—but at least you will have tried. Put a gate in the fence between the yards, with the word *Welcome* painted on their side of it. That should help.

If I had to plan my garden from scratch on a blank piece of land in the middle of a suburban subdivision, and I couldn't move, the very first thing I would do would be to put up a fence or a hedge before I even met my neighbors, so they couldn't take it personally.

Fences provide instant gratification, because a fence immediately turns a blank piece of land into a framed enclosure. I can't think of any change in the landscape that is more dramatic, short of strip mining. My problem would be the cost. Unless you have a wealthy relative or generous friend whom you can torture into helping pay for it, a fence can be very expensive, especially if you want a beautiful fence. (And who doesn't?)

A beautiful fence with details that harmonize with the architecture of the house is an asset to any landscape. Of course, there are cheap fencing materials and lots of ugly ones. If I couldn't afford to fence my entire yard in beauty, and that would seem likely if I were living in a subdivision out in the middle of nowhere, I would buy cheap fencing, such as unfinished palisades or plain boards, and plant vigorous vines to grow on both sides of it. Wisteria, silver lace (*Polygonum Aubertii*), and red trumpet (*Campsis*) vines come to mind. Any one of these would obscure that fence in two or three years. Vines on a fence are a good idea in any case, since a fence is properly put up with the good side out. By custom and law, the owner is the one who has to look at the horizontal stringer boards. One way to disguise an ugly fence (or the backside of a decorative one) is to paint it dark green or brown. Further obscured by foliage, it's practically invisible.

I don't know why, but hedges seem friendlier to me than fences. My lilac hedge is so high and wide that it provides a definite sense of enclosure to the side garden, but there are one or two places where my neighbor and I can get through to visit. After all, the lilac hedge is not a formal clipped hedge at all, but only a collection of ancient lilacs planted in a row. But isn't that the definition of a hedge? A hedge is a collection of shrubs planted in a row, spaced closely enough to give the appearance of a wall.

If a hedge is tall enough, it effectively creates a private place, and if it is a tall clipped hedge, it is as though the space were a room with living green walls.

A good hedge, like a good man, is hard to find. The quickest way to get one is to buy suitable evergreens, such as yews or hemlocks, that are already ten feet tall, and have them planted professionally. The effect of a ten-foot-tall yew hedge planted this way is as stately, handsome, and instantaneous as any item that only the really rich can afford. For most of us, such instant gratification is out of the question financially, and there are a couple of other problems, as well.

The trouble with a yew hedge is that it is a gourmet delight to deer. Unless you live in an area where there are no deer, it is foolish to plant it. (I don't know if there is such a place. Deer are everywhere just now, even in very populated areas. Last week, I saw a couple of fawns shopping in Kmart.) Deer have been known to enjoy a meal of hemlock, too, but given the choice of yew or hemlock on the menu, they'll pick the yew every time. I'm told they don't like to eat arborvitae or rhododendron, but I don't believe it.

There are sprays on the market you can apply to a plant or shrub that will prevent deer from eating it. One brand name that comes to mind is Hinder, but there are others that are also environmentally safe, so far as I know, and they work. It tastes like liquid fire. The reason I know this is because Walter accidentally got some on his tongue one day and spent the next half hour with his mouth under the kitchen faucet. He didn't die, although the label is full of dire warnings. Lucky Walter. Read the label.

The great advantage of an evergreen hedge is that it is an effective screen all year round, but a deciduous hedge can be quite wonderful, too.

Any shrub can be made into a hedge. Shrubs that lose their leaves in the winter are not good for screening out ugly views, but they enclose a garden just as well as evergreens in spring, summer, and fall, and since most gardens are not occupied that much in the winter, this is not so bad. Besides, a three-season hedge is better than no hedge at all, and flowering shrubs add a spectacular few weeks to the garden while they are blooming.

Some of the nicest hedges I've ever seen, aside from my famous white lilacs, have been ones made up of flowering shrubs. I've seen forsythia, kerria, shrub rose (*Rosa rugosa*), spirea (*Spiraea prunifolia* cv. 'Plena'), and rose-of-Sharon (*Hibiscus syriacus*) hedges blooming at various seasons around the local countryside. The taller ones, such as the rose-of-Sharon at eight to ten feet, and the kerria, at eight feet, grow neatly and thickly enough to make very fine garden walls. Deciduous shrubs are very amenable to being clipped and shaped, although it isn't necessary to square them off like formal hedges. For the most part, flowering shrubs look and flower much better if given enough space to form their own natural growth pattern.

There are a couple of ways to obtain a beautiful hedge without spending a fortune. One way to do it is to buy very small shrubs from a catalog or nursery. A bundle of a dozen hemlock seedlings can be obtained for about ten bucks. The bad news is that these babies will have to be nursed along for several years before they look like anything. The good news is that the wait will give the neighbors time to get used to the idea. By the time the hemlocks are ten feet tall, the neighbors will have forgotten that they don't like fences, or they'll be too senile to care.

The other method is free. Ask a friend or neighbor who already has a large shrub to let you take suckers off it.

About two years ago, a young couple, perfect strangers to me, approached me in the front yard and asked if they could take some suckers off my lilacs, since they wanted to make a pretty lilac hedge like mine in their new home. I was flattered, and they seemed like a nice couple so I said sure. The following Saturday they arrived with a pick-up truck! I felt lucky they didn't bring a bulldozer. What nerve! They took about twenty suckers from around the edges of the lilacs. I couldn't very well throw them out of my yard, because they kept thanking me and blessing me and complimenting me the whole time they dug up and pulled at my beautiful hedge. I followed them closely, standing over their shoulders like a bad conscience. It was nerve-wracking, but to tell you the truth, when they were done, the missing suckers were not noticeable. They had taken only two or three from each plant, so there were no obvious gaps, and I never missed them. After they left, I didn't miss the couple, either.

Any shrub that has many branches that grow from the roots is suitable for this treatment, the aforementioned forsythias, kerrias, and spireas, for example. There are plenty of others. All you have to do to find them is to look at the shrub and see how it grows. If the shrub increases in width by putting out new growth next to itself, then it's a candidate. I suspect that some of the beautiful hedges I've seen around the countryside were made in just this way, by replanting shoots from the original plant.

Shrubs that seed themselves freely are also good candidates for hedges, like the rose-of-Sharon. I have one in the side garden that has produced at least a dozen babies in the nearby flower borders. Instead of weeding them out, I've been saving them to transplant between the driveway and the shady side of the house.

To clip, or not to clip, that is the next question. Graceful flowering shrubs, like the forsythia, look very peculiar when they are tortured into unnatural shapes, but privet was made for cutting and only improves with each trim. Other shrubs, like hemlock, can be pruned or not, depending upon personal preference. Some shrubs need to be clipped a lot, and some don't need to be clipped at all.

If you think that I'm about to tell you the proper way to clip a perfectly straight formal hedge, you're wrong. I like badly clipped hedges. I'm not talking about unkempt hedges, with wayward branches sticking up from the main growth so that they look as if they've stuck their fingers into an electrical socket. We've all seen those. No, by imperfect I mean a hedge that is not perfectly square. Some of the most beautiful hedges I've seen were not squared off at all, but undulated with all the whimsical imperfection of the gardeners' own hands. I especially like tall hedges clipped in this way. I've seen pictures of hedges like that in England, and they were extremely charming, not to mention lush, or maybe the gardener was the lush, which is why he couldn't clip a straight line. Then again, all pictures from England are charming and lush looking.

The only important point to remember when clipping a hedge is to make sure that the top of the hedge is narrower than the rest of it, so that the lower branches are not shaded out. Making the top larger than the bottom will make the bottom lose its leaves and look scraggly. If you were looking down the spine of a properly pruned hedge, it would form a wedge shape with the widest part at the bottom. In other words, a hedge should be a wedge. There. That's clear and easy to remember.

So, what would I do if I were faced with a blank piece of land in the middle of a subdivision and very little money? I would buy the cheapest fencing I could find, paint it dark green, and plant trumpet vines every six feet along the bottom. (Incidentally, trumpet vines root easily in a container of water.) For the first couple of years, until the trumpet vines got big enough, I would train annual vines, like morning glories, on strings to hide the fence. In the meantime, I would get a few bundles of hemlock cuttings and plant them on both sides of the fence. If that fence is as cheap as I think it should be, it will be ready to fall down by the time the hemlocks are grown. After the fence fell down, I would clip the hemlocks into a graceful hedge, the kind that rich people can order in ten minutes, and inside this enclosure, I would dwell contentedly with Walter and Sam in the prettiest cottage garden you ever saw.

Good fences make great gardens.

A Visit to the Los Angeles Arboretum

For a gardener in the Northeast, February is a good time to leave town and go south. Take a break, catch a few rays. Although a cruise to the Caribbean is not in my budget, I did get to go to Los Angeles last February to give a lecture. I admit, driving around the freeways of L.A. is not the same thing as basking on the Love Boat around the Bermuda Triangle, but at least it's warm.

One of the joys of being a gardener is that you can bring your love of plants with you wherever you go, and that makes every trip more interesting. It's hard to be bored when there are so many new flowers to see! Since I had a couple of days to spare in Los Angeles, I wanted to get out into the countryside and explore the unique flora of the American Southwest.

My friend, Pam DuBois, had invited me to stay at her apartment for a couple of days to do a little sightseeing after my lecture was finished. Pam was raised in Los Angeles and had mapped out a Hollywood tour for me, starting with Universal Studios and ending with a visit to Graumann's Chinese Theatre. To her disappointment, I told her I wasn't really interested in watching television shows being made or touring the homes of the Rich and Famous by bus, much less walking around on cement casts of their feet. What I really wanted to see was the flora of the area. She was nonplussed. "Flora who?" she quipped.

"No, no, not a person. Plants and trees. Is there a botanical garden in Los Angeles?"

She wasn't familiar with one. The closest thing to a botanical garden that she knew of was Forest Lawn Cemetery. It contained lots of flowers and lots of dead stars! That sounded like a good compromise, so we went to Forest Lawn.

I wouldn't exactly call Forest Lawn Cemetery a mecca for horticulturists. First of all, it was much more "lawn" than "forest." The entire hillside was swathed in perfectly manicured grass and resembled a fantasy version of an English eighteenth-century landscape dotted with memorial statuary and temples. This was quite a feat when you consider that Los Angeles is naturally a semiarid desert. But at Forest Lawn, they throw water around as if it were . . . water.

There were a few enclosed gardens with benches and plantings, mostly of the "privet and bedding-out annuals" school of public garden design.

There were stone "walls" surrounding the plantings, but they were actually the repositories of the ashes of the Dearly Departed, especially the Rich and Famous Dearly Departed. (There were lots of cute euphemisms for dead people in Forest Lawn, like Dearly Departed and Heavenly Traveler. It really was right out of *The Loved One* by Evelyn Waugh, may he rest in Eternal Slumber.)

We sat down on a stone bench, in front of Walt Disney. We knew it was Walt's vault because a metal reproduction of his signature was affixed to the wall. I was surprised to see him at Forest Lawn, because I had read somewhere that his body had been frozen through cryonics. But no, there he was—nothing left of his body but a brass nameplate and ashes. It was depressing. Not because he was dead, although I loved his work as a child, and still do, but because he had been cremated. As an organic gardener, I think that cremation is a waste of good compost.

Judy Garland's remains were across from Walt Disney's. I knew it was her repository without looking because a guy with a boom box was standing in front of it, dressed in a red dress and hat, lip-synching to "The Trolley Song." I thought he was very good.

The chapel at Forest Lawn was one of the highlights of my trip, containing reproductions of religious artworks by the great masters of Europe. I especially remember the reproduction of Michelangelo's *Pietà*. It looked as if the Hollywood carver had definitely improved upon the original. I would estimate that he had taken a good twenty pounds off the Virgin and given her a nose job that made her look a lot more like Elizabeth Taylor than Michelangelo had been able to do. Jesus looked fabulous as well. According to the printed information on the wall that hyped—excuse me, described—the exhibition, over the years millions of tourists, religious fanatics, and the ignorant from all over the globe have flocked to Forest Lawn to admire these Great Works of Art. How can you top "improved masterpieces"? We left the chapel and started for home.

I still wanted to see some of the native flora of the area, so the next day, Pam found the telephone number for the Los Angeles Arboretum by dialing "0" and asking the first person who answered, namely the operator, who by chance was interested in horticulture. She even gave us directions from Pam's apartment. It was not far, by Los Angeles standards—a mere two-hour drive away.

The arboretum was beautiful, although not nearly so well attended as Forest Lawn. (No dead movie stars here.) In fact, the place was almost deserted, except for one kindergarten class and a few foreign tourists taking pictures, whose paths we crisscrossed throughout the afternoon. This was what I had come to see, the landscape of the southwesternmost part of the United States, as exotic and far away from the Northeast as I could get. Unlike Forest Lawn, the arboretum specialized in collecting plants from arid regions of the world, with climatic conditions very similar to that of Southern California before the importation of water and estate gardeners. One large area was dedicated to the flora of Australia and, as you might expect, there were a great many drought-tolerant gray- and blue-leaved plants, as well as succulents and grasses. This kind of planting might not sound as exciting as an English flower garden, but the different textures and the subtle blues and grays, sage greens, and burgundy reds of the leaves looked like a sophisticated border that could have been designed by Gertrude Jekyll herself. And the best part about a garden like this was that all these plants thrived in an arid environment. Any gardener in the Southwest could grow these plants and laugh at the water meter man.

We turned a corner and walked into a magical place. There was a field of giant aloes (sometimes called century plants) that were all higher than my head! There seemed to be hundreds of them. It was like walking through a Martian landscape. Some of them had enormous orange and red flowers that looked like the tails of giant scorpions. They made me nervous, but I loved them. Again the question arose, Why would anyone want to fuss with things like hybrid tea roses in Southern California when they could grow these amazing plants so easily?

The desert plantings were exotic, at least to me, and thrilling. After seeing them, I knew I was really in the American Southwest and nowhere else. But it was in the orchid greenhouse that I knew I was in Los Angeles and nowhere else.

The orchids were as gorgeous as orchids usually are, but the most beautiful living thing in the greenhouse was the horticulturist. He was about twenty-four, moderately tall, with dark hair, blue eyes, and long black eyelashes—as handsome as a movie star. I suddenly found myself consumed with a nameless desire to learn as much about orchids as possible! Overcome by the humid torpor of the greenhouse, Pam went outside, leaving me alone with the orchid god, except for a couple of elderly orchid lovers taking pictures (and probably pinching cuttings, if I know orchid enthusiasts).

I'm a happily married middle-aged woman, but I'm not dead and I'm certainly not blind. Wasn't I there to admire the wonders of nature in Los Angeles? Wasn't he a wonder? I asked him the name and origin of every orchid in the place, and he very sweetly told me. I learned more about orchids that day than I will ever remember. He showed me the moth orchid (*Phalaenopsis*) from Burma, the one used in bridal bouquets, *Miltonias* from Brazil that resemble large pansies, the vulgar *Cattleyas* of prom corsage fame, the *Cymbidiums* that grow so well in Southern California, and the gorgeous butterfly orchids (*Oncidiums*), almost all of them in full February-in-the-tropics bloom. I didn't remember most of what he told me five minutes later, to tell you the truth, but in my mind, the beauty of orchids will always be inextricably intertwined with the memory of the beauty of the young man in the greenhouse.

After only a few minutes, which Pam swore was an hour, she came in and interrupted us, saying she desperately needed to find the ladies room. Thudded back to reality by Pam's mundane bodily concerns, as opposed to my high-minded aesthetic ones, I thanked the horticulturist and left, wishing I had a lei to throw to him as my ship headed out to sea.

We wandered around, looking for the ladies room. The arboretum had originally been a country estate, and there was still a very charming Victorian house on the property, surrounded by a thick grove of palm and eucalyptus trees, oleander shrubs, and a small pond full of frogs. It turned out that the house was closed, although it was intact, because we could see the original nineteenth-century furniture in the parlor through the porch windows. I found it more engaging than Pam did. We walked back through the grove of trees, I lingering and exploring, Pam trotting and yelling, as tropical birds sang overhead.

Suddenly, I heard the roar of a crowd, the thunder of horses' hooves, and a man on a loudspeaker calling the races! I could hear it all as plainly as if I were sitting in the stands at a racetrack. Boy, was I annoyed! Is Los Angeles crass, or what? It was bad enough that they exploited the famous dead in the cemetery, but to violate the little bit of nature that remained in this land of six-lane highways and endless parking lots by sticking Santa Anita racetrack right next door to the arboretum was really too much!

As I walked on, musing and fuming, Pam was urgently making her way toward the entrance building, and inspired, perhaps, by the announcer, she broke into a gallop. I followed more slowly, but I spotted her coming around the turn and into the home stretch. Just as she approached the arboretum exit, she found a bush with a tag on it marked "Women"! She looked at it in horror for a moment, but then realized it was connected to a small bathroom, which she dove into. The crowd cheered! Pam had won the race! I think that was the high point of her trip.

After we came out of the bathroom, we decided to start for home, but just before we reached the parking lot, we came upon a low adobe building. It was an old Spanish mission, where local tribes and Franciscan friars had lived hundreds of years ago.

The place was completely deserted and unattended, except for Pam and me, and the ghosts of the ancient Americans who once lived there, now wiped out by disease or dispersed to parts unknown. It had a poetic feeling about it. Just us, and the voice of the man calling the fourth race at Santa Anita.

Comfortable now, we sat down on the rim of an old well in the center of the clearing and tried to imagine what it had been like to live here when the mission was in full swing. We saw ourselves drawing water from the well, weaving rugs, blowing chaff and praying to Santa Anita (the one without the loudspeaker), and living a peaceful, contemplative life, separated by the wall of time from the all-conquering machines that now laid waste to the land. Pam had to admit that it was beautiful.

Could the people who lived here ever possibly have imagined the kind of world that now surrounds their little mission? What would they think of it? How would they cope? Would they find it as repulsive as I do? Probably not. In many ways, their lives were pretty grim. They'd probably be thrilled to have an air-conditioned bungalow with hot and cold running water and a car to drive to the supermarket in. Who could blame them?

I have to admit that I also enjoy the comforts of modern life. But as we drove back in the automobile, breathing the smoggy air only half-filtered by the weak dribble of the car air conditioner, past the endless strip malls, fast-food joints, gas stations, photo stands, construction sites, drive-in banks, and dry cleaners, all floating on a vast sea of blacktop and cement, as though the earth underneath were something to be stamped out and killed, I wanted to blow the whole thing up.

I'm glad I was there. I am. Not only did I manage to get away from winter for a few days, visit with my friend Pam, and see the *Pietà* with a nose job, I had a beautiful day at the arboretum, a lovely moment of tranquillity, and a great horticultural adventure; by the time I got back to New York, it was almost March.

MARCH

*If Mrs. Greenthumbs is attacked by a tree,
she will attack back!*

Pruning Trees

There are days in March when the sun warms the earth, and we can smell the sweet odor of stirring life. We linger outdoors for an hour at a time with nothing much to do, bent over double while gazing downward looking for the first emerging spring bulbs, like misers looking for pennies. Then the weather turns ugly and we catch a cold. This happens every year. But there is at least one useful project we can accomplish this month, and that is to prune trees. Fortunately, pruning trees is not as complicated as a lot of people think.

It took me a long time to learn to enjoy pruning trees. For years, I hated it, because every time I made a cut, I thought I could hear the tree screaming in pain like a victim in a horror movie. I was so guilt-ridden and sensitive that every log we burned in the fireplace seemed like a little Joan of Arc. Even when I cut down the weedy ailanthus and maple tree saplings to make my garden, I felt like a mass murderer. I told myself that I was cutting down all those weed trees for the good of the whole garden, but then a little voice inside me whispered, "Adolf Eichmann thought so, too." It's very difficult to get any gardening done when you're in that frame of mind. You become like the Jains, an orthodox Hindu sect, who take only baby steps because they're afraid they're accidentally going to kill a bug.

Then I studied the art of pruning and education has eased my conscience quite a bit. I learned that there are basically two types of pruning: one is for the benefit of the plant, the other is for the benefit of the gardener. I resolved to stick to the former type and only resort to the latter when absolutely necessary.

Actually, correct pruning helps a tree to grow properly and makes it more resistant to disease, as well. For example, if you did nothing else, removing dead branches would be very helpful to a tree. A dead branch is a haven for insects, fungi, and bacteria, so cutting it off cleanly at a point where the bark can heal over the cut is a good deed.

Prune away any branches that are crossing each other, especially if the branches are touching. As the branches move in the wind, they will rub against each other and wear away the bark, which like our skin is a protective covering, thereby making another entrance for disease.

Small branches that are crossing may not touch each other yet, but trees grow, and in a few years, they will become a problem, so the sooner you can do it, the better. It's also easier to cut a small branch than a large one, especially if you don't have a power saw, which I don't. The chain saw Walter used to clear the land was borrowed from my brother, and we promptly returned it four years later.

A tree also grows better if it is not in conflict with other trees or creatures. A case in point is the *Magnolia stellata* that I planted too close to a wild cherry tree a few years back. Rather than move the magnolia, which is probably what I should have done in the first place, I have pruned the wild cherry to grow away from the magnolia. This type of pruning may not be included under the heading of pruning for the benefit of all the trees, but it has done the cherry no particular harm. You might say that in this case, I have been pruning the wild cherry in favor of the magnolia. I wouldn't say this in front of the wild cherry, but my intention is to have the magnolia eventually replace the cherry tree in that corner of the yard.

A tree with a branch growing so low it keeps hitting the gardener in the head when she walks by is not going to be loved as well as one with branches arching gracefully overhead. I remove any branches that will aggressively attack a passerby, because if this passerby is attacked by a tree, she will attack back. And I've got the saw!

I have previously mentioned that when I bought my house, there was one very large and 100,000 small Norway maples in the yard. That second figure might be a slight exaggeration, but the first one is absolutely correct. These maples are the most aggressive Norwegians since the Vikings. Not only do the winged seeds have a germination rate of 125 percent, but the tree itself is a very poor neighbor to other plants. To put it plainly, nothing grows under a Norway maple tree. Okay, maybe ivy and pachysandra will give it a try. The broad leaves cast the densest shade of all the trees in my yard, and the roots are so shallow, they grab all the nutrients and moisture from anything struggling underneath. In my lectures, when people ask me what to put under a Norway maple, I tell them, "Flagstones."

And the Norway maple is not small. It is not small compared to any other tree you can think of, and it is not small compared to a brontosaurus. The Norway maple next to my driveway is probably about forty years old and it's three stories tall. My Norway maple would look lovely growing next to a fjord in its native land. I wish it were there right now.

I must confess that the maple tree does have some advantages. For six or seven months of the year, the abundant foliage obscures the view of the parking lot next door from the upper story of my house, which is a blessing. And it does turn a beautiful yellow in the fall, just before it drops all its leaves on the driveway. So I have not only maintained it, I have encouraged it by arbor-friendly pruning. The first thing we did was to take out some of the lower branches so we wouldn't bump our heads when we got out of the car. You'll notice that, once again, I have switched to the first person plural. When it comes to some of the heaviest work, "we" includes Walter, the big guy. Walter sawed off the largest branches, while I held them so they would come crashing down where we wanted them to.

When to Prune a Tree

Prune a tree in late winter or very early spring. That is the time when a tree has its greatest food reserves, all stored up from the previous summer. In spring, the tree is getting ready to put forth the tremendous effort of growth and regeneration, so a cut made at this time will have the best chance of healing over quickly. If you prune after the leaves are out, the tree has exhausted much of its reserves, and it will be months before the tree gets around to attending to the wound. Please don't consume yourself with guilt if you must remove a broken limb in the summer or fall, however. There is no great harm done if you cut properly.

How to Cut a Tree Properly

Always remove a branch where it joins the trunk or the next larger branch. Do not, do not, don't, do not cut a branch halfway down. This will leave a cut that the tree will not be able to heal.

Until fairly recently, the prescribed, kosher way to prune a branch was to cut it off flush with the trunk and paint the cut with some kind of tree ointment. My landlady in Brooklyn used to put cement in the holes in her tree. I guess she wanted them to match the ones in her head. This kind of thing is no longer necessary, if it ever was, because tree surgeons, like plastic surgeons, have come up with more effective methods.

Instead of cutting the branch off flush with the trunk, cut it just outside the bulge where the branch meets the trunk. This bulge is called the branch collar. To get a clear visual image of just what the branch collar is, think of an elephant. The skin of an elephant resembles the bark of a tree. Now think of the wrinkled bulge of skin at the point where the elephant's leg meets its body. Well, trees have that same wrinkled bulge at the base of each branch. This is what we mean by the collar. To help a tree heal as quickly and completely as possible, always make the cut so as to leave the branch collar intact. The cut wound will leave a little bump on the trunk, but you don't have to paint the cut with any chemicals, since the extra skin, or bark, will be able to seal up the wound by growing new bark around it.

It's impossible to prune with a carpenter's saw, and don't ask me how I know. Use a pruning saw and make the first cut beneath the branch to avoid stripping the bark when the branch falls.

What to Prune

1. *Take out dead branches.* Your tree will thank you for it.

2. *Take out crossed branches.* Even if they are not rubbing against each other—yet. They will.

3. *Take out branches that do not follow the natural pattern of the tree's growth.* The way to figure out the natural pattern of growth is by looking at the tree. This was very easy to do with the Norway maple next to our driveway. It had never been pruned, so it was rounded, full, and had retained its natural form. Not everyone is so lucky. Sometimes a tree has been previously pruned by someone who didn't know what he was doing. Such a tree can be so badly mangled, it's difficult to tell what its natural shape would have looked like had it been left alone. This kind of vandalism is more common with shrubs, but we will deal with them in another chapter.

You can determine a tree's natural shape by consulting a tree guide, or you can observe the new growth arising from the cut area. This new growth is called *reiteration*, which means that each regrowth copies, or reiterates, the genetic growth pattern of the tree. Any tree will reiterate itself when it has been damaged, and bad pruning will damage a tree. So when you look at the new growth, it is fairly easy to see whether this tree ought to grow in a vase pattern, a rounded pattern, or an oval pattern. You'll also be able to tell whether it should have one main trunk with smaller branches growing out from it, like a Christmas tree, or several main branches that divide and redivide as they grow, like my Norway maple.

Once you have determined what nature meant the tree to look like, prune to encourage that shape. Like Michelangelo, who sculpted a piece of marble by taking out anything that didn't look like David, take out anything that doesn't look like the proper shape of the tree.

4. *Take out branches that interfere with people, houses, or other trees.* Try to be artistic about this. If you just chop away at the annoying branch, instead of removing the whole thing neatly, it will only grow back and hit you again.

5. *Walk away.* You're done. If you have any doubts about whether to remove a particular branch, leave it alone. You can always take it out later, but just try and put it back. And if you have any doubts about whether or not to prune a tree at all, leave it alone. Billions of trees all over the world are growing perfectly well without your help.

Number 5 is my favorite rule, because it's the easiest to follow. And we have followed it. The Norway maple was the first and last tree in our yard that we have seriously attempted to prune. It's not that we don't have any other trees. The small wooded area at the back end of the property is just loaded with young trees, but I confess, we haven't touched them. It's best to leave major tree pruning to professionals, and we have taken this advice gratefully. Tree pruning can be dangerous, both to humans and trees, and that seems as good a reason as any for avoiding it.

When working on the Norway maple, Walter did not attempt to prune above the height he could reach by climbing a ladder, not even with me holding it while nagging him to be careful. Nobody should try to prune higher than they can comfortably reach, especially when using a power saw. Never work with the power saw over your head, either. I know a man who does this all the time, but this guy also enjoys sky diving, auto racing, and eating fried foods. For most of us, the only thrill we want is the joy of having a healthy, shapely tree, and the only limbs we want to remove are the tree's. A kid can get injured falling out of a tree; an adult can get killed.

The New York Flower Show

The year's at the spring,
And day's at the morn;
Morning's at seven;
The hill-side's dew-pearl'd;
The lark's on the wing;
The snail's on the thorn:
God's in his heaven—
All's right with the world!

Robert Browning, "Pippa Passes"

. . . And the flower show is in town.

In March of every year, my friend Bobbie and I meet each other at the New York Flower Show. By the end of the winter, we are so garden-starved, we trek to the flower show like trail-dusty cowpokes heading for the saloon. We go religiously, like Moslems making their hajj or the sick stumbling hopefully to Lourdes.

It's always lousy weather on the day we journey to the flower show. There's not been one day of nice weather in all the years I've gone there to meet Bobbie. In March, Old Man Winter gets panicky and tries to use up any weather he might have overlooked during December, January, and February—like icy sleet or sixty-mile-an-hour winds. The winter throws the last of its armaments like the departing volleys of a retreating army. In past years, I have walked through slush and snow. This year it was the wind—the temperature a balmy forty degrees, and the windchill factor minus ten. Nice day. But I say, "Winter, do your worst, you miserable season. The flower show is in town and your days are numbered."

The New York Horticultural Society sponsors the flower show, which takes place at Pier 92 off Twelfth Avenue, not the most convenient place in Manhattan to get to. If you can't find the right bus, it's a half-mile walk from the nearest subway.

Pier 92 is as romantic as its name. It is, architecturally speaking, uninspiring, a huge Quonset hut on a platform as large as a football field, which extends out into the Hudson River. The facility is also used for cat and dog shows, but the flower show smells much better. In the beginning of March, the inside of this unprepossessing site is transformed into a spring wonderland. This year's show was called "A Fantasy of Flowers," a title that pretty much covered the ground. (That pun was not intentional, I swear.)

As I came up the escalator that leads from the street level to the exhibit hall, I could see the tops of potted palms hanging over the open space above, and my heart thumped. The entry was banked with scores of pink and white azaleas—no magentas! I generally dislike magenta azaleas, but at this time of the year, even if there had been a hundred of them, I wouldn't have cared; I was so grateful to see so many flowers in one place.

Bobbie was there ahead of me, since it had taken me longer than expected to miss the bus and trundle the half mile bowed down by strong head winds. I bought a program on the way in. Normally, I would not have sprung for the five bucks, but since the trip was, technically speaking, research for this book, I figured it was deductible.

Bobbie and I were hit in the face by the scent of hundreds of hyacinths as we entered the main exhibit hall. They had been planted near the door by the Horticultural Society and seemed to be saying, "Welcome to Heaven, Beauty Seekers!"

The crowd at the flower show is a pretty nice bunch of people. There are lots of suburbanites, as well as professional landscapers, couples with babies in strollers, elderly artists, and youthful artisans, looking, sniffing, milling, talking among themselves, and generally having a good time.

The main exhibits consisted of a series of gardens set up around the hall, laid out like decorator rooms in a good department store. In the center of the room there was a parklike scree of unusual trees and spring bulbs, set up by the Matterhorn Nursery of Spring Valley, New York. There were also several other exhibits that were designed to look like natural woodlands, rather than cultivated gardens. They contained lots of unusual shrubs and trees, including beautiful dwarf evergreens, uniquely formed andromedas, and lots of rhododendrons. A mass planting of *Viburnum* x *Burkwoodii*, with small white blossoms, was so sweetly fragrant, my nose thanked me for smelling it. I swore on the spot that, this year, my shrub border along the fence next to the parking lot would include a *Viburnum* x *Burkwoodii*.

The New York City Department of Parks and Recreation featured plants for shade that will do well in the city and even thrive, in spite of dogs, soot, and air pollution. If I had a city garden, I would have made a list of every plant in the display.

As you might expect, it was the flower gardens that fascinated Bobbie and me the most. One of the flower gardens featured the front of a Georgian-style house flanked by flower borders and surrounded by a white picket fence. It was so pretty and nostalgic, it resembled the set of *It's a Wonderful Life*, when Mr. Potter did not have control over the town. The border on the left was for shade and the one on the right was for sun. The daintily colored shady border had pink and white astilbes, ferns, and hostas—the usual assortment of shade perennials—and the sunny border was bright with pink and red hollyhocks, blue delphiniums, apricot lilies, and yellow irises. It's a miracle how the exhibitors got all those May and June flowers to bloom in March, especially the irises, and we were very impressed. It wasn't that the choice of planting materials was so unusual; what delighted us is that they were there at all. But the most interesting thing, from a gardener's point of view, was how well the shady and the sunny borders (two different borders really) looked together in this symmetrical design.

We also loved a tiny cottage garden that surrounded a primitive wooden shed. The shed seemed charmingly realistic, with peeling paint on the shingles and an unpainted wooden window box on the sill. It was enclosed by a simple fence, behind which was a blue and yellow garden of violas, daffodils, and white English daisies. In front of the fence was a collection of small shrubs. A particularly fragrant little citrus bush had been planted on the forward corner, just so everyone would be sure to smell it as he or she went by. A narrow path led to the shed door, paved with mosaic tiles made from the shards of broken dishes in old-fashioned Blue Willow and flower patterns.

A gallery of a dozen tiny town-house gardens (four by four feet), executed by famous interior designers, was very chintzy, and I mean that as a compliment. Against backdrops painted to look like the backs of town houses, the interior designers had placed garden furniture, pots, and plantings to resemble small city gardens. Homey items like teacups, books, garden clippers, and exercise gear were left out as though the owner had just stepped out of the scene for a moment. These interior designers used many more fancy pots and topiary, garden structures, gates, and flowered cotton than a plain old gardener like me would ever use. We gardeners know what mud and rain will do to chintz, and it's not a pretty sight. Everything looked fresh and new in the exhibit, of course. But then again, the exhibit was indoors. I must say, though, the crowding together of these elements into those tiny plots gave the small spaces an importance they wouldn't have had otherwise. They were genuine, albeit teensy "gardens," and lovely, too.

Actually, Bobbie and I learned a lot from the interior designers' displays. The use of structures was very effective. A beautiful urn is a great complement to even the dullest bush, and there was one decorative effect that I especially liked. The designer had made instant topiary columns by placing chicken wire around a post and sticking boxwood cuttings in the openings in the same way as one might stuff tissue paper into a Rose Bowl float. Such "faux topiary" would not last long outdoors, but it would be sensational used as decoration for a wedding or an affair, or a wedding following an affair, or an affair following a wedding, or any experience that doesn't last long but is splendid while it lasts.

One exhibit that got a lot of attention consisted of a beautifully made wrought-iron gate with masses of *Malva sylvestris zebrina* planted behind it. *Malva sylvestris zebrina* resembles a hollyhock. It is about four or five feet tall with striped flowers in white and rose-pink. One *Malva sylvestris zebrina* plant would have been attractive. A clump of them was a knockout. I counted thirteen plants in just one of the clumps, proof of the fact that you need many more plants than you think to make a generous display.

The dramatic juxtaposition of a big clump of one variety of flower against the strong structure of the fence was an example of design that I think every gardener could profitably copy.

The *Malva sylvestris zebrina* exhibit was not only a lesson in the value of structure and the massing of plants, but especially in the dangers of pride—the kind that goeth before a fall. This variety is not very well known, so everyone in the crowd kept asking, "What is it? What is the name of that flower?"

Trying to be helpful, I said, *"Malva sylvestris zebrina."*

More people came over. "What did she say?"

"Malva sylvestris zebrina," I explained, "is a sort of hollyhock. Very easy to grow from seed." As more and more people asked me about the plant, I began to feel pretty important and puffed up, especially when some of the crowd began to take notes. I came down with an instant case of galloping hubris. I started to expound on malvas in general, the prodigious height of my own specimens, the need for more gardeners in the world, and was just starting to segue into a discussion of the imminent destruction of the planet by an overly industrialized society, when Bobbie grabbed my arm.

"You sound like a total fruitcake, Cassandra. Let's go." Then she dragged me away to the next exhibit.

The New York City Street Consortium featured a display of the sort of gardening that can be done around the bases of conventional street tree plantings. Pink hyacinths, azaleas, and tulips burst out of the squares around the trees in great abundance. It looked like a dream of what a city street ought to look like in the best of all possible worlds. Of course, it would have looked more realistically like New York City if they had scattered some garbage around the hyacinths and dogs had been allowed in the hall. But we weren't there for realism, anyway.

After the *Malva sylvestris zebrina* incident, the next dramatic event on our journey occurred at a garden ornament exhibit that occupied a large area in the center of the hall. These ornaments were not the usual plaster gnomes, jockeys, and religious statuary one sees for sale at roadside garden centers. Instead, they had benches, urns, and fountains copied from the classic gardens of France, Italy, England, and upscale places like that.

These ornaments were manufactured out of a composition stone that does not have to be taken in every winter, because frost will not crack it, as it will cement or plaster. There were Roman and Etruscan vases, dolphin garden benches, Moorish fountains, statues of naked putti, and Gothic urns (I loved those).

The exhibit was presided over by two Englishmen in Savile Row suits. According to their identification badges, one of them had a hyphenated last name, and the other had a hyphenated first name. Innocently, I asked the price of the Gothic urns. This was obviously a mistake. Wordlessly, the one with the hyphenated first name handed me the price list, turned his back on me, and walked to the other side of the exhibit. I looked down at the paper; three-, four-, and five-figured numbers danced in front of my eyes like ants on a hot tin roof.

"We do have a complete catalog, but it costs five dollars," the hyphenated last name said through his nose in a "good school" accent, every syllable implying that I didn't look as if I could afford it. As he glanced at my clothes, his eye rested on a bit of tuna fish that had landed on my coat during lunch. I know when I'm being high-hatted! This was snobbery! Outrageous! I wasn't about to be outdone by a pair of English twits, even if they did have great accents! This is America. This is the flower show given by the New York Horticultural Society, whose one qualification for membership is an abiding love of gardens and the desire to learn more about them! Gardens, for God's sake, not Fabergé eggs! I love gardens! I even know what a *Malva sylvestris zebrina* is! I belong!

I looked him up and down right back, my eyeballs aggressively seeking a grease spot or a piece of lint on his clothing. No such luck, so I settled for a wen on his cheek. I smiled slightly, acknowledging the blemish. He smiled back, never once taking his eyes off the tuna fish. Our eyes dueled like rapiers in the silent, international language of Attitude.

Finally, Bobbie interrupted. "Excuse me," she said, "have you a card?" The other salesman gave her one. "Oh," she murmured, examining the card, "so you're 'in trade' in New Jersey! So convenient to bridges and tunnels." Devastation! Thank you, Bobbie. They nodded an unspoken touché, and we moved on. *Veni, vidi, vici.*

The various specialty plant societies were well represented. There were excellent displays of begonias, orchids, gesneriads (African violets and their cousins), and other favorites. Some of the exhibits were eccentric. The Rare Pit and Plant Council was run by a clown with a collection of plants grown from the pits of fruits and vegetables found in New York City's ethnic markets. These plants reminded me of the houseplants I used to grow in Brooklyn. The clown, who was dressed like Ronald McDonald, complete with plastic nose, had an avocado plant, a small nectarine tree, an allspice bush, as well as plants started from mango, guava, chestnut, sweet potato, peanut, kumquat, lime, pomegranate (in flower!), and pineapple. He even had a coconut with an obscenely large sprout coming out of the top. I liked this exhibit very much. Growing plants from fruits and vegetables is a great way for kids to start gardening, and the lack of pretension of this display was a balm after the stoneyard boys.

No flower show would be complete without awards. Most of the exhibitors were given citations and medals; some even got two. Then there were the contests—ribbons were given out for the best window-box plantings, single specimens, and, of course, flower arrangements.

The winning flower arrangements were displayed in niches set into the walls. They were dramatically lit, and the inside walls of the niches were painted in colors that harmonized with each arrangement, so they all looked their best. Who wouldn't look good, sitting in a niche with flattering light and background? I'd like to get my picture taken in a setting like that some time.

Some of the arrangements, or floral designs, as they are called, were terrific. My favorite was an enormous vase overflowing with lilies, Rembrandt and parrot tulips, pussy willows, and lots of smaller but lovely backup fillers. It looked like seventeenth-century Dutch floral painting. Apparently, the judges liked it, too, because there was a big blue ribbon hanging off the bottom.

Toward the back of the hall, various companies had rented space, and there were booths with plants, seeds, botanical prints, books, and other gardening-related supplies and novelties for sale. To their credit, not one of the concessionaires sold T-shirts. I would venture to say that the flower show is one of the few public functions in America at which no one was selling T-shirts, which is why I liked it. Go to any church bazaar, school playground, street fair, state fair, rock concert, corporate convention, or war, and there's a guy selling T-shirts decorated with somebody's logo or opinion. Must every event be commemorated by a T-shirt? What's next? Guys selling T-shirts at funerals with "R.I.P." and "Death is nature's way of telling you to slow down" emblazoned across the front? I only mention this to emphasize how much I appreciated the Horticultural Society's restraint.

Bobbie and I shopped. Well, browsed, mostly, but we bought some seeds and bulbs at the New York Botanical Garden concession. They had some nice unusual vegetable and flower seeds, like mustard greens, arugula, and Italian sunflowers, as well as packaged dahlias, canna lilies, calla lilies, and amaryllis bulbs. I was looking for *Malva sylvestris zebrina* seeds. The truth is, I had never actually grown *Malva sylvestris zebrina*; I had only read about it. I had to have some seeds to try in my own garden, just to see if they were as good as I'd told all those people they were. I looked all over and couldn't find any.

At the counter, as I was paying for some other seeds, I couldn't resist giving it one more try. "Excuse me," I asked the boy at the register, "do you have any *Malva sylvestris zebrina* seeds?" I felt sure he would have no idea what I was talking about.

"You know," he said, "it's very funny that you should ask for those particular seeds. They're easy to grow, you know."

Taken aback, I said, "I know."

"We had lots of them," he continued, "but a while ago, a herd of about fifty people came in here and bought them all up. It seems there was a saleswoman over by the exhibits who lectured about them for half an hour."

Maybe I didn't sound like such a total fruitcake after all.

GARDEN PATHS

Finally, it is the end of March, and it looks like spring has arrived at last. The witch hazels and the crocuses are in flower, the sap is rising in the trees, the sun warms the earth, the rain waters it, and all is well except that the ground is a slimy sea of mud. Not so romantic, eh? It is the time of year when every flower garden needs to have some sort of path.

Some gardeners avoid laying stone or brick paths by placing the flower beds around the perimeter of the yard and leaving a patch of lawn in the center. There is nothing wrong with this design. It's pretty basic, and grass makes a perfectly good walking surface under most conditions. It's not so hot if you need to cross it in high heels, or like now when it is a sea of mud, or if it's in an area that gets a lot of heavy traffic at all times of the year, such as the path between the backdoor and the garage. But other than that, grass makes a terrific path (even though it has to be mowed every week).

Since I have a cottage garden, I have lots of flowering perennials and shrubs and very little lawn, so garden paths are a necessity. The decision that Walter and I faced was not whether to make paths or not, but what kind of paths to make. We wanted to use a material that would be as beautiful and as inexpensive as possible, in that order.

Beauty is a function of harmony, as the great world philosophers—Confucius, Aristotle, Yogi Gupta, and Yogi Berra—would tell you. Our first consideration was to make sure that the garden paths would harmonize with the style of the house.

It seems as good a time as any to talk about style and how to choose a style when constructing garden features. No consideration of style would be complete without a discussion of taste. What is good taste in gardening? How do you know what kind of paths or style of fence is right for a particular place? What kind of garden ornaments will be pleasing, and what kind will look awful? And don't you wish your next-door neighbor had asked those questions before he put that plastic burro and those classic American icons—pink flamingos—on the lawn? These are difficult questions to answer, but answers do exist.

I have compiled a short list of my own rules of what constitutes good taste in gardens and garden ornament, which I have gleaned from numerous authors, such as John Brookes, Christopher Lloyd, Russell Page, and, of course, Gertrude Jekyll, as well as from study and observation of the best gardens I could find. These rules are a compendium of advice from all of these sources. Take them for what they are worth, and feel free to flout them if it suits you. *"De gustibus non est disputandum."* (In matters of taste there is no dispute. At least not with me.)

Rule 1: *A garden should suit the place where it is located.* In other words—where are you? Are you living in temperate downtown Seattle, the arid desert outside Phoenix, or in a suburb of Cleveland? Wherever possible, the climate and history of the area should determine the kind of plants that you grow, as well as the overall style of the garden. For instance, the aforementioned famous flamingos would not look so bad in Florida or Louisiana, especially if they were alive, but they are in bad taste in Las Vegas, Nevada, where the last flamingo flew south during the Jurassic period when the Great Nevada ocean receded. I take that back. Everything in Las Vegas is in bad taste, so flamingos would be entirely appropriate.

Rule 2: *The style of the garden should be compatible with the style of the house.* Rule 2a: *The style of the garden should be no more formal than the style of the house.* Rule 2b: *The style of the garden can be less formal than the style of the house.* For example, you have a small suburban Cape Cod cottage on a quarter acre of land. You are a person of modest means but very good taste, an assumption proven by the fact that you have bought this book. Following Rule 2, you can do one of three things. First of all, you can make a traditional Cape Cod cottage garden, with a white picket fence, a brick path, symmetrical plantings, and an arbor with roses 'round the front door. By enhancing the architecture, and not making it more formal than the house, the garden will be in harmony with the Cape Cod. This approach may not be exciting and avant-garde, but at the very least, the property won't be funny looking and might even have a great deal of charm.

Rules 2a and 2b offer other alternatives. You could make the yard less formal than the house. This means that the garden could have an unpainted wooden fence, asymmetrical plantings, and paths made of stone or gravel instead of brick. Or you could go wild, literally, and plant an informal hedge, with trees and a shady ground cover underneath. This type of planting would make the Cape Cod look like a cottage in the woods.

Let's assume, for a moment, that you are the same person but with limited means and bad taste—one of millions. You are unhappy with the charming but humble Cape Cod. You wish you were a big shot, a big cheese, a big wheel, a big wheel of cheese, a mogul, a mucky-muck, a somebody, a star. You're not content to be a mere mortal who's lucky to have a decent life with a loving family and a house of your own.

So what do you do? You try to make your house look like more than just a Cape Cod on a quarter acre of land; you want a palace. You say, "Isn't every man's home his castle?"

I say, "Every man's home is his home." Nevertheless, you go ahead and landscape that quarter acre as if it were the last place on earth. Assuming that you have left the house alone, which I doubt, you dress the yard up for an International Expo. You put a circular driveway in white gravel leading to the front door, because white gravel seems Japanese and Zen. In the center, you place a large cement copy of the Trevi Fountain in Rome, so Continental. You clip the four shrubs in front of the house in the shape of gumdrops to resemble the topiary at Chatsworth. You mow the rest to imitate the parklike expanses of an English landscape, only smaller. You add an American flag, just in case the neighbors have forgotten what country they're in, and a few gnomes and saints just for luck. These garden "ornaments" are cheaper than shrubbery, and you figure no one will notice that they're plastic. You put realistic plastic daffodils in the window boxes even though the neighbors get suspicious when the daffodils are still blooming in August. It is a front garden only the visitors to the World's Fair could appreciate.

Horrible to relate, the yard I just described really exists across the street from my Aunt Dotty on Long Island. Really. My description of it contains no exaggerations, except for literary purposes. This family has created a monument to bad taste. You should see how these people dress.

This leads me to Rule 3.

Rule 3: *Don't use plastic in the garden.*

Rule 4: *When in doubt, clean, comfortable, and well maintained is always tasteful.* Healthy-looking trees, shrubs, and flowers are always a pleasure to see, even without an effort at a particular style, and some of the nicest gardens I've seen had nothing more to recommend them than a sense of order. Trees of the same varieties planted in rows along a lane or driveway are always beautiful (especially if they are cherry trees in bloom!). Shrubs planted in rows give form to the landscape. Even flowering plants in rows look better than when they're dotted at random all over the yard. When in doubt, keep it simple and neat.

Now let's assume that you are the happiest of creatures, a person with piles of money and the taste of Coco Chanel. You have acres of land, a lake with an island in the middle of it, a rose garden, a kitchen garden with espaliered fruit trees against the walls, a flower garden with a seventeenth-century sundial in the center, and a staff of ten to keep it all looking wonderful. I say good luck to you, best wishes, and I hope you feel very guilty. The money you are spending on those gardens would probably feed the poor of Bangladesh for a year. Think about that the next time you send the maid out to cut flowers for a cocktail party.

Since our house is a nineteenth-century cottage, we decided to make the garden path out of flat stones rather than brick, which I associate with eighteenth-century houses. We originally wanted to use large squares of slate or Vermont bluestone, but after pricing them, we decided that food was more important. We would have to make do with crazy paving, which is fine, according to Rule 2, since it is less formal than the style of the house. Crazy paving is an assortment of irregularly shaped flat stones of different types fitted together like a jigsaw puzzle. When properly placed, it can be very artistic and as neat and straight as any brick path.

It's hard for me to describe a crazy paving path, exactly, but it was no trouble at all to lay one—Walter did it. To minimize expense, we collected flat stones from along roadsides all over the county. People riding in the car with us thought we were crazy. Everytime we passed a flat stone along the highway, I would suddenly shout, "Walter, stop the car! There's a rock!" My mother, sitting in the backseat, would say, "A rock? I wanted a restaurant." Walter would stop the car and we'd take the rock and put it in the trunk. After a couple of years of lugging large flat stones in the back of the car, we had enough stones for Walter to make some very nice crazy paving paths, and we'd saved enough money to fix the shocks.

Most garden experts say that you should make paths at least four feet wide. Four feet is wide enough for two thin people to walk abreast, if they are very friendly. That is also wide enough so that when the flowers spill out onto the path, you won't be tripping over them as you pass by. It is also a good idea for a path to go somewhere, such as to and from the house or to another part of the garden. Use the shortest route possible. I know many people think that curving paths are romantic, and they are, but not in winter. Nobody wants to go meandering along an icy path when there is a more direct route available, and they won't. If the path is picturesque and circuitous, everyone, especially dogs and children, will take the shortest route even if it is across a flower bed. The smartest thing to do is to put the path along the shortcut and design the garden accordingly. We made the paths along straight lines going from the front to the back of the house and between the flower borders. We figured that the flowers and the irregular stones would provide enough visual movement without having the paths going all curvy as well.

Walter was a great layer of paths. He had to be, given the wide variety of flat, and not so flat, stones he had to deal with. Laying a crazy paving path is a lot like making order out of chaos and he went about it in a very orderly, rational manner. He used tools, like a spirit level, a chisel, and a hammer, stone-age innovations I would never have thought of using. I would have simply thrown the rocks down in a frantic effort to get them to land within a straight line and after a couple of hours, I would have been ready to kill myself, thereby making a Sylvia Plath path.

Before hoisting a single stone, Walter stuck twigs in the ground to mark off straight parallel lines along the length of the path and tied string between them to act as visual guides. Then he removed the sod down to a depth of six inches and threw it into the wheelbarrow. I took it away and used the sod to fill in some low spots in the lawn or piled it up for use as topsoil later.

By the next morning, Walter had a straight trench that was four feet wide and twenty feet long. Our next-door neighbor on the side opposite the parking lot had recently dumped a load of gravel onto his driveway, and he had extra, so we had a good supply of drainage material on which to set the crazy paving stones. We put a level bed of gravel down in the trench, about three or four inches deep. A couple of inches of gravel or builder's sand under a stone or brick path will make the difference between having one that sits where you put it for many years, or one that shifts and wobbles every spring like a ten-year-old at church.

Walter began to fit the stones together. He placed the largest stones first and then those with the straightest sides along the edges of the path. Then he filled in with the smaller ones. If a stone did not butt up perfectly with its neighbor, he chiseled off a bit of the edge to get a tighter fit. He didn't try to get all the stones to fit together perfectly. Part of the charm of crazy paving is having a few tiny plants pop up between the cracks here and there, but too much of that and you leave the idea of ''path'' and enter the world of ''mess.''

Every six feet or so, Walter placed a row of paving bricks that we had found in a landfill at the edge of town. The row of paving bricks, laid perpendicular to the path, divided it into sections, made a frame for the stones, and gave order to the pattern. It looked marvelous.

Since the stones were of unequal thickness, Walter used a spirit level to make sure that they were even across the top and made his adjustments by removing or adding gravel underneath. It took Walter a lot of time and effort to lay paths that summer. And I must say that our son Sam and I did help. We were the apprentices. We brought the stones from the pile next to the driveway around the house to where the Master was working. It was a wonderful family experience. We all learned a great deal, especially young Sam, who found out what to say when a large stone lands on your foot.

Flowers growing off in a border by themselves look good, but flowers growing along a stone path look great. It was the same with the arbor. Flowers growing along a stone path look great, but flowers growing along a stone path leading to an arbor covered with roses and clematis look like poetry. And an arch, being sort of a doorway, immediately establishes the garden as a separate room.

After finishing the paths, Walter built a rusticated arbor using the trunks of the ailanthus and maple tree saplings we had cut down when we first cleared the yard. Rusticated garden structures, like rusticated furniture, are made of unfinished, unvarnished wood. Usually, even the bark is left on, so the entire effect is that of pieces of trees fashioned to form a man-made object. Rusticated structures are considered informal, so they were very appropriate for our cottage garden. It would have been just as appropriate to use Gothic arches made of expensive finished lumber, painted in the same dark green as the house trim, but one guess why we didn't.

Building the arches was a breeze compared to laying the paths. We had houseguests the weekend that Walter decided to make the arbor. Mary and Jimmy are city people. Mary is a comedy writer, not a carpenter. Jimmy is a novelist. His idea of outdoor activity is playing baseball in Central Park, not digging holes to erect garden arbors, but he and Mary seemed to be eager to help and, as good hosts, we couldn't very well refuse them. Mary held the branches while Walter sawed, and Jimmy dug four holes, each one a foot and a half wide and two feet deep. I was indoors at the time, making my famous gourmet hamburgers. They have ketchup on them.

We wanted the arbor to form a rusticated Gothic arch, so Walter found curved branches and cut them to size. With Mary's help, he then nailed them to four upright sapling trunks and used smaller pieces to give the whole thing stability. When they were finished, the structure was about ten feet tall. After Jimmy had finished digging the heavy clay soil out of the holes, they sank the whole structure a couple of feet into the ground and put gravel around the trunks so they wouldn't rot too quickly. When the arch was finally in place, it was eight feet tall at its highest point.

The whole project took no more than six or seven hours. Afterward, I brought out lemonade and hamburgers. Our guests would have enjoyed going for a swim, but we don't have a pond or a pool, so they had to settle for a hot shower and a nap. I think Mary and Jimmy enjoyed their weekend very much. My only regret is that in the five years since then, they have always been too busy to come back.

With an arch to define the space and paths to act as visual frames for the flower pictures, the planting I had already done looked as though it had always been there and all I had to think about was how to improve and refine the plantings. My husband, my son, and my friends had all done their part, and I was grateful. But I began to detect a definite waning of enthusiasm. After spending two vacations laying paths and building structures, every time the word *garden* was mentioned to Walter and Sam, they cleared out of the room as though somebody had dropped tear gas. I suspected that from now on, I would be working on the garden alone.

APRIL

*Spring cleaning the garden is a lot more fun
than spring cleaning the house.*

Spring Cleaning the Garden

Spring cleaning the garden is much more fun than spring cleaning the house. As I rake up the old remains of last year's garden and the leaves that have collected over the winter, little green growing shoots are revealed. Finding green living things growing after the debris of winter is swept away is a delightful discovery. Fortunately, it is a discovery that happens only occasionally inside the house.

For me, the time to clean the garden is spring rather than fall. There is some dispute about this, which I'll get to in a minute. Clearing the area around the plants allows the spring sun to get to the roots faster, the whole garden looks better, and it gives me something to do in early April. I cut down the dry empty stalks and gently nudge the dead refuse from around the newly emerging leaves, using my old gap-toothed lawn rake. The dead leaves come off easily, and the little plants, which are attached by roots, remain. The green shoots underneath are as cute as infants. I bend down to examine them more closely and am shocked to see that many of the lovely green shoots that have emerged are actually perennial weeds. But after a long winter, I'm glad to see even them.

I pause a moment to contemplate the wonder of spring and the joy of renewed life, then I heartlessly pull the little fellows from the soft tender earth, like a Hun pulling a babe from its mother's breast. I have a certain amount of guilt about this, but I, too, am a part of nature, and my nature is to pull weeds.

Some compulsively neat gardeners tell you to remove all the spent foliage and stems of perennials in the fall rather than the spring. If you don't remove all trace of the previous year's growth, they warn, you will be encouraging hideous pests and dangerous diseases. I have no patience with such fastidiousness. Oh, horrors! All those contagious stems! All those poisonous dead leaves! Typhoid Mary! They ignore the fact that the whole natural world has had old stems and leaves on it every winter since time began. Who raked the forest primeval every fall? Dinosaurs? I think their real reason is more aesthetic than antiseptic. It looks neat and morally upright to have bare ground in front of the house, swept and scrubbed, like a clean kitchen floor.

Taking my cue from nature, I have always assumed that the old leaves remaining on the garden served some important purposes, namely, to cover and protect the roots of the plants from heaving out of the ground as the earth freezes and thaws during the winter, and to break down and become humus. So I leave the leaves alone. Standing stalks add "winter interest" to the landscape, especially when the snow covers them and they look like funny animals. The critters get pretty beat-up-looking after a blustery winter, but the dead stems serve as markers that make it easy to find the plant while the roots are still dormant.

In the fall, I remove only the debris of plants that I know for sure really do have diseases that would cause the plant to suffer if the leaves were left to rot.

I do have a few plants that hold fungi and pests in their leaves from year to year, plants that would be reinfected by diseases if the leaves were left on the ground. For example, the peony is notorious for harboring *Botrytis*, a fungus that causes the leaves to wither, and in really bad cases, destroys the flower buds. I've never heard of *Botrytis* actually killing a peony. Nothing short of dynamite could do that. In my garden, *Botrytis* does some minor damage to the leaves and that's it. My personal preference is to ignore any disease that doesn't actually kill a plant, but since some of my peonies are in the front of the house, vanity prompts me to make the effort to keep them looking as well groomed as possible.

There are basically two ways to control *Botrytis*. One is to spray with a fungicide on a regular basis, and the other is to cut the stems and leaves right to the ground in the fall and burn them or throw them out with the trash. The first alternative is out of the question. I refuse to spray my garden with any chemical that has the suffix "-cide" in its name. "-Cide" means kill, as in herbicide, meaning to murder a plant; insecticide, to murder an insect; homicide, a person; regicide, a king; patricide, a father; fratricide, a brother; matricide, a mattress . . . and so forth.

Botrytis lives in the old leaves from year to year, so discarding them controls the *Botrytis* without committing fungicide. I chop the peony down to the ground in October, pick up every bit of leaf or stem I can find and throw it out with the trash. This precaution has really worked. My peonies look as dainty and fresh as debutantes all year.

Phlox is prone to mildew. Don't ask me the difference between fungus and mildew. I'm not at all sure that there is one. All I know is that fungus grows between your toes, and mildew grows on the shower curtain. By the end of a humid summer, mildewed phlox are covered with a matte gray finish, similar to thick dust on furniture. I tolerate dust on the furniture, so why not on the phlox? Mildew does not kill the phlox, just gives them a ghostly appearance. There are several remedies for dusty phlox. One recommendation is to spray with a mildewcide. Forget that. Another is to keep the air circulating around the phlox so that the leaves dry quickly. I do this by cutting out all but five shoots per clump in the spring shortly after they emerge. There are fewer flower clusters per plant, but the fewer the stalks, the more magnificent the blooms, since all the plant's energy will go into making those flower clusters as luscious as possible.

Keeping plenty of air circulating around each plant usually stops mildew from forming, but during a particularly hot and humid summer, sometimes the leaves turn gray anyway. If that happens, I give up. If anyone asks me about them, I say they're called "Silver Phlox," a rare gray-leaved variety. If the person I'm talking to is a knowledgeable gardener, at least it's good for a laugh.

Irises and hollyhocks get cut down in the fall for the same reason as peonies and phlox; old leaves can reinfect the plant if left to overwinter on the ground. Otherwise, if a plant looks clean and healthy, I leave it alone. I let the old stems stand to make artistic patterns on the snow and the old leaves to act as winter mulch, just like in nature.

Nobody ever walked into a forest and said, gee, what a mess! And nobody who has ever walked into my garden has said that, either. At least to my face.

DAFFODILS—A LOVE SONG

I wandered lonely as a cloud
That floats on high o'er vales and hills,
When all at once I saw a crowd,
A host, of golden daffodils;
Beside the lake, beneath the trees,
Fluttering and dancing in the breeze.

William Wordsworth, "I Wandered Lonely as a Cloud"

I know just how he felt. Since reading that poem at the age of twelve or so, one of the ambitions of my life has been to have a host of golden daffodils blooming in my yard. How many daffodils are in a host, anyway? Later in the poem, Mr. Wordsworth goes on to tell us that he saw ten thousand at a glance. Allowing for poetic hyperbole, we can probably knock that figure down to about six thousand. Six thousand daffodils would be something worth seeing in April. (It would be even more extraordinary in September!)

If I had six thousand daffodils, I would plant them thickly under the lilac hedge, naturalize them under the trees on the embankment at the rear of my property, and continue them along the driveway leading from the garage to the street. Naturalizing is planting bulbs or other plants in and among trees, in woodlands and meadows to resemble the way they would look if they had grown there themselves. In other words, I would have great swaths and drifts of them growing like wildflowers all around the perimeter of my yard. They would be so welcome in early spring, I would want to go out and hug and kiss them for being the only really brilliant, colorful thing in the landscape. Between you and me, I probably *would* hug and kiss them, when no one was looking.

What a springtime abundance those daffodils would make, raising their heads in a song to the vernal equinox like the Mormon Tabernacle Choir hitting a high note. A "host" indeed. Yes, about six thousand ought to do it.

The only thing that stands between me and my Wordsworthian dream is money. A quick calculation tells me that six thousand daffodils would cost $2,700—wholesale. That figure is just a little over my daffodil budget, about $2,650 over, to be exact. I can only afford to plant about a hundred daffodils a year. At that rate, it will take me sixty years to plant six thousand! I don't need the roof to fall on my head to realize that I have just dreamed another impossible dream.

Or have I? Daffodils, unlike tulips, tend to increase each year. If you've ever grown them, you've noticed that after a couple of years, there are four or five flowers where you planted one. A daffodil bulb will divide and redivide endlessly. That's why, like the peony, it is one of the few flowers you can find around abandoned farmhouses, still blooming and increasing in numbers fifty years after the farmer and his wife have moved to heaven, or the other place, Boca Raton. If you dig up a clump when no one is nearby and there is no danger of being shot, you'll find that there are scores of little bulbs in each clump, the progeny of a dozen or so planted by the farmer's wife in 1942. If you take these home, separate them, and plant them in your own yard, within a couple of years, you'll have a hundred daffodils for the mere price of a trespassing fine or imprisonment or both. I had this adventure once, and I consider it one of the great cheap thrills of my gardening career. I am not advocating trespassing, especially on my property, but there is no law against having a shovel in the trunk of your car.

Although I dream of naturalizing daffodils around the perimeter of my property, I would not plant them in the flower beds. There are a couple of reasons for this. I dig in my flower beds all the time, and I hate the thought of slicing through a dormant bulb in the middle of the summer. The second reason is that the leaves of the daffodil have to ripen and wither away without interference in order for the bulb to store enough energy to bloom and increase the following year. In practice, this means that you have to let the leaves turn brown and look as attractive as overbleached hair for at least a month and a half. The leaves also have a tendency to flop over during this time, and a good size clump can smother its emerging neighbors for a foot around. I've seen this happen and the results can be tragic, as the following story will illustrate.

My friend Bobbie had planted daffodils in her perennial border. Fortunately, she had not planted many, only about five or six of a variety called "February Silver." After a few years, "February Silver" had established five enormous clumps with twenty-five flowers to a clump. This was lovely in early spring, but by June, these clumps had flopped over the delphiniums and before it was noticed had *killed* them. Tragic. Okay, maybe this isn't as tragic as a fire in an orphanage, but it's damned annoying. I suggested that we braid the ripening leaves together like a little girl's pigtails, a technique I had read about in one of my English gardening books. This would prevent the leaves from flopping as they matured, and at least they would look like neatly coifed overbleached hair. We started to braid, but after fifteen minutes we realized that this was one of those stupid make-work gardening tasks only a heartless employer of a large staff of servants or a seriously anal-retentive personality could love. Compassionately, I offered to dig the clumps out of the border for her and get rid of them by taking them home and planting them in my own yard. Rather ungratefully, I thought, she only let me have one clump.

I took the clump, separated all the little bulbs, and planted them along with my other daffodils under the lilac hedge. This gave me an idea. If I could dig up and replant other people's daffodils, why couldn't I do that with my own? By now, the daffodils I had planted when I first bought the house had themselves formed clumps, and since they were conveniently in my own yard, I even had the luxury of waiting until fall to dig them up. Digging the bulbs in the fall would allow the plants to go through their normal cycle, so they would be moved with the least possible disturbance.

So this spring, while they are blooming and are uppermost in my mind, I have marked each clump of daffodils with a small stake so I can find them in the fall when it's time to dig them up. Using a fork, I'll gently lift each clump, separate the bulbs, and replant them in long S-shaped trenches. At the bottom of the trench, I will add compost and bonemeal to feed the little pipsqueaks. Some of the larger ones will bloom next spring; the rest may take an extra year.

If I replant old clumps and buy a hundred new bulbs each year, I will have annually increased my daffodil collection by two hundred instead of one hundred. That means it will take me only thirty years, instead of sixty, to accomplish my dream! No, wait—less! After five years, each of the older clumps can be redivided into drifts, so that the population will not increase arithmetically, but exponentially! By the tenth year, the first hundred daffodils will have increased not times ten, but to the tenth power! Like cats! My mother-in-law had two cats that she had neglected to spay, and two years later, she had fifty-two! Oh, beloved daffodils, that reproduce like cats but smell much better. How wonderful you are.

If the daffodil population can be increased exponentially, why not keep going? Why not fill up the neighbor's yard? The neighborhood? The Hudson Valley? Imagine the entire Hudson Valley covered with a million hosts of ten thousand golden daffodils, white daffodils, pink daffodils . . . daffodils everywhere, on roadsides, in woodlands, surrounding parking lots, schools, condos, everywhere except in flower borders! Each spring would be as golden as fall! And every fall, thousands of daffodil lovers would be out digging up old clumps and replanting them. Down the Hudson Valley, through New Jersey and Pennsylvania and on to the Midwest! Today the yard, tomorrow the Northern Hemisphere!

Arbor Day: How to Plant a Tree

Very few activities in life are as rewarding as planting a tree on Arbor Day. It's one of the nicest holidays of the year, but you don't hear much about it lately. Tree planting is work, but it is also an act of hope and faith in the future. I suspect that the reason we don't hear very much about Arbor Day anymore is because (a) Earth Day gets most of the publicity, (b) department stores don't have Arbor Day sales, and (c) hope and faith in the future are in short supply nowadays.

Although Arbor Day is a national holiday, the actual date varies from state to state, depending on the local climate. In New York State, it is always celebrated on the last Friday of April, which is a good time to plant trees in my area. Arbor Day was first introduced by an agriculturalist named Julius Sterling Morton in 1872 and by the end of the nineteenth century was observed in every state and territory of the Union, as well as in Canada, Spain, Britain, France, Norway, Russia, Japan, and China. It was still religiously observed in the 1950s in my grammar school in Brooklyn.

I remember a chilly, rainy April morning when I was in third grade. The school principal, Miss Hamilton, called all the classes out of doors to witness the planting of a tree next to the playground. The school custodian had dug a large hole, and next to the hole sat a little tree, not much taller than I was then.

There was a ceremonial quality about the occasion, like an ancient rite of spring. In our ceremony, Miss Hamilton was Demeter, the goddess of the earth. I wish I could say that she was as beautiful and compassionate as that deity, but in fact Miss Hamilton was a stone pillar of moral rectitude. She had steel gray hair, which she wore in a very short tortured bob, a large wardrobe of man-tailored gray suits, and support stockings that she wore with an equally impressive selection of sensible shoes.

Miss Hamilton wasn't married. Marriage would have been too frivolous an occupation for her. Of course, she never had children of her own. Unmarried ladies didn't have children in those days. Miss Hamilton was a serious person of the old school, my old school. She was the first really serious person I had ever known.

When Miss Hamilton spoke, we listened. Before the planting of the tree, she gave a little speech. She said that the planting of trees, like the education of children, was a gift to the future. We do not plant trees for the pleasure of those who are here today, but for those who will come after. This young tree, she said, which looks so small and puny sitting with its roots tied up in its little rag of burlap, would one day be great and tall, with branches over the heads of the people passing by underneath. It would, she promised, one day be taller than the school itself.

I'm not sure I believed her. How could a stick become a tree? But she looked like a true believer as she unwrapped the burlap and placed the tree in its prepared hole. Some of the girls got a chance to take a spadeful of earth and fill in the hole, and some of the boys got a chance to stomp on the earth once it was in place. Afterward, Miss Hamilton took a bucket and carefully poured water all around the little tree, and that was it. The ceremony was over, and we went indoors.

Last year, Walter and I drove past the school yard on our way to someplace else, and there it was, the tree I had helped to plant so many years before. The neighborhood around the school was as run-down and decadent as the world has become in the thirty years since my grammar-school days. And I'm sure that many of the children Miss Hamilton educated, as her gift to the future, would be a sore disappointment to her. But the tree, the tree! The tree was in full leaf, broad and majestic, pure as a Grecian temple dedicated to Demeter, and sure enough, it was taller than the school.

I loved that tree-planting ceremony. Perhaps I remember it so vividly because it was the first time I realized that one could actually plant trees, that a tree was more than just something that grew, spontaneously, along the sidewalk. Perhaps it was the first time I had ever even noticed the earth or the trees. And then, of course, there was that magic promise—an ugly little stick would turn into something grand and beautiful. Without a doubt, that day affected me profoundly, because that was the day I first discovered nature.

The wonder and amazement that I had felt, as a child on Arbor Day, was nothing compared to my absolute astonishment the first time I saw the countryside. I was in my early twenties.

Amazingly, I had never actually seen trees and plants growing wild until I was a young adult. I know it's difficult to believe that I had never been out in the country, but it's true. It was not that my family was so poor that I was a candidate for the Fresh Air Fund. I'd been around. I had seen Long Island. I was familiar with the lawns and shrubberies of suburbia, and I assumed, without thinking about it, that you had to do something to make a plant grow, like placing it in the ground, watering and pruning it. Of course, I knew that there were such things as forests and meadows and wilderness. I'm not an idiot. I had read about them and seen them in Walt Disney movies, like everyone else. But it was not until I was about twenty-one that I actually walked in wild woods and golden meadows, met nature on its own terms, and surrendered completely.

I had been invited out to the country to meet George and Paul, friends of Ron and Bobbie. These two guys had acquired an old farm in a remote part of Pennsylvania that had not been worked in many years. They were later to turn the place into an extraordinary series of gardens, but at the time, the farmhouse was surrounded by woods and in front of it stretched an enormous meadow.

I remember the first time I strolled through the meadow. Strolled is an understatement. I danced, I sang, I was inebriate of air that I could not see, for a change. I was mad for it.

It was late summer; the meadow was full of goldenrod and asters. I picked some, amazed at the abundance of it all. I had never seen so many flowers in one place before. All these flowers and no one took care of them? How was that possible? Is this what the earth was really like? Did everyone know about this? Oh God, how beautiful it all was! How beautiful! How beautiful! It left me gasping and breathless. I ran through the meadow, singing selections from *The Sound of Music* and dancing like Isadora Duncan, until I was exhausted.

It was a moment of epiphany, similar to that described by James Joyce in *A Portrait of the Artist as a Young Man*, when he saw a young girl bathing in the ocean and knew at that instant he wanted to become an artist, except that my moment took place in a meadow in Pennsylvania instead of by the sea in Dublin, and I was a young woman who wanted to become a gardener.

By discovering nature so relatively late in life, I had been given the opportunity to appreciate it as though I were an alien from another planet. I was an alien from a world of brick and stone who had been dropped onto the green and golden earth to explore it for the first time. It was all new to me, and I took nothing for granted.

I still plant trees. Although I removed the weedy trees that had grown up around the house, I left the ones growing on the slope in the back to encourage the small woodland that is only one hundred feet wide and fifty feet long, and I add a new tree each year. Last year, I planted a white pine in the corner behind the garage. The year before that, I planted some shrubby dogwood (*Cornus alba* 'Siberica') to hold the slope's earth in place, and this year, at the bottom of the slope, I added an oak that will mature as the shorter-lived weedy locust and ailanthus trees die off. Right now the oak is only five feet tall and I'll be a very old lady by the time it will be visible from the house, if I ever live to see it at all. But my son will, and I believe in both of them.

As Julius Sterling Morton said: "If you seek my monument, look around you."

How to Plant a Tree

1. Dig a hole twice as big as the size of the root ball. The old adage, "plant a five-dollar tree in a ten-dollar hole," is correct. (If you can find a five-dollar tree, let me know.) Stuffing a tree into a too-small hole is mean.

Loosen the soil at the bottom of the hole, and fill in with the best earth you have available; a mixture of compost or manure and topsoil is wonderful. There is a small controversy about this among some horticulturists. One school of thought believes you should use the same soil as the surrounding area without adding anything extra, so that the tree doesn't get too used to such a rich diet and will be encouraged to send its roots out in search of nutrients. The other school of thought says that a newly transplanted baby needs the extra food to grow and establish itself properly. I belong to the latter, or the "Jewish mother" school of arborists. It couldn't hurt to pour a little tepid chicken soup into the hole, either.

2. After you've replaced the soil in the hole so that the young tree will sit an inch or two lower than the surrounding area, place the tree on top and pour in half a bucket of water. The earth under the tree will compact slightly, so add some more, and gently lift the tree until the soil has settled nicely around the roots.

If the tree is balled and burlapped, make slits in the burlap and don't remove it. The burlap bag retains moisture around the roots, and keeps them from being damaged by the planting procedure. Of course, if the burlap is actually plastic, take it off. If the tree is in a large pot, remove the pot, but keep as much of the soil intact as possible.

Sometimes, when a plant has been in a pot too long, the roots have grown in a circular pattern around the bottom (looking for a way out!). If you find this to be the case, you'll have to untangle the roots, gently separating them with your fingers like a comb on a child's knotted hair. Then you can go ahead and arrange them in the hole properly. If you don't do this, the roots will continue to grow in the circular pattern and will eventually strangle themselves, like a boa constrictor committing suicide.

3. Once the tree is in the hole, make sure it is straight and not leaning drunkenly over to one side. This is also the moment to step back and take a look at it from the place where you will see it most often, like the kitchen window or the front door. Adjust the tree so that its best side is facing you.

4. After making sure that the tree isn't too high or low, fill in the hole to about two inches from the top, and then run your fingers through the soil to eliminate any air pockets. It isn't such a good idea to stomp on it, unless you are as small and light as a grammar-school child. I'm not.

5. Water it all in. Add some more soil if it settles. The two-inch depression around the tree will make a little well to catch extra rain, and make watering easier. To help conserve water even more, it's a good idea to mulch.

6. This is the hardest part of all. After the tree is in place, prune off about one third of the stems and branches. I know it hurts, but you want the tree to concentrate on establishing new roots the first year. It puts a lot of stress on the plant to have to support more leaves than the shocked root system can handle. But if you plant that tree as carefully as I think you will, the top will be twice as large by the second year anyway.

7. There are a couple of other points to remember. First, do not give a newly planted tree any chemical fertilizer at the time of planting. It's too strong. Stick to the compost and the chicken soup. Second, water the young tree a lot in the first year. A bucket of water per week is about right, more if the weather is particularly hot.

It is not absolutely necessary to stake a tree with wires at the time of planting unless it is very tall, or in a windy location, or a spot where it is likely to be jostled, such as next to the sidewalk. If you do have to stake it, be sure to protect the bark by wrapping the wire, where it comes in contact with the tree, with a piece of rubber hose or thick burlap. And don't forget to remove the wires after a year or two, or the tree will try to grow around them for a while and eventually die. Horrible thought after all this trouble.

MAY

Everyone knows how to prune a shrub, right?

ANNUALS TO GROW INSTEAD OF MARIGOLDS

It's May tenth and I'm standing in the middle of a display of this year's offerings at Mike's Garden Center, the local nursery out by the mall. Everything is laid out at arm's reach on a series of large plywood tables, like the buffet at a wedding reception. Gazing out over the sea of display tables, I can see trays of pink, purple, red, white, blue, and even yellow petunias, already blooming, even though they are only one and a half inches tall—amazing! There are hundreds of geraniums in shades of red, orange, and pink; gray dusty miller; coleus in every leaf color known to man; blue lobelia; maroon and pink nicotiana; red, orange, white, and pink impatiens; purple, blue, and yellow pansies; red salvia; orange marigolds, small pale yellow marigolds, large fiery yellow marigolds, orange and brown marigolds, mixed giant marigolds, and some more marigolds in the back.

I look at all of this and say to myself, "Well, there's nothing here," and go home.

Some nurseries have a somewhat larger selection of annuals than Mike's, but not much. As Eleanor Perenyi pointed out in her book *Green Thoughts: A Writer in the Garden*, the only annuals that you are likely to see for sale at local nurseries are those that have been commercially bred to bloom in the seedling pot. The reasoning behind this strategy is that the average person will be more likely to purchase a plant that is already blooming, so he can see what it looks like. There must be some justification for this rationale, because Mike's business is booming. Customers are buying these plants as if they were lining up for a wedding buffet and the food is free and this is their last meal before execution. Mike is no fool; he gives the public what it wants and he couldn't care less if he bores me to death.

It's not that I have anything against petunias, marigolds, or coleus as such. I can honestly state that I am not a horticultural snob. I think any plant can look great if it is in an appropriate setting. Small-scale annuals like geraniums, petunias, dusty millers, and lobelias make terrific window-box plants; their bright colors are just the thing to zip up a house front. They look very classy in containers next to the front door or planted in drifts in front of taller and more substantial perennials.

I don't even mind the marigolds. They would add a lot of charm to a

93

vegetable garden and repel nematodes in the soil, as well. When I plant my vegetable garden, I will use them. But even then, I'll be darned if I'll buy marigold plants from Mike's at two or three dollars a six-pack. I'll grow them from seed, the way I do most of my annuals.

You might well ask why I bother growing annuals at all, since there are so many great perennials available. The virtue of annuals is that they can be relied upon to carry the garden through the August doldrums. Most perennials like to bloom either in the spring and early summer or in the early fall when the weather has cooled off a bit. So in August, there is usually a deadly lull.

The big-time, glamorous perennials that bloomed in June and early July, like peonies, irises, lupines, and delphiniums, have finished blooming and, like Norma Desmond in *Sunset Boulevard*, have started to look like aged movie stars past their prime. There is only one remedy left for them, cosmetic surgery. I cut and snip like a Hollywood Doctor Lookgood, removing the old, telltale wrinkled leaves and sagging seed pods. These plants may be past their sexual peak, but at least they look well preserved. It's just around this time that the annuals, the horticultural equivalents of this year's bombshell, come into full bloom.

As you probably know, an annual is a plant that grows from seed, blooms, and dies in one season, as opposed to a perennial, whose top dies down each fall, although the roots remain alive over the winter. The other germane fact about annuals is that there is a difference between tender annuals and hardy annuals. You might have noticed the letters HA or HHA printed on a packet of seeds. (I used to read those letters as ha or ha-ha, the joke's on you.) Actually, they mean Hardy Annual or Half Hardy Annual and they're telling you that the seeds of these plants will survive over the winter and make new plants the following year, because they're hardy in cold climates. They also mean you can plant newly purchased seeds before the last frost date in your area. Half Hardy Annuals will survive in half-cold climates, I suppose. Most of the plants sold at the local nursery are Tender Annuals (ta-ta!). They are native to Mexico, Africa, or other warm places, and their seeds will not survive a northern winter. Tender Annuals usually have to be started in a greenhouse or on an indoor windowsill every spring because a cold climate will cut their growing season short.

This information means a lot to me, because I can't afford to spend fifty bucks at the nursery every spring. I need that money for more important things—like daffodils. Neither do I have the patience (or the luck) to start tender seedlings on my windowsill. So I have to confine myself to annuals that I can plant directly in the ground in the spring. These hardy annuals tend to reseed themselves every year without replanting, and after the first season, I don't even have to buy new seeds. In fact, they come back so enthusiastically that I have to weed most of them out, or they'll take over! This may sound bothersome, but I would much rather pull out plants for free than spend a lot of money putting them in.

Here are my three favorite Poor (or cheap) People's Annuals that I would never be without. I think they ought to be listed on the seed package as PPA. (Papa!)

1. *Nicotiana alata*
2. *Cosmos*
3. Spider flower (*Cleome*)

Although nicotiana, or flowering tobacco, is often offered at Mike's Garden Center, I never buy it there. The cultivar he specializes in is called Nikki Mix. It comes in shades of pink, maroon, and white, as well as an odd lime green, which I find interesting but some people dislike intensely. I grow an older variety, *Nicotiana alata*, originally started from seeds I ordered from Thompson and Morgan several years ago. It reaches a height of three feet and has white lilylike flowers that will perfume the air at night. The flowers close up during the day in sunshine but stay open in the shade.

The fact that the *Nicotiana alata* closes up in sunshine sounds like a flaw; but on the other hand, this habit makes it a terrific annual for shade, and if you've ever tried to find an annual besides impatiens to grow in a shady spot, you know what a virtue that is. I've also discovered that it is great for cutting. The flowers stay open indoors, smell wonderful, and they last for weeks in a vase.

I had bought the *Nicotiana alata* seeds on the recommendation of my friend Richard, who assured me that they would return faithfully each year without further effort on my part. This sounded like my kind of plant. I'll buy anything that requires no effort and costs almost no money. Who wouldn't? Imagine my disappointment when the next April rolled around and there was no *Nicotiana alata* coming up! I immediately called my friend and politely inquired, "Hey Richard, what the hell happened to the nicotiana, huh?" He was reassuring.

"Cassandra, my dear," he said, "once you plant nicotiana, you'll always have nicotiana, believe me." He chuckled softly, with an ominous touch of irony.

Indeed, I needn't have worried. About three weeks later, the nicotiana began to emerge with a vengeance. It had seeded itself around the garden like a capitalist's dream of international expansion. There were enough flowering tobacco seedlings to fill a small woodland. I planted about fifty of them in the shade under the lilac hedge, among some ferns and ripening daffodil leaves. I gave some away to my neighbor Ross and pulled the rest like weeds. I do the same with them each year, and rather than curse them, I bless them, and my dear friend Richard, as well.

Planted in the spring, cosmos will grow to about four feet tall by August, with large but delicate-looking flowers that resemble daisies in pink, white, and maroon. They are easy, easy, easy to grow. I like the name cosmos. It reminds me of astronomy and Carl Sagan, and the Big Bang theory of the Cosmos. I think the Big Bang theory must have been invented by a man. A woman would have wanted it to take longer and insisted on a commitment.

Cleomes are also tall and easy to grow. The flowers look like six-inch fireworks going off in shades of pink, lavender, purple, and white. I like to use both cosmos and cleomes as fillers in newly planted perennial beds. I sow them between the baby perennials to have some flowers the same season, until the babies grow up and start to bloom the second year.

I recommend *Nicotiana alata*, along with cosmos and cleomes, to my gardening students, and sometimes it is I who get the poison phone calls.

"Hey, Cassandra, I planted those cleome seeds you gave me last year and they were terrific, but this year, they're coming up all over the place! What do I do now?"

"What do you do now?" I reply testily. "You have hands. Pull out the ones you don't want, and thin out the ones you do want to about a foot apart. That's all."

As I've mentioned before, pulling out seedlings is a whole lot easier and cheaper than buying and planting new ones. And you have enough to give away to neighbors and enhance your reputation as a wonderful human being. Now that beats marigolds from Mike's any day.

PRUNING SHRUBS

Everyone knows how to prune a shrub, right? Wrong.

On a beautiful day in May a couple of years ago, I was out in Bobbie's garden, and, as is my wont, I wonted to do some gardening. Bobbie had a Japanese flowering quince that she told me had been annoying her because it had overgrown the spot she had allotted for it, a corner of her lily garden next to a low stone wall. My mission, should I decide to accept it, was to decrease the size of the quince and get it back in bounds.

May was the perfect time to do the job because the quince, like other early spring-blooming shrubs, had just finished flowering and was getting ready to make its growth for the year. It was a simple job. Using my trusty lopper, I cut some of the older, longer branches right back to the ground so that the quince looked much smaller without looking as if it had been given a crew cut. Then it occurred to me that, really, the shrub would look even better if I could train the branches to grow over the stone wall, rather than into the garden. That would keep it out of the way of the lilies and visually relate the garden to the wall. I was aiming for a graceful, stylized, artistic effect. You know, something like what you might see on the set of *Shogun*—I loved that show. I imagined a few perfectly formed flowers blooming against the gray stone of the low wall, one or two droplets of dew caught in their delicate petals. I fantasized beautiful plinky-plunky Japanese music playing in the background and a lovely kimono-clad damsel wearing tons of white makeup, carrying an umbrella, and stabbing herself because she was caught sleeping with Richard Chamberlain. Romantic stuff like that.

Japanese gardens are known for their elegantly pruned trees and shrubs. Over centuries, the masters of this technique have achieved the art of miniaturizing plants. With miniaturization, they are able to fit woodland trees, flowers, ferny paths, a stream with a bridge going over it, a pond, and a rock garden all in an area the size of my dining room. The secrets of this art have been refined and passed down through generations. The skill takes years of patient concentration to learn, and only a select few ever master it completely.

What the heck, I figured, ignorance is bliss. I gave it a whirl.

I started by cutting out all the branches that were growing away from the wall. The quince now looked like half a bush. Encouraged, I then removed all the smaller branches at the base, so that nothing would conflict with the graceful line of the remaining branches. With an iron discipline better used toward my efforts at dieting, I carefully removed one branch at a time and left only those branches that were heading for the top of the wall. When I was finished, there were two branches left, and the whole operation had taken only ten minutes. It was quick and easy! I couldn't imagine why Japanese gardeners made such a fuss about it.

I dragged the unwanted branches to the brush pile and had a good look at what I'd done. Not bad, I thought. A bit sparse, perhaps. Well, okay, it was ugly, but I could see that with time, the branches would eventually arch gracefully over the wall the way I wanted them to. This might take five years or so of rigorous pruning, but wasn't that the Oriental way, the patient way, the Zen way? Do we not live in the dimension of time as well as space? With my third eye, I saw that pruning the quince was more than just yard work, it was a living lesson in Eastern philosophy.

Serenely, I showed Bobbie the results of my efforts when she came out of the house to tell me that lunch was ready. I suspected that Bobbie was not as impressed by Oriental philosophy as I was, although there was a long contemplative moment of silence, just before the scream.

To make a long story short, this quince bush is now growing in my yard! That very day, Bobbie gave it to me. "Take it out! Get rid of it!" she suggested in a very loud, high voice. So I took it, and I must say it was easy to move because there were so few branches in the way. I dug it up, wrapped the roots in wet newspaper, and threw it in the trunk of my car.

Upon returning home, I planted it next to the kerria at the back of my flower garden. These shrubs serve to separate the side yard from the backyard, or at least they will, when the quince grows out in about five years. At the moment, it looks like a drowning man with his arms up over his head. But that's okay. To me, that Japanese quince is more than just a shrub; it is a Zen Master. And I thank Bobbie for it. It was a lovely gift and well earned, if I do say so myself.

Anyone can prune a shrub, right? You just cut off the part that's sticking out. If the shrub is too large altogether, you keep cutting until it's as small as you want it, right? Wrong. The results of lousy pruning are all around us, and not just in my yard. The countryside is filled with for-sythias, spireas, lilacs, weigelas, and even roses that look like giant gum-drops. Any relation to the natural shape of the plant is purely coincidental. Whenever I see this type of pruning, often crowded against the foundation of the house and surrounded by miles of mown grass, I get the feeling that the owner is at war with nature, a war waged with power tools and lawn tractors, the armaments and tanks of a *Wehrmacht* calculated to guarantee him military superiority. Such a yard is not a garden, it's a dictatorship.

I am not entirely unsympathetic to these militant, power-tool-crazed horticulturists. Really. I dislike them intensely, but I understand their plight, especially when it comes to pruning shrubs. Their desperation stems from the fact that the shrub has grown larger than they expected, and they don't know how to keep it in proportion without mangling it. It's just another pathetic case of ignorance leading to violence.

So, in the interest of world peace and to make amends for my own wanton destruction of Bobbie's quince, I learned a few useful tricks for pruning shrubs of all kinds.

One of the most common questions people ask me on my radio show is when to prune a particular shrub. Sometimes it happens that I am not familiar with the plant, so I always ask this question: "When does it bloom?" If the people say that it blooms in the summer or fall, I tell them to prune in the spring. If they say it blooms anytime before June, I tell them to prune it right after it blooms. Most spring-flowering plants bloom before they make their growth, and most summer- and fall-blooming plants flower after they make their growth. I can tell the audience thinks I'm a genius. I'm not a genius. If you think about it, this principle is just common sense. Who wants to prune a spring-blooming shrub (like Bobbie's quince) just before the flowers come out? What a waste! You wind up cutting off all the flower buds. On the other hand, shrubs that bloom later in the summer usually bloom on new wood, the growth that they have made since the spring. Pruning them in spring will encourage them to make more new growth and therefore more flowers.

The proper way to prune lilacs, for example, is in late May, right after the blooms are finished, to prevent the bush from setting seed and to force it to compensate by making more flowers the following year.

Old lilacs tend to get leggy and only bloom on top of the tallest branches, because that's where the sunlight is. (Everyone with an old lilac in his or her yard has had this experience.) To correct this, you're supposed to take out one third of the oldest branches each year. In other words, if an old lilac has fifteen very tall branches, you should take out five. This treatment allows sunshine to reach the smaller branches, so they have a chance to fill out and bloom a year or two later. After doing this for three years, the bush will be completely renewed.

Obediently, I have always pruned my lilacs right after they bloomed, although I've never had the patience or the time to cut each spent panicle individually to prevent it from setting seed. There are thousands! But last year, I wanted to cut a lot of lilacs for the house because I was having a birthday party for Ron. On the theory that more is more, I figured that if one bouquet of white lilacs is lovely in a room, eight bouquets, set all around the room in the corners, on the tables, and dripping from the mantelpiece, would be even better. That's when I decided to prune the lilacs while they were blooming.

Because I like the height of my lilac hedge, I generally prune it sparingly. I take one or two trunks out each year instead of one third, and then only if they look really rotten. But on this occasion, I removed the trunks while they were laden with flowers. In short, I did the same pruning while the plant was in bloom as I would have done afterward. I cut off the flowering branches, slit the woody stems, and put them in water. I hauled off the rest of the branches to be used as firewood.

Did this do any harm to the lilacs? No, no, of course not. Pruning them while in bloom not only served the purpose of opening up the plants, it allowed me to have lots of free party decorations.

But the best part is that nothing was wasted. When the party was over and the flowers faded, I put them on the compost heap and threw the water onto the garden. The branches that were used as firewood became ashes, which I spread on the ground under the dormant lilacs during the winter. Lilacs love fresh ashes because they provide potash (which promotes bloom) and lime (lilacs prefer slightly alkaline soil). These nutrients quickly leach into the ground. This sort of thrifty recycling fills me with a warm glow. I know I am working within the laws of nature; I am cooperating with the inevitable; I am part of the cycle of life; I am a great human being and an all-around good sport. It's wonderful how gardening raises your self-esteem.

That's all very well, but what do you do when you have a shrub that has overgrown its allotted space and attacks you everytime you walk out of the house? If you get hit in the face enough times by the luxuriant growth of a lusty forsythia, the gumdrop starts to look good.

I'm not sure if my method is the officially approved one or not but I use the same principle on all shrubs as I use with the lilacs. Since I want to make the shrub smaller without losing its natural shape, I take out the longest stems right back to the ground, especially if the shrub is of the type that grows from multiple stems, like lilacs, forsythias, flowering quinces, deutzias, et cetera.

After the oldest, largest branches are removed, the smaller branches will grow to fill in, just as they do with lilacs. Plants that have one main stem, like my *Magnolia stellata*, are really small trees and I prune them accordingly. (See the chapter on pruning trees, beginning on page 57.)

This method has worked wonderfully on an old spirea in the side yard that was ten feet across when I bought my house. It took up too much of my garden, so I kept cutting the longest branches out until the thing was about two feet across, one fifth of its original size. I never cut a single branch in half! (Start from ground level. This is an unbendable rule.) When I was finished, the gracefully drooping branches of the spirea looked completely natural, as though it had never been pruned! Isn't that amazing?

I prune roses, which bloom in June, the same way I treat any other summer-blooming shrub. In early spring, I walk around and cut off any branches that have died over the winter and any branches that are crossing each other. I go one step further with the hybrid teas and cut any branches that are sticking out at an odd angle down to the nearest outward-facing leaf bud. This helps give the otherwise ungainly plant a rounder shape. Other than that, I leave them alone. If you are trying to grow exhibition-size roses, you have to prune the hybrid teas down to three or four branches and cut them halfway to the ground every year. The result of such drastic pruning is a short rosebush with relatively few, but very large, blooms.

So what have we learned here? First of all, prune shrubs to follow their natural form, taking out the longest, oldest stems to allow sunlight and air to penetrate the interior. Second, cut whole stems, unless we want to turn the shrub into a hedge or a gumdrop. And last, it's perfectly all right to prune a shrub while it is blooming, especially if we want flowers in the house.

There is another lesson to be learned here: Never prune somebody else's shrub unless you are in perfect agreement with the owner or you want to take it home. It is a dangerous venture but an excellent way to acquire new shrubs, especially if you know that the owner loves you anyway.

Five Classic Rules for Flower Arranging

We have finally reached that time of the year when the garden looks stunning. One of the nicest by-products of having a cottage garden in full bloom is having the indoors in full bloom, as well. There is no room so dreary or so badly decorated that a container of fresh flowers won't add a note of beauty, especially if it's a really big bouquet, big enough to hide the wallpaper, maybe.

As a city dweller, the idea of having fresh-cut flowers in every room always seemed to be the height of luxury and extravagance. In New York City, flowers are expensive. A small nosegay costs four or five bucks, and anyway, seven boring carnations stuck in a Woolworth's vase was far from the gorgeous floral fantasies I secretly dreamed about. I wanted bouquets like the ones I had seen in paintings at the Metropolitan Museum of Art, urns full of roses and peonies, Chinese ginger jars loaded with huge spiky red chrysanthemums, sunflowers by Van Gogh, roses by Fragonard, Dutch Masters' paintings with striped tulips, poet's daffodils, peonies, and primroses so luscious they spilled out of the blue and white delft pottery that was supposed to contain them. I wanted flowers as art, flowers as icons, flowers as metaphors for the exuberance and joy of life.

In the city you need the big bucks to be able to afford that kind of thing on a regular basis. Masses of flowers are not for the masses. This is unfortunately true of other, less extraneous aspects of life in the city, as well, like food, clothing, and shelter.

So, as soon as I had a garden of my own, even before we started decorating the inside of the house, I used to cut bouquets. With flowers in the room, even my bare bedroom with its peeling paint and falling plaster had a romantic allure. It reminded me of the boudoir of a degenerate southern aristocrat, scented with lilacs, magnolias, and sin. It was around that time that I began to call Walter Stanley Kowalski.

I can't tell you how many people I know who hate to cut flowers out of the garden. And they all have different reasons, some of which are quite legitimate, and some of which are cockeyed.

Reason 1. *There aren't enough flowers in the garden. If I cut these, there'll be none left!* This sounds like a pretty good reason, until you examine it more closely. First of all, who says that you have to cut all the flowers? When I can't bear to lose the beautiful drift effect in the border that I have worked so carefully to achieve, I only cut one or two of my favorites and then add wildflowers, leaves, or grasses to fill out the vase. Professional florists use this trick all the time. Why do you think florists' bouquets of roses include all those ferns and those little white things? It's a way of stretching out the merchandise. The green fern leaves and the little white things set off the red roses nicely, but they also fill out the box and prevent it from looking skimpy. Imagine a guy sending a dozen roses to his wife or girlfriend (or both) and having it look skimpy? What would it imply? "I love you, dear, but not too much."

Almost anything is grist for my flower arrangement mill. I cut shrubs in bloom or in berry. Rose hips look just as beautiful in a fall arrangement as roses do in June, and more unusual. Tree leaves are wonderful additions, especially if the flowers themselves are dramatic. One of the most artistic flower arrangements I've ever seen was the combination of dark green oak leaves and apricot trumpet lilies in an earthenware jug. It was put together by my friend and former client Remi. Remi is one of those people who hates to cut flowers out of the garden. The only reason she had the lilies in the vase was because their stems had broken due to inadequate staking. (She blamed me.) Unwilling to cut more lilies, she added the oak leaves just to fill things out. Gorgeous.

I have a couple of old quince trees among the white lilacs in the hedge. The fruit is useless to me, because I don't make jelly, but boy are they decorative! I like to cut the branches with the fruit attached and use them to fill a pair of urn-shaped vases in the living room. It looks almost like art.

Reason 2. *It will hurt the flowers.* This is ridiculous. Almost all flowers last longer indoors than in the garden, exposed to wind, sun, and rain, not to mention the amorous attentions of insects who want to fertilize them. Remember, once a flower is fertilized, its job is done, and the petals fall off. Unfertilized, it will hang around for hours or days longer, hoping for a dance, so to speak. The flower's sexual frustration is my interior decoration.

Rain, especially, beats the heck out of most blossoms. Every year, when the peonies are in bloom, there is at least one day of torrential rain that turns the blossoms from pouffy spheres of scented pink petals into sodden lumps as romantic as wet toilet paper. The peonies inevitably come crashing down to the ground around the plant, and no amount of shaking to dry them out will make them stand up again.

Peony hoops, metal rings designed to fit around the whole plant to keep the flowers from falling over, are worse than useless. I actually bought three of them from one of those fancy gardening supply catalogs, at six bucks apiece plus postage and handling. It would have been worth it if the hoops worked, but after the first rain, the soaked flower heads leaned over the rails like drunks at a race track. I realized then that there was only one way to turn this disaster into a triumph. Now when the inevitable spring rain threatens to destroy my beauties, I run out in the rain and cut as many as I can to put in vases around the house. If I have a lot of them, I give them away to grateful friends and neighbors. It is especially satisfying to give peonies to my city friends who don't know anything about horticulture. The more ignorant they are, the better. Presented with a dozen peonies the size of Refrigerator Perry's fist, they naturally assume you must be a fantastic gardener to grow carnations that big.

Reason 3. *Cutting the flowers will hurt the plant.* Oh, come on, now, grow up! Cutting the flowers will actually encourage more bloom on an annual. And even if the plant is a perennial that blooms only once each year, removing the flowers will save the plant the trouble of setting seeds, thereby leaving more energy that will go into root, bulb, or leaf growth. Sometimes the grateful perennial will even bloom twice. This goes for shrubs, as well. As I have mentioned earlier, lilacs are supposed to be pruned right after they bloom. But if I prune them a few days earlier, *while* they bloom, I get to have the flowers for the house.

Reason 4. *I'm scared.* This reason is usually unspoken. I call it fear of flowers. It is not quite as psychologically significant as fear of flying, but it is nonetheless very common. It is a fear that the flower arrangements one attempts will turn out badly.

I have enormous sympathy for the fear-of-flowers syndrome, because the truth is, I, myself, have absolutely no talent for flower arranging. I have no natural eye or artistic ability. I'm not just saying this because I want to bolster your ego at the expense of mine or to manipulate you into making a fool of yourself by trying to create elaborate floral arrangements that turn out badly. I'm saying this because it's true. I have made some of the most boring flower arrangements you've ever seen. They were cliched, stupefyingly trite floral designs that I wouldn't send by wire to my worst enemy. My arrangements bore the same relationship to the paintings in the Metropolitan Museum as a statue of a jockey on the lawn bears to the *Winged Victory*. All of my early attempts at bouquets, using whatever cleverly garnered materials I could find, were shapeless and crude. I could have put on a blindfold and thrown the flowers at the vase, and it would have looked just as well, if not better.

That being the case, I read up on flower arranging, to learn to do by craft and knowledge what I could not do by art and talent. From my reading, I gleaned about five basic rules of flower arranging, which, when followed faithfully, helped me make some sense out of even the most eclectic assortment of vegetation.

Before I tell you what the rules are, thereby building suspense and making them seem more important, I'd like to tell you how to gather flowers. As with everything else in life, there's a right way and a wrong way, or at least there used to be before they invented no-fault divorces. The wrong way is to go around cutting on a sunny midafternoon, placing the cut flowers in one of those adorable flat baskets that you see in magazines. It looks good but works badly. The right way is to go around in the morning or late afternoon, when the sun is not so strong, with a bucket of tepid water, plunging the cut stems into it immediately. Tepid water helps keep the capillaries of the stem open, so they can take up the maximum amount of water. The first time I took this advice, I made the water too hot. I wasn't aware that anything was wrong until I began to notice an odor similar to that of steamed broccoli coming from the bucket. I had cooked the bouquet.

It also helps the stem to soak up water if you cut it on the bias rather than straight across. Woody stems, like those of lilacs or quinces, should be slit before placing them in the tepid water.

After filling the bucket with plant materials, get a couple of attractive containers, like vases or pitchers, fill them with tepid water also, and away you go. You're ready to begin an artistic adventure in the world of floral design, following my Five Classic Rules for Flower Arranging.

1. *Flowers should blend or contrast, but not clash with the colors of the room.* The first thing to do is to separate out the different colors to match

the room in which the bouquet is to be placed. This can be done mentally, while leaving the flowers happily soaking in the tepid water. By colors that blend, I mean yellow flowers in a yellow room; by contrast, I mean yellow flowers in a blue room. By clash, I mean yellow flowers in a hot pink room. (What are you doing with a hot pink room anyway?)

Of course, all bouquets are not monochromatic. Some of the most beautiful have both blending and contrasting colors in the same arrangement. But unless you have the color sense of a Matisse or more self-confidence than I do, it's best to stick to one or two main colors per container and perhaps just a touch of contrasting color to set them off. For instance, if you have mainly yellow dahlias, yellow black-eyed susans, goldenrod, and blue bachelor's buttons in one bouquet, it's best to leave it alone, except for some brown grass or green or gray leaves to fill it out. Adding red salvia and magenta phlox is not going to make it look better, believe me. I am constantly tempted to add just one more thing, and the results are as inharmonious as only the arrangements of the truly untalented can be.

Here's another hint about color. For nighttime viewing, use light and warm flower colors. Blues and purples look gray and are lost under incandescent lights.

Now you're ready to actually put the flowers into the container. I tend to be conservative about my choice of containers. I use standard vases for the living room and the dining room and earthenware pitchers for the porch or kitchen. A battered tin pitcher doesn't go with formal furniture, although I've seen very talented designers use them to good effect. There is a very famous floral designer who uses old valises, yes, valises—luggage. (I assume he inserts watertight containers inside.) He fills them with the most romantic flowers imaginable—lilies, roses, delphiniums, foxgloves, phlox, and so forth—and arranges them so they seem to be spilling out of the valise like underwear. It's actually very beautiful, though just a little too, too, too divine and decadent for my taste, but it shows what you can do if you have The Eye.

2. *The height of the flowers should be one and a half times the height of the container.* If the container is one foot tall, measured from the tabletop, the tallest flower should be eighteen inches from the tabletop. Once again, I have seen this rule flouted successfully many times, but

when I try to make the flowers much taller than this proportion, the arrangement looks like a short woman in a big hat. Sometimes it's desirable to cut the flowers less than one and a half times the height of the container, when you're making a table centerpiece, for example. Centerpieces should be less than a foot high, so the dinner guests won't feel like they're talking to each other through camouflage, ducking and craning their necks just to see each other through the jungle.

3. *Darker, larger, or brighter flowers should be close to the center and bottom of the arrangement. Lighter, smaller-flowered, airier material should be at the top and sides.*
Heavier objects sink and lighter ones float. We humans know this scientific fact deep in our unconscious, and that's why it is disconcerting to see a large, round flower, such as a peony, German iris, or cabbage rose, floating in space above delicate flowers, sprays of spirea, or dancing columbines. When you place the larger flowers in the center and toward the bottom, they act as a base, the place where the eye rests before going on to explore the delights of the rest of the arrangement. This is especially true of arrangements that will be viewed from one side only, but even if you're doing a bowl of flowers, the substantial ones should have shorter stems than the delicate ones. This will also make the bouquet look three-dimensional instead of flat.

4. *The arrangement should have a form.* It should not look like a blob of color. One of the simplest yet prettiest shapes is an isosceles triangle, with the tallest flower at the top and another one the same length going out to one side. This is less formal than a fan-shaped arrangement, the kind you see at weddings and funerals. More subtle and absolutely gorgeous is the elongated S-shaped curve, Hogarth's famous "line of beauty." The tallest flower is placed to one side of the perpendicular, and flowers spill over the opposite side of the vase, roughly forming an elongated curve. There are many other shapes in the art of floral design, but these two give the greatest amount of no-fail beauty for the least amount of effort. Besides, they're my favorites.
Lack of form is usually the reason that a lot of flower arrangements come out looking funny. When that happens to me, I adjust the flowers to make some sort of overall shape, and although the difference is subtle, it turns a messy-looking effort into a pleasing one. Usually. Sometimes,

if things really turn out badly, there's nothing to do but to take everything out of the vase and start all over again. Or leave it. Probably no one else will notice. Probably.

5. *Have a few flowers, tendrils, or leaves trail over the edge of the container.* This makes a visual relationship between the vase and the flowers. It also immediately gives the impression of abundance, as though the arrangement were saying: "There's so much life and beauty here, this vase cannot contain it." Vine leaves, berries, and grapes are especially good for this purpose, since they have a natural tendency to trail downward.

In my efforts to satisfy my passion for flowers, flowers, everywhere, I have gone to great lengths. I have never believed that less is more. More is more! Tasteful restraint is not my cup of tea. If you want taste and restraint, go to Japan and drink a cup of tea. Don't come to my house.

I try to treat each bouquet, large or small, as though it were a little garden inside the house. I don't intersperse them in the container, the way that professional florists often do—a dozen chrysanthemums interspersed with a dozen statice, for instance. I try to put them in a vase the same way I would grow them in the garden, in groups or drifts. To do this, I place the same flowers together in groups of three or five. (Odd numbers of flowers, especially groups of three, look more pleasing than even numbers, but don't ask me why.) So when I'm out cutting, I try to cut at least three of any one flower.

Some people use special florist's supplies to support their flowers, like frogs, pins, marbles, or that green spongy stuff. I think they're fine, although I never use them. To use them would mean that I have to buy them, and I hate spending money on unnecessary accessories. I have an alternate method, a cheap trick that I invented myself, one of so many. I cut a twiggy stem and stick it in the bottom of the container. The twigs hold the stems upright as well as a frog does, and they have another advantage—they can be thrown onto the compost pile along with the spent flowers after they have faded. In practice, however, I generally use so much plant material in the vase that there is no need for extra supports of any kind.

I feel this way about flower arranging: If you have a garden, cutting flowers and bringing them into the house is an added pleasure. And even if the arrangements don't come out exactly the way you thought they would, even a badly arranged bunch of flowers is better than no flowers at all. At my worst, no one ever came to my house and said, ''Oh, what ugly flowers,'' at least not while I was in the room.

If you are a victim of fear-of-flowers syndrome, start with a few daisies in a pickle jar. Or cut a lot of one thing, even if it's only leaves, and put them in a vase, just to get the feel of it. In a little while, you may have works of floral art that any painter would be proud to put on canvas. Or maybe not. But the wonderful thing about flower arranging is that your disasters, as well as your victories, will only last a few days.

JUNE

What a gorgeous creature this lily is,
and virginity has nothing to do with it.

A Petunia Named Desire

This is the month that I dream about all year, the month that rhymes with spoon and moon, the month of flowers, the month of midsummer madness, the month of ecstasy. June. Yippee.

I dreamed about flowers when I was a teenager. In my dream, I was walking hand in hand with my boyfriend, Hank, the first boy I ever loved. We were walking down a street of suburban tract houses, all of which resembled my Aunt Dotty's home on Long Island. In reality, these houses were uniformly planted with shrubs around the foundation, had a lawn adjacent to a driveway, and were surrounded by a cement sidewalk. In my dream, however, there were no lawns. Front yards were filled with flowers, rose arbors covered the paths leading to the front doors, and in each of the gardens, irises were about to bloom. As my boyfriend and I walked by, we touched the irises and they burst into bloom. They were cobalt blue, true blue, like no real iris ever was. I woke up filled with longing, and not just the longing for a garden, either.

Anyone who has studied high-school biology knows that flowers are the sexual organs of plants. We all remember that diagram of a buttercup, or some other simple flower, with stamens and pistils neatly indicated by a thin line connecting the part to the word. At the age of sixteen, which I was at the time, I would have found it impossible to associate that drawing with anything resembling what I would have called sex. But fortunately, my copy had been annotated the year before by Jimmy Carlino, the book's previous owner. His marginal notes and drawings indicated an intuitive understanding of the metaphor implied by the organs of the flower, and his translations of the obscure Latin terms into clear Anglo-Saxon added the folksy, human touch that the science editor at Houghton Mifflin had omitted.

Jimmy Carlino had the right idea, although I doubt if he passed the final. Flowers are all about sex, and not just some dry scientific kind of sex, like an in vitro fertilization procedure. Flowers are full of sensuality, passion, aching desire, abundance, and erotic love. The perfume of some flowers is so heady and intoxicating that throughout history human females have stolen it and worn it themselves so that men would want to make love to them.

Walk into the garden, when everything is an orgy of color and scent and nodding blossoms, opening buds and buzzing bees . . . Does it look like they're doing banking transactions? It's beautiful! It's joy incarnate and love eternal and life undefeated. It's a wedding day.

Now, don't get me wrong. I'm not suggesting that I believe in some primitive form of animism, with gardens full of flowers sighing with love, making clandestine trysts, or having orgasms. We can leave all that to us gardeners. But it seems to me that any life that grows and blooms and reproduces has more in common with our own feelings of love and desire than we might think. Where did this human emotion come from, anyway? Human beings didn't invent sexual passion, although each culture seems to have its own method of expressing it. How could anything as pervasive and universal as love and marriage come from anywhere except nature? It exists, and has always existed, because it is a part of our animal life, and we are a part of all other life on this planet.

It is no accident that flowers are beautiful. They are beautiful for the same reason that humans make themselves beautiful, to be attractive enough to get fertilized and reproduce successfully.

Think of the lily, the pure white fragrant *Lilium candidum*, that in European tradition is associated with the Virgin Mary. In Renaissance paintings of the Annunciation, at the moment when the angel tells Mary that she is going to be a mother, there is always a Madonna lily somewhere in the picture. It's not there because the painters always had Madonna lilies lying around the studio, along with a few madonnas. It's there because it represents fecundity and new life. Only later did it become associated with virginity and death, in that order, and only then by the ultraconservative religious fanatics who hated sex and thought that the best thing you could do in life was to get out of it as soon as possible.

Now, let's stop thinking of the lily as a symbol and look to the lily sitting in a vase on the table in front of me: "It toils not, neither does it spin, but Solomon in all his glory was not arrayed like one of these." What a gorgeous creature this lily is, and virginity has nothing to do with it. I look into the trumpet-shaped petals. The male parts, the anthers, exude a pollen so abundant and virile that it will permanently stain anything with which it comes in contact, like my clothing or my cheeks, when I lean in too close to smell the perfume.

There is nothing passive about the pistil, the female part of the lily, either. It is thrust outward from the center of the trumpet, and the entrance to the oviduct is wet, sticky, and eager to be fertilized. I'm blushing. If Solomon in all his glory had been arrayed like one of these lilies, he would have gotten a lot of dates, believe me. Come to think of it, he did get a lot of dates.

The objects of desire that flowers wish to attract are not other flowers, of course, but insects, like bees and butterflies, and it works beautifully for them. Most people tend to assume that the bees have no knowledge of the plant's use of them and are only after the nectar. In other words, they are a bunch of unwitting stooges, slavishly servicing the carnal appetites of the flowers and getting no fun out of the experience at all. I don't think so. I have observed bees going from flower to flower in the garden, and they seem to be enjoying themselves enormously. I wouldn't presume to know the thoughts and feelings of bees, but if I saw a bunch of teenagers sipping nectar, rolling around with their feet up in the air, covered with fragrant pollen, and then racing off to do it again and again, I would assume that they were having a wonderful time and would probably call the police.

Some plants, like some people, are sexual anomalies. They become active only under stress. Fear excites them. This phenomenon is the horticultural equivalent of a baby boom right after a war. It might also explain why people who live in poverty have more children at an early age than those who are well off. When life is short and death is all around you, reproduction is the only way to ensure that the species will survive. Not all plants (or people) react this way to stress (thank heavens!), but there are some plants that not only reproduce more prolifically under stress, they positively require it. You might call them the sadomasochists of the vegetable kingdom.

A perfect example of this perverse type is the wisteria vine on my garage, which has not bloomed since I bought it. At the time of purchase, it had been grown in a large black plastic pot for three years and had long, white, grapelike racemes of flowers. I took it home and planted it, lavishing it with compost and a large root run next to the wall of the garage. The result after five years is that, although it has covered the ugly garage with a satisfying graceful green mantle, it has not produced even one panicle of flowers. Not one! And it won't until it runs out of room or nutrients, or until I hack away at the stems and break the roots by digging four feet around it, thereby causing it to fear death and release the hormones that will make it bloom. This treatment is similar to having the gardener put on a leather body suit and mask and tying the wisteria to the bed posts. Call me Dominatrix Greenthumbs.

Shocked? The garden as a place of innocence and repose is strictly a human idea and a pretty fey one at that. The garden is a place of conflict and competition, but we are not aware of it, because it all goes much too slowly for our time sense. The resolution of a war between a small maple tree seedling and the roots of the daylily in which it has insinuated itself is a matter determined over the course of two or three years. We can't sit still that long. When it comes to watching a conflict, our attention span is about the duration of a football game. But the contest between the daylily and the maple is far more dramatic than a game between the Los Angeles Rams and the New York Giants. It is more than a matter of winning the Super Bowl; it is a matter of life and death. At least until the gardener comes along and pulls out the maple seedling while serenely weeding her flower beds.

Passion and life or death conflict are all excellent subjects suitable for a novel, Academy Award–winning film, Pulitzer Prize–winning play, or made-for-television movie. But all of this goes on in the apparently bucolic peace of my cottage garden in June. It consists of drama, tragedy, and lust—the stuff that my dreams are made of.

The Magnificent Seven

Anyone can make a garden look good in June. That's when most of the showiest garden flowers bloom: roses, peonies, irises, daisies, campanulas, columbines, and many more. Most of those gorgeous garden photos that you see in *Architectural Digest* and *House and Garden* magazines are taken in June. Photographers run all over the countryside during this month, taking pictures for inclusion in next year's March issue. So don't be fooled by those photos. It's fantasy. Pure theater. Just for spite, I like to imagine what those same gardens would look like in July when all the showstoppers have gone to seed and far fewer flowers are in bloom. They'd look like everybody else's garden.

So the whole trick of a perennial cottage garden, which is, after all, nothing if not a flower garden, is to keep it blooming before and after June. You have to have enough different kinds of plants so that something is flowering every month of the gardening season. That can be quite difficult when you don't know when each plant blooms. When I first started to garden, I tried to discover the blooming times of different perennials by reading the descriptions in the garden catalogs.

The main thing that I learned, however, is that most catalogs lie like dogs. Here's a typical example of horticultural baloney: "Blooms from June to frost!" What a lie! No perennial blooms without letup from June until frost except a plastic poinsettia!

Just once, I would like to read a catalog that tells the truth for a change: "Blooms for two weeks in May and looks like hell for the rest of the summer." That would be honest. "Will kill its neighbors!" Or, "Did spectacularly in our trial gardens, but will drop dead in yours."

So to clear up the mystery of what the catalogs are actually saying in their descriptions, let me give you a few examples of "catalogese," along with a free translation, based upon my own experience. Here are a few of the most frequently used terms:

CATALOGESE	PLAIN ENGLISH
New Introduction!	We got these cheap when an old nursery went out of business.
Multiplies quickly!	Pestilential weed.

CATALOGESE	PLAIN ENGLISH
Twelve-inch blooms!	Four-inch blooms!
Stunning vertical accent!	Will fall over in a light breeze.
An outstanding breeding accomplishment!	Short with weirdly colored flowers.

Descriptions of Colors

Blue	lavender-blue
Intense rich blue	dark lavender
Intense violet-blue	purple
Brilliant purple-pink	magenta
Charming lavender-pink	magenta
Glowing rosy pink	magenta
Rosy carmine	magenta
Luscious clear pink	magenta
Pink	magenta

Descriptions of daylily colors

Melon	orange
Peach	light orange
Apricot	medium orange
Mustard yellow with pink flush in ribs	bright orange
Deep red with a golden yellow heart	looks like orange from two feet away

So, because of the unreliability of catalogs, I have prepared a list of my favorite, most reliable perennials for you, my friend, a list that will carry you through the gardening season from May to November! Really! (For March and April, I use every sort of early bulb, including daffodils, hyacinths, species tulips, puschkinias, fritillarias, crocuses, and Siberian squills.)

I call my list of perennials "The Magnificent Seven," plants that no cottage garden in a temperate climate should be without. They are:

Columbines (*Aquilegia*)
Peonies (*Paeonia*)
Irises (*Iris*)
Hollyhocks (*Althaea rosea*)
Daylilies (*Hemerocallis*)
Phlox (*Phlox*)
Asters (*Aster*)

Needless to say, they are all easy to grow and will flourish in sun and decent garden soil. If you had only a dozen of each of these (a hundred would be better), you'd have a pretty terrific flower border, even if you grew nothing else. All of these flowers come in many colors that can be mixed and matched endlessly according to taste.

If you have room for a few more plants, here are some other indispensables, all of which bloom from August onward, just when most perennial gardens look their worst:

Sedum 'Autumn Joy' (*Sedum*)
Chrysanthemums (*Chrysanthemum*)
Oriental lilies (*Lilium orientalis*)
Japanese anemones (*Anemone japonica*)
False dragonhead (*Physostegia*)
Black-eyed susans (*Rudbeckia fulgida* 'Goldsturm')

I would like to have added all these perennials to the original list, but then I couldn't have used the catchy title "The Magnificent Seven." "The Magnificent Thirteen" just doesn't have the same evocative ring. Inspired by the title, I have asked my friend Mary to compose a short poem about "The Magnificent Seven." I must warn you not to try to memorize it, even though it would be helpful when you go to the nursery. It's the sort of inane doggerel that will haunt you, like the Doublemint gum jingle, cursed be the person who wrote it. You won't be able to get it out of your mind, you'll find yourself reciting it like a mantra while doing the dishes, driving the car, and especially when you're trying to think of something else more important. It can be extremely annoying, and don't ask me how I know.

THE MAGNIFICENT SEVEN RAP

Columbines, peonies, irises, phlox,
Daylilies, asters, and giant hollyhocks.
Seven plants you'll love to grow;
They will grow for any schmo.

Columbines all bloom in May
Right through Independence Day.

Irises, they bloom in June
With peonies, they'll make you swoon.

In July it's very hot,
But not too hot for hollyhocks.

And when those hollyhocks are through
Garden phlox picks up its cue.

Daylilies bloom all summer long.
With plants like these you can't go wrong.

Asters bloom in September.
This rhyme will help you to remember.

Columbines, peonies, irises, phlox,
Daylilies, asters, and giant hollyhocks.
Seven plants you'll love to grow;
They will grow for any schmo.

WHY I GROW PERENNIALS

Yes, June is the month of the glorious perennials. Each day something new comes into bloom, the peonies open at intervals, the early, mid-, and late-season irises are in various stages of development, the roses go from leaf to bud to maturity, the daisies pop, and the Asiatic lilies burst open. At last, there is one perfect day when everything catches up, and the whole garden is a grand bouquet. There is no place on earth more delightful to be than ten feet outside my kitchen door.

On this morning the plumber came to fix the hot-water heater. When he was finished with his work, he stood outside the kitchen door and looked around the garden. I thought for a moment that he was going to burst into song or poetry or at least say something rhapsodic. But as he handed me his bill, he only remarked, ''Boy, I bet all these posies cost a fortune, huh? Yeah, this place looks like real money.''

I was knocked off my pins. I'd never heard anything so crass in my life! ''Real money?'' I shouted at him as he picked up his toolbox and sauntered over to his Mercedes-Benz 235. ''Your bill comes to more than I've spent on my entire garden!''

He chuckled as though I had made a pleasant joke, revved up his motor, and cruised off with his elbow out the window. What a Philistine!

In truth, I grow perennials because I'm cheap. No, thrifty. I'm thrifty. Although a perennial plant costs three or four times more than an annual initially, it is one of the few things in life that grows (literally) in value the longer you have it. You start out with one plant and keep dividing it, and pretty soon you have a dozen, then four dozen, then a regiment, and then a whole army.

Sometimes callers to my radio show complain that the trouble with perennials is that they bloom for only a few weeks each year, unlike annuals that bloom continuously all summer. That's a fair criticism. The way around this problem is to grow enough perennials so that when one is finished blooming, another one is just starting up. That's where my ''Magnificent Seven'' plus six come in. These plants bloom sequentially, so you only have to buy thirteen plants once, and theoretically at least, you never have to spend another dime to buy flowering plants for the rest of your life. Of course you will and you'll want to buy some shrubs and trees as well. That's normal. But confining ourselves to the flower border,

I thought it would be instructive to look at a cost breakdown between perennials and the annuals you might buy in the garden center every spring.

Just for the sake of argument, let's assume that as a gardener, you will live to be ninety years old, and you are now thirty-five. Here's what thirteen perennials would cost you for a lifetime of flowers:

$$13 \text{ perennials @ } \$5.00 \text{ each } = \$65.00$$

Now what if you bought a few flats of annuals each year (say $100.00 worth) for the rest of your life (fifty-five years)?

$$\$100.00 \text{ worth of annuals } \times 55 = \$5,500.00$$

You don't have to be a mathematical genius to see that there is some lollapalooza of a discrepancy between those two figures. And I haven't even included the value of the perennials after they have multiplied. After the first year or two, it is no big deal to divide each plant into the drifts of three or six that make a flower garden look so lush, thereby making their net worth approximately $325.00. After fifty-five years of dividing and redividing the original thirteen perennials, there would be hundreds, in some cases, thousands of new plants with a net value of several *millions* of dollars!

Okay, maybe not millions. But definitely a lot. Suffice it to say that the annuals you buy at the nursery every spring are a gyp.

Economy is one thing, beauty another. I think perennials have it all over annuals in that department, too. Annuals can be boring. Once you set out the petunias in the spring, what you see is pretty much what you'll get for the rest of the summer. Perennials that come in and out of bloom create an ever-changing canvas. A garden of perennial flowers reminds me of the paintings of the master Impressionist, Claude Monet. I love that guy.

Me and Claude. I feel as if he and I are kindred spirits. Even though he was a great painter, which I'm not, he was also a dedicated gardener, which I am.

I first encountered Claude's garden in my first mad flush of gardening passion. I wanted to find as many pictures of beautiful gardens as I could, and so I pored through tons of magazines from all over the world: *Ar-*

chitectural Digest, House and Garden, House Beautiful, House and Garden Beautiful, British House and Garden Beautiful, French Maison et Jardin Magnifique, Italian Casa i Giardino Inamorata Buon Giorno, Spanish Jardin y Guacamole. I can't remember all their names, and I didn't (couldn't) actually read them all.

I didn't actually buy them, either. I would stand for hours in the magazine store, browsing. Luckily, I was friends with Lotte, the owner. I would flip through the magazines while she told me all about her granddaughter, a child of remarkable gifts, and I agreed heartily with everything she said, just so Lotte wouldn't notice that I was getting drool all over her expensive magazines.

Through the windows of the magazine photos, I got to see a great many gardens in every style imaginable, from severely clipped Louis XIV parterres in France, to wild meadow gardens in the Midwest, to Japanese Zen gardens, to hillside terraces in the Himalayas, to town gardens in San Francisco, and everything you can think of in between. But to me, the most beautiful garden of all, my favorite garden in the whole wide world, is the garden of my friend, Claude Monet—Giverny.

You know why I like Giverny so much? It's not overly tidy. It doesn't look like one of those gardens in which the owner has tried to control nature with an iron fist, everything clipped and planted in rows like soldiers in a Stalinist May Day parade. Giverny looks as if Claude were madly in love with nature and did everything he could to tenderly embrace it. This garden celebrates the beauty of flowers and trees and light and air. It's sexy. Even in photos, you get the explicit sensuality of the artist's passionate ardor for beauty, his voluptuous enjoyment of life, his willing surrender to the caress of nature. Claude and I are very close, really.

There are a couple of Giverny photos I remember very well. I think I saw them in a French magazine, one of many I looked at while Lotte gushed over her grandchild. One showed the garden in May. Fruit trees were in bloom, their pale pink blossoms falling softly on blood red wall-flowers, and pink, white, and "black" tulips. In the middle distance was a beech tree with dark maroon leaves, exactly the same shade as the "black" tulips. Gorgeous.

The other photograph was of a large portion of the garden, taken in June (of course). There were full-blown roses and peonies in luscious shades of pink and red spilling all over each other in abandoned profusion. Between them were blue campanulas, violas, and foxgloves standing like phalluses in a novel by D. H. Lawrence. You could almost smell the perfume of them all. Ooh, la, la. *C'est magnifique.* Wow.

This was a man who knew how to live.

My other great perennial influence was, of course, Gertrude Jekyll. I'd like to point out that when Gertrude Jekyll started her perennial cottage garden, in the late nineteenth century, she was being extremely unfashionable. The trendy people of her day—that is to say, the newly rich industrial barons—were crazy for exotica. They weren't interested in growing the quaint cottage plants that would flourish in any English peasant's yard. Heavens, no. They wanted rare, strange, nonhomey floral oddities that could only be obtained by some compulsive British botanist who was willing to risk his neck to make his reputation and possibly knighthood by hanging off a cliff in the Andes. They wanted tropical stuff that you'd have to build a greenhouse for, that you'd require a full-time staff of nurses for, that your neighbors would die for.

The Victorian craze for exotica had much more to do with showing off than communing with nature. The prevailing landscaping style was to dot variously shaped island beds all over the lawn and fill them with tender annuals in the brightest colors possible. I don't have to tell you what kind of exotics they were; we all know them too well. They were in the same infernal annuals that are still sold every year in the local nurseries! Orange and magenta celosias, fire engine red geraniums, Kool-Aid acid orange marigolds, and psychedelic red salvias were bedded out every year in combinations to make your eyes bleed. Here's a quote from a Victorian taste-maker:

> Contrast of colour—The rule . . . is to put one of the primitive colours—red, blue, or yellow—next to another of these colours, or some other colour formed by compounding the other two . . .*

. . . and the louder, the better. I'm surprised he didn't recommend magenta as a neutral. And this from Victorians, the folks who brought you sexual repression and the corset. They should have worn it over their heads.

Gertrude Jekyll (and her pals in the Arts and Crafts movement) didn't

*McIntosh's *The Book of the Garden* (1853), quoted in David Stuart, *The Garden Triumphant: A Victorian Legacy* (Harper & Row, New York, 1988).

like all those exhibitionistic plantings. She thought they were ugly. I think they were, too. For inspiration, Miss Jekyll took long walks around her Surrey countryside and observed the gardens of the cottagers, people who were too poor or too busy (or possibly too lazy) to buy and plant annuals every spring. She admired the subtle colors and unique forms of the old-fashioned perennials, their ease of culture, and their ability to flourish in the local climate. She and her friends also had a social ax to grind and it was decidedly anti–industrial revolution, as I will explain shortly. So she made herself a cottage-style garden. Of course, her garden encompassed several acres and needed lots of gardeners to keep it up, but its effect, however expensively maintained, was simple and charming and looked as though it just happened to be planted there by a sweet old gray-haired lady. Miss Jekyll was, in fact, a sweet old gray-haired lady, but her garden was a perfect example of art concealing art and lots of money, as well.

Gertrude Jekyll's style of gardening has become accepted in the twentieth century and is growing in popularity, even as we speak. But the Victorian legacy of bedding-out annuals is still with us in force, in public parks and along driveways all across America. There has been a strange sociological twist, however. A hundred years ago, the poor grew perennials and the rich grew annuals. Nowadays, the rich and the comfortable middle class hire gardeners, like my friend Jim Miles, to put in perennial English cottage gardens, and the working class goes all out for the marigolds and the red salvias every spring! You figure it out.

The use of annuals in Victorian gardens had social and political overtones, as well. As I alluded to before, many of the tender annuals had been recently discovered in parts of the world that were then colonies of Great Britain, so in a way, the plants were symbolic trophies of triumphant conquest. Annuals also represented the triumph of industry, since they required an artificially heated greenhouse and a fair degree of technology to produce them. The bright hues of the flowers echoed the new colors of textiles, made possible by the use of recently invented artificial dyes. Prior to this, fabric colors were made from vegetable dyes, which had soft colors, very much like the colors in a perennial garden.

So the use of annuals had much more than a horticultural significance. They represented the triumph of science, industry, and empire. The war between industry and nature was a central issue in Victorian England, and I don't need to remind you that this conflict is still with us today. So far, industry has won and never mind that it is the sort of victory that brings disaster on the winner.

I plant perennials because they make me feel like a true follower of Miss Jekyll and a true lover of Claude Monet. Perennials are substantial, their colors are beautiful, they increase abundantly, they don't die every year, and they are constantly changing. I also grow perennials because I'm cheap.

HYBRID TEA ROSES, *MON AMOUR*

Anyone who has ever gardened in his or her life, or has even browsed through a garden center, is familiar with the hybrid tea rose. It is *the* modern rose. The most famous one is called Peace, appropriately named after the end of World War II. Thousands of new varieties have been bred since then, and for years, new introductions have been promoted by the large rose companies, most notably Jackson and Perkins. As a result, hybrid tea roses have become extremely popular, and practically everybody in the country grows them. Everybody except my favorite garden writers, that is.

Such horticultural connoisseurs as Pamela Jones, Thalassa Cruso, Allen Lacy, Graham Stuart Thomas, Henry Mitchell, Michael Pollan, and Thomas Christopher, to name just a few, all give modern hybrid tea roses the raspberries. They have hardly a single nice word to say about them: hybrid teas are disease-prone, they have to be constantly sprayed with chemicals, they must be pruned and watered with clockwork precision on pain of imminent death (either theirs or the gardener's). They lack charm. Some of them have downscale, vulgar, show-biz names like Bing Crosby, Dolly Parton, and Tropicana. They aren't reliably hardy north of zone six and must be grafted onto hardier root stock so there is always the possibility that unwanted, unhybrid, rugosa rose suckers will arise. A lot of them don't even smell like roses. And worst of all, the plant itself is ungainly. A hybrid tea rosebush looks like flowers stuck on a piece of barbed wire.

Nobody's perfect.

Of course, the garden writers' objections are all valid. Many hybrid teas are unnatural products of too much hybridizing, fussing over looks, and not paying enough attention to character. The scent, health, and gardenworthiness of the whole plant have been sacrificed for one thing only, the shape and color of the flower.

Instead, my favorite writers suggest that we plant older roses, such as the gallicas, the musk roses, and the damasks, all sturdy plants with softly colored, heavily scented June blooms and the most romantic names imaginable—Zéphirine Drouhin, Reine des Violettes, Boule de Neige, Nuits de Young, Madame Hardy, Albertine, and Souvenir de la Malmaison.

Most hybrid teas lack evocative French names. Because I am from Brooklyn, the one place in the world that not even foreigners consider exotic, I was always a sucker for the allure of anything Continental. Foreign names do have a certain je ne sais quoi. I used to feel sophisticated and beautiful when I smeared my face with Clinique, but I would have been worried if my dermatologist had recommended that I use a cleansing cream called Clinic.

But I have ceased to be in awe of the foreign ever since the time I ordered a haute-cuisine item called cassoulet in a French restaurant and was served a crock of beans. So now, when I see a listing for the antique rose called Boule de Neige, which is white, I know it means "snowball." Now, "Snowball" is a tacky name that you might find on a regular old American hybrid tea rose—the kind that you see wrapped in tinfoil in any supermarket.

Being an avid reader of gardening books, I took the current distaste for hybrid teas very much to heart when I first started my garden. I swore that I would never grow a plant that had to be sprayed and coddled and fussed over like a wealthy maiden aunt who has not yet named her heir. So, following the advice of the gardening cognoscenti, I ordered some old-fashioned roses from Roses of Yesterday and Today, a California nursery that specializes in them. To be on the safe side, I chose a couple with German names.

I ordered five, confidently expecting a bumper crop of antique beauties, all of which were, according to my sources, horticulturally, poetically, and politically correct. One was called Camieaux, a pink-and-white-striped rose that looks very medieval for the two weeks in June that it blooms. Not only is its blooming period disappointing, but every July it gets black spots on its leaves, just before they fall off.

Another dud was Frau Karl Druschki, a lovely, delicate white. It's dead now.

The other three were successes. Paul Neyron, a magnificently healthy Hybrid Perpetual bred in the nineteenth century, has large, fragrant, bright pink blossoms that really do recur intermittently, if not perpetually, throughout the summer. The Bourbon rose Mme. Pierre Oger, named after the wife of the famous M. Pierre Oger (who?), is a large shrub with eight-foot canes that I have tied to the latticework of the porch rail. Mme. Oger dresses up the porch with her flat, many-petaled blooms for six weeks starting in June, with intermittent flowers thereafter.

My favorite old rose of the batch is called Gruss an Äachen. (It means salute to Äachen, which is a town in Germany.) It is a floribunda that grows to only about three feet tall, with flowers that are pale warm pink—almost apricot. Because it is hardy, I was able to propagate it the old-fashioned way. In the fall, I cut a few twigs about six inches long, removed all but the upper leaves, stuck them in the ground, and covered them with quart-size mayonnaise jars. By spring, one of the cuttings had rooted, and I now have two Gruss an Äachen bushes.

Until a couple of years ago, I was fairly content with my collection of old roses. True, some of them had failed, but gardening has taught me to be philosophical about that sort of thing. I'm willing to admit that it might have been my fault that two fifths of them had done badly. So I would never have planted hybrid tea roses at all, if only I had been able to resist a bargain.

One of the local nurseries had a clearance sale of pot-grown hybrid tea roses. Since it was July and the nursery wanted to get rid of them, instead of twelve dollars apiece, they had been marked down to two. Two dollars. Two dollars! How could I resist? Could you resist? Thanks to forbearance, admirable restraint, and the fact that I had to carry it home on foot, I bought only one. It was apricot pink with a very heady, strong rose fragrance, and it was called Helen Traubel.

"Wasn't Helen Traubel a Metropolitan Opera singer in the thirties and forties?" I asked myself. A Wagnerian motive resonated inside my head. This rose had not been named after a pop singer, a country western singer, or even the nightclub where Ricky Ricardo sang "Babaloo"! This rose was named after an opera singer! That was at least as classy a name as the wife of the mysterious Monsieur Oger!

I took it home and planted it in the side garden, right among the pink and blue and white perennials in the flower beds. It looked wonderful.

In fact, Helen Traubel has proven her worth in my garden. She not only looks marvelous and smells like my mother, who always wears Chanel No. 5, she's never had any diseases, and her leaves are healthy and green all summer. She died back to the ground when the temperature reached minus ten in the winter of 1989 (who wouldn't?) but came back that spring to sing another day. With proper pruning, even her figure doesn't look too bad, for an opera singer. The ungainly branches are further hidden by her neighbors, the daylilies, peonies, irises, and Japanese anemones.

I don't know why my local nursery was selling Helen Traubel. It's pretty rare nowadays. Like so many hybrid teas, it was popular for a while but has long since been replaced by newer varieties in the larger rose catalogs. The only place I've ever seen it listed is in the back of the Stocking Rose Nursery catalog, along with some other hybrid tea has-beens. As soon as I spotted it there, I ordered a second one and planted it on the other side of the flower border, opposite Helen the First. In spite of my prejudice against hybrid teas, I had to admit that this was a great plant.

I was reading a back issue of *Horticulture* magazine recently, and it contained an article by rose expert Rayford Raydell. It was a critique of the All-American Rose Selections, an award that has been instrumental in promoting hybrid tea roses over the years. To give you an idea of the article's point of view, the blurb on the cover read: "All America Rose Roast." It was not full of compliments. The article also contained a list of the winners, and, to my gratification, I discovered that the Helen Traubel was a recipient of the AARS award in 1952. I now feel vindicated. I had loved my politically incorrect hybrid tea in secret, but now I feel it can be shouted to the world: "My name is Mrs. Greenthumbs and I grow hybrid tea roses!"

There, I said it, and I feel so much better for it. I even bought another hybrid tea, Mr. Lincoln, an admirable American if ever there was one. He was dark red with a great rose fragrance. I planted him in the front border with the bright colors. Unfortunately, the cool blue-red of the rose clashed with the warm reds and yellows of the other flowers, and I had planned to move it to the cool-colored side garden, but history repeated itself. Mr. Lincoln was assassinated by the winter of '89. Oh, captain, my captain, you can't win them all.

But I will continue to try different hybrid tea roses as they present themselves to me—on sale. Because when they're good, they're very, very good, and when they are bad, at least they're cheap.

So I say, with all due respect to the great garden writers, let us not throw out *le bébé* with *l'eau de bain* and give up on the hybrid tea out of some romantic ideal or linguistic snobbery. Like any other plant, the hybrid tea is wonderful when it is healthy and placed in the right setting. The whole trick with hybrid teas is to camouflage their faults and enjoy their virtues.

The virtues of hybrid teas are their many colors, the beauty and size of their flowers, and their ability to bloom repeatedly throughout the summer and fall. The main aesthetic flaw is that the shrubs themselves are ugly. We all know people with good-looking faces and bad bodies, and we love them anyway. To disguise their unattractive physiques, I plant the roses behind leafy perennials. I don't grow them in the traditional way—off by themselves in a rose garden, like debutantes in a limousine. I grow them democratically, out in the flower border, just like all my other plants. In other words, my hybrid teas ride the bus, or they don't go. All they get is the same good earth, sun, air, and water as my other plants. If they get diseased or damaged, I cut out the bad part. If the plant dies, I sigh and throw it on the brush pile. I don't have time to do all the stuff that dedicated rosarians are supposed to do to keep the "rose garden" looking perfect. All that spraying, mulching, and fussing is more than I do for Walter and Sam.

Anyway, I don't think it's such a good idea to abandon a whole group of roses just because some of them are stinkers, or because they are out of style. As I have discovered, some of those old roses are stinkers, too. It was fashion that caused hundreds of varieties of antique roses to be abandoned in the last century, the good along with the mediocre. How we miss them. And how we mourn the loss of so many other old garden flowers and vegetables! The genetic diversity of these plants has been lost to us, because people stopped growing them in favor of the next horticultural fad.

So I will continue to grow Helen Traubel in the flower border, enjoy her beautiful apricot color, smell her heavenly perfume all summer, and imagine that she is singing the *Liebestod* from *Tristan und Isolde*. And next year, who knows? For two bucks, maybe I'll even give Bing Crosby a try, *buh, buh, buh, boom.*

JULY

A shady garden is a great place to fall asleep.

One Hundred Bargain Daylilies

In July, the roadsides are loaded with daylilies (*Hemerocallis fulva*). They are by far the showiest wildflowers we have growing here in the Northeast. And when I read that, in fact, they are not native wildflowers at all, but escaped garden plants brought over by the Pilgrims, I wasn't surprised. They *look* cultivated. They grow in neat clumps with large grassy leaves that give them a civilized appearance. The large lily flowers are not bright orange like a pumpkin or a glass of Tang, but slightly muted, like the color of a good wool Chanel suit. They are so classy and attractive, they fairly beg to be planted in a flower garden.

Needless to say, they *have* been planted in flower gardens all over the country. Almost everyone who is just starting to garden goes out and digs up a few clumps from the roadside and plants them near the house. People have been doing this ever since the time of the Pilgrims, and now daylilies are all over the place. As a result, during the month of July, you can hardly turn your head in any direction around my area without seeing huge masses of orange daylilies, tastefully adorning houses, roadsides, parking lots, farmyards, schoolyards, lumberyards, cement plants, and even garbage dumps. God bless them, those daylilies grow anywhere. And they're very colorful, if you like orange.

I do. I would wear a muted orange Chanel suit to a tea party at the Plaza, if I ever got invited to one. I would be horrified, however, if every other woman also turned up wearing the same orange outfit.

Even the prettiest objects get tiresome if you see them all over the place. So, although there is absolutely nothing wrong with the common daylily as a garden plant, I felt I wanted something a bit more unusual, perhaps the same thing in a different color. So one of the first things I did when I started my garden was to buy some hybrid daylilies.

Luckily, I found some on sale in one of the more arcane garden catalogs I received when I sent away for every one listed in *Horticulture*. And what a sale it was! One hundred bargain daylilies for $29.95! That's about thirty cents each. The catalog was from a small nursery in Florida, owned by a sweet elderly lady with a decidedly religious bent. It consisted of an eight-page mimeographed list (no photos) of daylilies, giving the name of the variety and a brief, affectionate description of the color. No money wasted on frills, like printing costs, here. Enclosed with the list of daylilies was a list of prayers and blessings, also mimeographed, and for free!

The plants sounded great. All the cultivars had up-tempo names like Young Contessa, Heavenly Dawn, Flamingo Surprise, and Bubba. According to the catalog descriptions these daylilies came in colors like melon, cantaloupe, burgundy wine, pineapple yellow, cinnamon red, pale peach, apricot, cherry, grape, and persimmon. They sounded delicious. Imagine, daylilies in every color of the rainbow except blue! I anticipated them with joyous anxiety.

When they arrived, I was surprised to see what a small package they all came in. I had assumed that a hundred of anything would take up at least a large packing case, but they all fit neatly into a two-foot-by-two-foot cardboard box. The plants were much smaller than I had expected. Each one consisted of a cut green stump with something that looked like a handful of fleshy peanuts attached to it. Those were the roots, I realized. A wooden name tag had been ruthlessly wired through each green stump. Young Contessa, read one of them. It didn't look like a young contessa to me. It looked more like an old contessa who had been dead for three hundred years.

Undaunted by their puny appearance, I planted them according to color, matching the names to the catalog descriptions. The pale peaches, apricots, and lemons went in the side garden off the porch, and the burgundies and reds were planted in the borders leading up to the front door. Then I waited for two years.

That last sentence needs explanation. I did not spend two years of my life sitting around waiting for the daylilies to show up. I worked; I ate; I slept; I made love; I cooked for my family; I did the dishes, et cetera. I lived. But it was two long years before those stumps actually bloomed.

To make a long story a lot shorter than it was, the damned daylilies finally bloomed and they were orange. No, they weren't the same orange as the roadside daylilies. They were, after all, hybrids. Most of the varieties planted in the side garden that had been described as peach, apricot, or cantaloupe were indeed those colors—shades of light orange, the color of Tang. The yellow ones were really yellow, it's true, but a lot of them were brassy—a yellow with lots of orange in it. The burgundies, persimmons, and cherries were red, all right, but most of the red flowers had yellow centers. Put red and yellow together and any kindergarten child could tell you that makes orange. At least they looked orange from four feet away. I mailed the prayers back with a nasty note attached.

I managed to find six daylilies out of a hundred that were not Day-Glo orange, gave away some, and planted the rest along a roadside.

Okay, so buying a hundred bargain daylilies was a mistake, but was it really so bad? Granted, I wound up paying five dollars apiece for six of them instead of thirty cents, but I got the pick of the crop. Over the years, I have divided them so now I have many handsome clumps of six different varieties of daylilies. And anyway, it was fun. Seeing what the plants looked like when they finally bloomed was like opening birthday presents and, like birthday presents, most of them were clinkers, but a few were great.

There are worse mistakes than getting burned on daylilies—like marrying the wrong man, for instance. Gardening mistakes are rarely very serious. (The big exception is planting a willow tree over the plumbing system.) But almost anything can be moved if you do it carefully, and even a hundred shades of orange flowers look better than no flowers at all. Nature is beautiful and bountiful and endlessly forgiving, and may the Lord bless your garden, bless your weather, and bless your heart. Yes, that's the way it is in the daylily biz, at least according to the mimeographed prayer sheet.

JAPANESE BEETLES

It seems to me that good gardening is the highest form of cooperation with nature, a way of finding one's own place in the great plan of life. I see it as a game, one of give and take, sometimes you win and sometimes you lose, and the garden is the playing field. The idea is to win the ball game, without wrecking the stadium to do it.

I like to think that my attitude toward nature is a middle ground between two extremes. On one hand, there are the Animal Rights, Vegetable Rights, and Fungus Rights fanatics who believe that any interference with nature is a crime punishable by imprisonment, at least. Then there are the Life Haters who treat nature as a Commie conspiracy that should be exploited or snuffed out with extreme prejudice. Their enmity extends to anything that can't speak English, like insects, wildflowers, mammals, rain forests, trees, wetlands, oceans, and the upper atmosphere. If I were forced to choose between one or the other of these two attitudes, I would pick the first one—at least they're kind, although not always to people.

My mother-in-law, Gertrude Brett (not to be confused with Gertrude Jekyll, whom I've never met in real life), is a great nature lover. She loves animals of all kinds. She takes in stray cats. She is the one who had fifty-two of them. As I mentioned before, she hadn't actually taken in fifty-two cats, only two pregnant ones and, like well-grown perennials in the floral kingdom, they had increased by the second year. After spending another couple of years finding homes for kittens (she never had them destroyed), she knew that something had to be done, but she thought it would be cruel to deprive the mother cats of a normal sex life. So instead of having them spayed, she had their tubes tied. This unorthodox approach worked. There were no more kittens, but the mama cats were constantly going in and out of heat, and as a result, her house was always surrounded by yowling, spraying tomcats, which was a constant nuisance. Her cats, however, enjoyed a long and exciting lifetime of dating fun.

My mother-in-law's love of nature extends to other life forms, as well. If she finds an injured bird, not an uncommon occurrence with so many cats around, she nurses it back to health or takes it to the veterinarian to be mended at her own (usually enormous) expense. She literally would not harm a fly but tenderly ushers it out the kitchen door, with all the politesse of a head waiter leading a VIP to the best table. Luckily for me, her kindness toward all living things includes her daughter-in-law.

She has a green thumb and saves all her kitchen scraps for compost, but she is so kind and sentimental, she won't pull weeds or cut down volunteer tree saplings—weeds are wildflowers. Like Henry David Thoreau, she understandably feels that they have just as much right to her compost-enriched soil as do the cultivated flowers. The result is that, after forty years of natural growth, her yard is a dank forest of vine-covered maple and locust trees whose branches scrape her roof and whose roots undermine the foundation of the house. The neighbors, with their neatly mowed lawns, blacktopped driveways, and small minds, think that Walter's parents are crazy, or worse, lazy. But to my eye, at least, hers is the nicest spot on the block, a bit of wild wood in the desert of suburbia. If Thoreau had lived in Levittown, Long Island, his place would have looked just like Gertrude's.

I suspect that Gertrude would like to have a more conventional sort of garden, even if it were only in a small corner of the yard, but her ethics don't permit it. From time to time, I give her divisions of some of her favorite flowering plants to take home when she comes to visit. Inevitably, she reports back that the plant has not bloomed or has even died from lack of light.

"Why don't you take out one of those maple trees?" I invariably suggest.

"I couldn't kill a maple tree," she replies, heaving a deep sigh. I can't decide whether the sigh signifies a sad acceptance of my brutality or a wistful desire to do just that herself.

"Why would I do a thing like that?" she says, leading me on.

"Well, then you'd have more light and you could grow other things besides maples, like flowers and vegetables."

We've had this conversation hundreds of times. She sighs again and says, "Yes, that would be nice." But we both know that it will never happen. One of us kills, the other doesn't.

I admire my mother-in-law's position, but the truth is, to have a cultivated garden, you have to be prepared to kill *something.* You have to pull weeds, cut down weed trees, and scare off, fence out, or murder woodchucks, rabbits, deer, and destructive insects. This doesn't bother me. Actually, it does bother me. It fills me with ambivalence. But I tell myself that the law of nature is the survival of the fittest in the game of life or death. Everything that lives must push out the competition and make a niche for itself, or else it will be pushed out and die in its turn.

So I want to make a niche for my garden, but I want to do it tenderly, selectively, and most of all, inefficiently. For instance, I don't use chemical pesticides in my garden. Not because they don't work, but because they work too well. Chemical pesticides that kill all insects indiscriminately are both wasteful and cruel. It is wasteful because chemical pesticides are expensive. (That alone would make me look for alternate murder weapons, even if these chemicals weren't bad for the environment.) It is cruel, because these pesticides kill not only pests but also friendly bugs, and possibly even the gardener herself over time. And it's not worth it for me to put poison in the air, in the ground, and then in the groundwater, just so I don't have holes in my rosebuds.

The holes in my rosebuds remind me that this chapter is supposed to be about Japanese beetles, not philosophical digressions. Ever since I have learned to spritz soapy water on my aphids and thereby control them, Japanese beetles are the single most destructive insect pests I encounter. I've gotten to know them very well, and to know them is to loathe them.

On its home island, that is to say Japan, this beetle is not a serious pest. It has natural enemies and diseases there, and the population is kept in check. But when a few of them were inadvertently brought to this country on a shipment of plants in the early twentieth century, they began to multiply with an enthusiasm my mother-in-law's cats would envy.

The Japanese beetle is a very beautiful creature. It has a coppery, iridescent thorax and a jade green iridescent head. It would make a lovely brooch. However, this lovely creature has some of the most repulsive habits in the animal kingdom. It is immoral, degenerate, and greedy.

The most repulsive aspect of Japanese beetles is that they mate and eat at the same time, like Romans in a Cecil B. deMille movie orgy. It is common to see them lounging on a bed of rose petals, one on top of the other, eating and making love in careless abandon. Shockingly, I sometimes see three or four of them lying on top of each other, presumably mating, while the one at the bottom continues to eat. What I want to know is: If more than two are lying on top of each other, which ones are the girls, and which ones are the boys? Are they so depraved, so steeped in debauchery, so lost in cold-blooded green lust that they don't even care? I'm as tolerant as the next person, but I do think a little old-time religion would do these creatures a lot of good. Actually, I would be much more tolerant of their 1970s' commune life-style if they didn't eat so much.

Most of the time I don't hang around the hollyhocks, ogling the beetles like a voyeur. I just kill them on sight. I grab them between my thumb and finger and squeeze. Result: beetlejuice. Those who find this method distasteful may prefer other less violent means.

A couple of summers ago, when the Japanese beetles were especially numerous, I tried an old-fashioned remedy, one known to, but never used by, my mother-in-law Gertrude. I found an empty coffee can and poured about an inch of kerosene in the bottom. (Actually, soapy water in the bottom of the can would have done just as well.) Each afternoon, I went around and simply knocked the slow-witted orgiasts into the can. They drowned in the kerosene, making me as pleased as a Puritan drowning heretics. I did this all through the month of July and managed to keep the damage to my plants at a minimum.

I admit the can of kerosene method is strictly low tech and inefficient. That's why I like it; it's sportsmanlike. Knocking them in one by one is more like a game between me and the beetles. It gives them a fighting chance, like hunting deer with a bow and arrow instead of an Uzi, or like fishing with a pole instead of a net. It's a gentleman's sport.

There is a more drastic organic method of Japanese beetle control, a weapon worthy of a Middle Eastern tyrant—biological warfare. There is a Japanese beetle disease, called milky spore virus, which you sprinkle on the lawn. It is available through organic gardening catalogs and at some of the hipper nurseries. It attacks the larvae, known as grubs, the immature beetles that live in the ground. In other words, the disease kills only the children. Horrible, isn't it? It takes about two or three years for one application to infect the entire grub population of an area, but once you spread it around, you never have to do it again. All the local Japanese beetle babies will have died of the plague. Nice.

Unlike a poisonous pesticide, however, the virus is very species specific and has no effect on other insects like worms and ants living in the same ground or birds that might happen to eat the stricken grubs. If I had a very serious infestation of Japanese beetles, or if I grew a commercial crop that Japanese beetles love, like raspberries, I would probably use the biological control, and the heck with sentiment.

There is also a trap on the market that is specifically designed to kill only Japanese beetles and nothing else. It uses sex to attract them. Needless to say, this sort of come-on works very well on these licentious insects. The sex-lure trap is a container of Japanese beetle scent, an odor that affects Japanese beetles the way Obsession by Calvin Klein is supposed to affect those incredibly handsome guys in the television commercials.

I don't know whether it contains male or female scent, but from what I have observed about Japanese beetles' sexual proclivities, it doesn't matter. (It doesn't seem to matter in the Obsession commercials, either.) They all come running anyway. There is a bag suspended underneath the trap. Attracted by the alluring scent, the lustful Romeo or nymphomaniacal Juliet flies into the trap and falls into the bag, each murmuring its famous last word—"rosebud."

You bet these traps work. Sometimes they work too well, especially if you suspend the contraption in the middle of the rose garden, as one of my radio listeners did last summer. Japanese beetles came from everybody else's yard for miles around, like out-of-towners to Forty-second Street, looking for love in all the wrong places.

On their way, they often stopped to hang out in her garden and have some dinner and a couple of drinks before entering the trap for an afternoon of romance, so her roses were even more damaged than they would have been if the listener had done nothing at all!

Sex-lure traps work best if they're suspended from a tree or post *away* from the garden, like in a nearby field or across the street. Of course, this only works if there is no one with a garden across the street. Your neighbor doesn't want them partying in his yard, either. You could always point out that at least they don't play loud music.

I get tough with garden pests only if they are very obnoxious. Otherwise, I leave them alone. If I did nothing, the garden would still be pretty, even though a few plants might need to be discreetly pruned to hide the fact that they have been munched on. My secret of pest control is to have many plants of different varieties, so that no one pest can possibly wipe them all out. Even Japanese beetles don't eat everything in sight; they have definite preferences, at least where food is concerned. Their favorites in my garden seem to be roses, hollyhocks, raspberry bushes, and grape leaves. They never touch the evergreens. (The deer eat the evergreens.) When I go after an individual pest, I use an individual weapon to kill it. It is the difference between a duel at twenty paces and nuclear war.

In the realpolitik of natural law, the lion does not lie down with the lamb, it eats it. And the lamb sheds no tears for the blossoms she tramples underfoot, either. It seems to me that the secret of living within nature is participating in the struggle, but not winning too overwhelmingly. The trick to maintaining the balance of nature is to have your innings, but not wreck the whole ball game. That is, after all, the highest form of good sportsmanship.

Gardening in the Shade, Singing in the Rain

When July gets so hot I can't stand it, I envy people with shady gardens. It's unbearable to work in the sunny borders when it's so humid you could boil an egg in your hand. If I go out at all in the middle of the day, I confine my weeding to the front borders, which are shaded by the house in the afternoon.

This is the time of year when the idea of a shady garden sounds good to me. It's cool, green, restful, easy on the eye and the sweat glands. To paraphrase Shakespeare's Macbeth: A shady garden knits up the ravelled sleeve of care. It's sore labour's bath, balm of hurt minds, great nature's second course, chief nourisher in life's feast. In other words, it's a great place to fall asleep.

Oh, sure, it's easy for me to talk about the glories of shade. I have a sunny spot to grow flowers in. I admit that there are limitations. You can't grow a flowery English cottage garden in shade. It's just impossible; it can't be done. All the gardening books tell you so. A shade garden is not a flower garden, they inform us, so look for plants with interesting leaves and be content with that. In other words, if flowers are the sex life of a garden, be a priest.

Being a horticultural celibate is all right for those who have the calling for it, but as a woman who has been growing large, colorful, luscious flowers for years, I can assure you it's not for me. A garden without flowers is like a life without romance. I know a couple of people who complain about both problems. I'm not a psychotherapist; I can't do much about their romantic lives, but perhaps at least I can help bring a little zip to their shady gardens.

First of all, there's shade, and there's SHADE. Shade, like passion, varies in intensity. There is a world of difference between gardening under the filtered sunlight of a tree with delicate leaves, like an ash or a honey locust, and trying to plant flowers under a Norway maple. Norway maples have roots so shallow and shade so dense, you might as well be gardening in cement under the roof of an air-raid shelter.

My friend Rita is fortunate because she has a west-facing backyard plot behind her brownstone in Brooklyn. Its exposure should give it quite a lot of sun, except that there is a very large old cherry tree in the middle of the yard. As a result, her garden lies in dappled shade for most of the day and gets only two hours of direct sun in the afternoon when the sun is low. I consider this kind of garden a real challenge, one that makes me roll up my mental sleeves, gird my mental loins, and open my mental case.

A plot like Rita's that gets two hours of sun a day is actually a semi-shady garden. The usual plants that are recommended for an area that gets dappled light or a short period of direct sun are those perennials that either thrive in or tolerate some shade. Lenten roses (*Helleborus orientalis*), bleeding-hearts (*Dicentra spectabilis*), snakeroots (*Cimicifuga*), astilbes (*Astilbe* x *Arendsii*), Virginia bluebells (*Mertensia*), monkshood (*Aconitum*), foxgloves (*Digitalis*), goatsbeard (*Aruncus*), and many more can be found listed in plant catalogs or in any comprehensive book of perennials. These are excellent choices.

From personal experience, however, I have discovered that there are lots of plants that will flower in only a couple of hours of sun, even though they are not listed as shade-lovers in the books.

The area between my driveway and the garden shed (see map on page 11) is shaded by the house for most of the morning and by the trees on the opposite side of the driveway until late afternoon. It gets slanting sun from about four until six-thirty P.M. in summer, when the shadow of the garage creeps over it. It is a situation not unlike Rita's.

When I cleared the weeds from this area, I was amazed at what was actually growing there. There were shrub roses: an old Harrison's yellow and several old-fashioned pink ones whose pedigree I can't identify. There was a large stand of orange daylilies and a deutzia, a six-foot bush that is covered with white flowers in May. The amazing thing about those plants is that *they all bloom!* And not sparsely, either.

You may well ask, why do those shrub roses bloom in that shady spot? Don't roses need at least six hours of sun a day? That's a good question, but my answer will astound you and leave you gasping.

Plants, like nature in general and humans in particular, don't always behave the way they're supposed to. You may have already noticed the human part. That's why psychology is such an imprecise science. Well, so is horticulture. Sure, a rose is supposed to bloom in full sun, but the shrub roses next to the driveway don't know that! No one ever told them. They're happy there. What can you do? What could I do?

What I did was to look around for some other plants that would grow well in this spot. I began to experiment, and I came up with quite a few plants that flourish in a lot less sun than you'd think. Some of them are what *New York Times* garden columnist Allen Lacy would call "thugs." Thugs are weedy perennials that spread so greedily, they would take over the whole flower garden if you didn't keep pulling them. Planting them in the shade tends to keep them under control, which is good. The shade is as good for the greedy plants as sound federal laws are for stock-and-bond manipulators. And wouldn't we all have been better off if we had had some sound federal laws for stock manipulators in the 1980s? But that is a topic for another book, one that will not be written by me.

So here are a couple of plants that are usually grown in the sun but which actually behave better when grown in semishade:

Obedient plant (Physostegia) is a thug in the sunny flower border, a pussycat in shade. It has three-foot stems and flowers that resemble snapdragons in white or magenta. Its most endearing quality is that it blooms in August, at a time when other perennials are absolutely perishing. It's a native American plant, which means that it's almost foolproof. My obedient plant was blooming among the weeds on the day we bought the house, so I have a special affection for it. Great plant.

Old-Man or Old-Woman (Artemisia ludoviciana 'Silver Queen'). The common name of this plant depends on your sexual preference. Although this plant is not grown for its flowers, but rather for its attractive pale gray leaves, it is a real asset to a flower border. I include it here because it's also a real thug.

I should have been suspicious about this artemisia's behavior from the moment I bought it at a yard sale in front of the home of a local dysfunctional family. You could tell that these were not happy people—even their junk told a sordid story. The front lawn featured a display of broken motorcycle parts, including a helmet with a bullet hole in it, old gun racks, several striped shirts with numbers on the back, a tattoo-it-yourself kit, a box of forty-five-caliber bullets, reproductions of Nazi memorabilia, a broken whip, and a large collection of "Beer Bottles of the World" that still smelled of beer, just like the couple sitting in their underwear next to the display. It looked like Bonnie and Clyde's yard sale. I suspected that these people were not English cottage gardeners.

You can imagine my surprise upon seeing a large clump of *Artemisia ludoviciana* 'Silver Queen' flourishing next to a dead yew in the front yard. Its white-gray leaves were a spot of purity in the squalor of its surroundings. I admit, I should have been suspicious about a plant that could thrive in that family without winding up in the hospital, but I never imagined that the plant was as much of a thug as it turned out to be.

I got up the courage to speak to Stud. (I guess that was his name, since it was written across his knuckles.) Dauntless in the pursuit of plant material for my garden, I asked him if I could buy a small clump of that gray plant over there.

"Oh, you mean the *Artemisia ludoviciana* 'Silver Queen'? I got that little number at the Chelsea Flower Show in London last year. Lovely, isn't it?"

Wouldn't it have been amazing if he had really said that? I would have been floored. But he didn't. What he actually said was, "Whah, whah the fuh?"

". . . that pretty gray-leaved plant. I would like to please dig up a bit of it and buy it from you. Thank you, please, sir." It never hurts to be polite to someone with "hate" written across his forehead, literally.

After a moment of bleary confusion, he seemed to find my request funny. Laughing and wheezing amiably, he lumbered up to the clump and pulled out a large handful by the roots! Unwilling to correct a man who sells ammo at a yard sale on the finer points of horticulture, I took the handful, gave him a dollar, and fled back to the car where Walter was waiting for me.

I planted it as soon as I got home, worried because it had been treated so roughly. Ha, ha. What a fool I was! The next morning, the clump was already starting to spread! The soft, rich, luxuriant loam of my flower bed was ice cream and candy to this Old-Man.

By the following spring, the handful of *Artemisia ludoviciana* 'Silver Queen' had worked itself under and into the roots of its neighbors for four feet around. It took hours to lift out all the plants and sift through the soil beneath to remove all the roots. I knew that if one root remained, it would sprout and the whole business would start all over again! What a thug!

I almost gave it the extreme penalty of my pushy-plant law—death in the compost heap. But the plant was as beautiful as it was bad. I gave it one more chance to rehabilitate itself. I planted it in front of the deutzia between the house and the driveway, where it would only get about two and a half hours of sun a day. It does struggle there a bit, but I think that adversity has improved its character.

There are a number of other supposedly sun-loving perennials that have done well for me in my little experimental station between the house and the driveway, even though they are not thugs, bless them. They are:

Garden phlox will flower with little sun, or even in dappled shade.

147

Pink, red, white, or magenta August-blooming phlox looks great with *Physostegia*.

Black-eyed susan (Rudbeckia) has flowered well. Like the *Physostegia* and the phlox, it also blooms later in the season, from July until September. The bad news is that the color of black-eyed susans goes with the pink phlox and *Physostegia* like ignorant armies that clash by night.

Old-fashioned flags (Iris) are real troupers. I dug up a clump in front of the door of an abandoned farmhouse a couple of years ago. They were blooming under the dense shade of an overgrown hemlock tree. I've noticed, however, that the newer large hybrid irises do well only in sunny spots with great drainage. No, I won't tell you not to try them. They may work for you.

Lilies of all kinds are said to prefer morning sun, but they also do perfectly well with only a couple of hours of it in the afternoon. I've tried all of the three commonly available varieties—Asiatic, Aurelian, and Oriental. Lovely, lovely, lovely.

Sedum, that bastion of the dry sun-drenched garden, is also very accommodating in dry shade. *Sedum* 'Autumn Joy', with its grayish fleshy leaves and deep red flowers, has a lot of style, as well as substance. No garden should be without it. The trouble is, this sedum is so popular, practically no garden *is* without it! But even though they may not be exotic, drifts of sedum are a welcome sight in September.

There are many other flowering plants that will grow, if not flourish, in semishade, which my further experiments will discover, I'm sure. And I shall keep trying new ones whenever I have a spare plant in my hand and no place to put it. I'll give divisions of my successes to Rita.

Rita *can* have a flowery garden. All she has to do is prepare the ground with plenty of good compost and select her plants courageously.

Gardens that have really deep shade are the most difficult for those of us who love flowers, meaning me and you. Plants for deep shade are woodland natives with flowers in subtle colors, and most of them bloom only in the spring. The most popular shade-lovers, the hostas, bloom in the late summer but are used mostly for their "leaf interest," and they do have interesting leaves. The leaves are architectural and shapely, with clearly defined rounded and pointed forms, some large and tropical-looking, some almost grasslike. Hostas also come in several colors besides plain green. Some have leaves that are striped and stippled like green and ivory marble, some have white margins, some are yellow, and some are gray-blue.

But let's face it, most hosta flowers are a joke. A few varieties, notably *H. plantaginea* and its hybrids, do have large, fragrant white flowers that resemble lilies, but for the most part, hosta flowers are pale lavender or white bells on thin stems that flop over as soon as they start to open. Some hosta flowers are so out of proportion to the tropical-looking leaves, the plant looks as if it is sprouting hairs on its nose. There are sensitive gardeners who actually cut off the flower stalks as soon as they appear.

Professional garden designers usually ignore the flowers altogether when working with hostas. They treat the leaves as the main design element, using contrasting leaf forms and colors as if they were drifts of flowers in a border. For example, they might put a group of pointy yellow-leaved hostas next to a stand of large round blue ones, just the way you might plant a group of yellow columbines next to a stand of blue irises.

Hostas, ferns, and their woodland friends are the only way to go in all-day shade. Areas that get no direct sunlight at all are pretty unusual in the countryside, but there are a lot of dark gardens in cities, the shade being provided by tall buildings and tall trees, thank you very much. My cousin Helen has just such a garden, a tiny plot connected to her ground-floor apartment in Poughkeepsie, New York. She always complains about it.

"Oh, sure, Cassandra, you can grow lots of flowers in your yard. You have sun. But what about me," she whined during a recent telephone conversation. Like all truly tireless whiners, she is able to speak even on the intake of her breath, thereby leaving no pauses at all. ". . . I have a rotten little dump of a garden with eight-foot walls around it the walls are higher than the garden is wide I can't grow flowers I have no sun it's not fair everybody likes your garden but nobody likes mine especially guys if I had more flowers I would get more dates maybe I should get my nose done . . . and et cetera."

This went on for an hour and a half.

"Well, Helen," I finally got in, "I don't think your problem has anything to do with your garden or your nose."

"Well, what do you think I should do?"

I gave a standard Brooklyn reply. "I think you should take a long walk off a short pier."

"Yeah, but what about my garden?" she persisted. It's impossible to offend her, no matter how outrageous the remark. She never hears what you are saying anyway.

All right, what about Helen's garden? In a small garden, we want to keep things simple. First, I'd use a great trick that I read about in a magazine recently. Along the back wall, opposite the apartment door, I'd hang a full-length mirror, the kind you use to check out your hemline. A mirror reflects light and gives the illusion of space. All the planting would be done with reference to the mirror.

I'd plant two large shrubs on either side of it to obscure the edges of the mirror, but not hide it. The shrubs could be evergreen, like hemlocks or rhododendrons. I'd pick rhododendrons because they flower in June.

Next, I would plant a shade-tolerant vine to grow up the sides of the fence that encloses the area. Virginia creeper (*Parthenocissus quinquefolia*) would do the job, as would the many varieties of ivy (*Hedera*), but I would add a less well known one called climbing hydrangea (*Hydrangea petiolaris*). Unlike the other two shade vines, it has umbels of white flowers in June. Then, leaving a six-by-six-foot area in the center for a table and chairs, I would fill in the area along the side walls with more shade-tolerant shrubs. I'd plant two viburnums (*Viburnum* x *Burkwoodii*) to bloom in May and two roses-of-Sharon (*Hibiscus syriacus*) to bloom in August. These large plants will fill the garden and provide large amounts of flowers in their seasons. If they get too big, they can always be pruned back into bounds.

In the space in front of the shrubs, I would plant ostrich ferns and hostas. Because this garden is so small, I would use only one hosta cultivar, the substantial 'Krossa Regal' for its strong architectural shape. In the fall, I would plant as many daffodils and other early spring bulbs as I could afford in and among the other plants.

I would not put a lot of small plants in Helen's garden, and I certainly wouldn't desperately throw in just anything that looked good at the nursery. I know Helen has been doing just that, and frankly, the place looks like her life—a mess.

Lastly, I would start collecting pots—clay pots, glazed pots, Indian pots, or anything else I could find—and display them on plant stands or tables on either side of the door to the apartment. Displaying pots means placing them on different levels to give the illusion of different heights. Placing pots on ascending steps does this automatically, but if there are no steps available, wooden boxes, upturned flower pots, or smaller and larger tables will do.

I would plant the pots with shade-tolerant annuals, like impatiens, coleus, four o'clocks, and begonias, and with summer bulbs, like Peruvian lilies, canna lilies, calla lilies, caladiums, and Mexican tuberoses. The fragrance of tuberoses will make you faint. If Helen could cook (she can't) I would recommend putting culinary herbs in the pots.

That would be a very nice garden for Helen, and it would keep her busy. I hope she's too busy to call me and complain about the results of her manipulative behavior. Besides, gardening is great psychotherapy, and she can use it.

AUGUST

You'd think that a simple thing like getting the colors right in the garden would be easy.

Color Is My Middle Name

Most of us don't start out with a perfectly color-coordinated collection of plants. You know, the sort of beautifully thought-out planting that can be had with the services of a professional garden designer. Most of us acquire plants in a haphazard manner, at least in the beginning. We buy them from catalogs, a few at a time, pick them up in the local nursery, get them from friends, or steal them from strangers. This is normal behavior. I know that's what I did when I began gardening, and I think it is all to the good. As we go along, we are learning what plants and flowers we like and what will grow well in our yards. But by August, after we have been staring at a late-flowering orange daylily next to the magenta phlox for a month, we begin to long for something more subtle and elegant in the way of color.

You'd think that a simple thing like getting the colors right in the garden would be easy. It's not brain surgery, for heaven's sake. It's a matter of getting the flowers to look good together. I believe I'm pretty good at it, but just when I think I have everything under control, as novelist Joseph Heller says, "Something happens."

Here is what happened to me. My plan for the side garden off the porch is for pale-colored flowers, mainly pink, white, and blue, along with other pastels. This plan works beautifully in the spring and early summer. The white lilacs and pastel tulips rise from a sea of blue forget-me-nots (*Myosotis sylvatica*). The forget-me-nots have seeded themselves all over the place, and after a few years, they have literally carpeted every spare bit of earth in the side flower borders and even grow in the cracks between the stones of the path. During the months of May and early June, this sea of blue is a background to all the pinks, whites, mauves, apricots, and pale yellows of the other plants. It is heavenly, if I do say so myself.

As the tulips finish blooming, the columbines (*Aquilegia*) open. I have some soft yellow and white ones that I especially like, but even the red and yellow ones are delicate and subtle. Then there are the blue irises, twelve different varieties that I bought on sale from Schreiner's iris catalog. The blue of an iris always has a hint of lavender in it, no matter what the catalogs say, but mine are as blue as you can find in irises. I adore them. I even ordered one called Victoria Falls, which was not on sale, but is the ultimate blue iris. The stems are three feet tall, the flowers periwinkle blue and the size of grapefruits (okay, small grapefruits). I paid an extravagant five bucks for it.

Dame's rocket (*Hesperis matronalis*) has seeded itself in and around the irises, in shades of pale mauve and lavender, and the peonies, which open just after the blue irises, are various tones of pink and white. The old-fashioned roses are shades of pink, except for the hybrid tea Helen Traubel, and the delicious floribunda Gruss an Äachen, both of which are apricot pink, and Harrison's Yellow, pale yellow with a scent like lemon verbena.

In late June, the true lilies follow the peonies and the roses. I have white and pale yellow spotted Asiatic lilies, quickly followed by the Aurelian lilies Pink Perfection, and the white trumpet lilies Regale and Heart's Desire. Along with the lilies, there are ten-foot hollyhocks (*Althaea rosea*) in many shades of pink, from palest to deepest, a soft red bee balm (*Monarda didyma* 'Cambridge Scarlet'), clear yellow sundrops (*Oenothera fruticosa* var. *Youngii*), lots of white Shasta daisies (*Chrysanthemum maximum*) and white feverfew (*Matricaria*), both of which bloom continuously throughout the early summer.

By the end of July, the pale yellow and pink daylilies (*Hemerocallis* hybrids), survivors of the One Hundred Bargain Daylilies Fiasco, make their entrance. As the daylilies continue blooming, the summer phlox begin to open.

Then, in late July, something happens.

My summer phlox are pink and white. The white is called Mt. Fuji, and it's lovely. The rest of the phlox are pink, but not the pale, sweet pink of the peonies or even the apricot pink of the Helen Traubel or Gruss an Äachen. They are a hard, bluish-pink, the color of an acetate dress worn by the mother of the bride at a wedding in Brooklyn. Ultraviolet pink. Tacky pink—a violet shade, the color of lipstick slashed across the mouth of a gun moll. I call it "Slap Me Pink." You can call it magenta.

The annuals I planted in May in order to fill out the August garden didn't help, either. I had planted them in all innocence, thinking that they would continue the pale color scheme that was so well displayed in that beautiful month. I planted dahlias in pink, tall cosmos in pink, white, and maroon, and cleomes in white. When the pink perennials and the pink annuals all burst into bloom in August, the effect of the entire flower garden was overwhelmingly purple-pink! By late August, it got to the point that everytime I walked out the kitchen door, I had to shield my eyes to avoid the ultraviolet rays. My lovely pastel garden had become a Pink Nightmare.

Okay, something happened. But what?

Nature happened, that's what. In nature, there are very few low-key, sweet-colored perennials that bloom in August. Just look around the countryside, and you'll see that late summer flowers tend to be bright yellow, like goldenrod (*Solidago*) and black-eyed susans (*Rudbeckia*), or any of the many members of the sunflower family. (I use these plants to good advantage in the warm-colored front border.)

In late summer, most pink perennial flowers have a definite magenta cast. The coneflowers (*Echinacea purpurea*) are in full bloom. They are dark, dusty pink without a hint of warmth in them. The obedient plant (*Physostegia virginiana*) is definitely magenta-pink. Even the Oriental lilies, those gorgeous, late-summer divas, are all either pink or white. They don't come in any other colors.

In a way, it's understandable. All those August-blooming plants with pink flowers have to battle it out with the bright yellow show-offs. Put a pale pink flower next to a black-eyed susan or a goldenrod and you wouldn't even see it. More important, neither would the insects, so necessary to pollination, and therefore the survival of the species. I suspect that pink-flowered plants have had to rev up their color or perish. Instead of the demure, come-hither glance of the virginal pale pink of early summer, the ultraviolet pink of late summer is forced by circumstances to lean up against a lamppost, lift its skirt, and yell, "Hey sailor, over here!" Figuratively speaking.

By late August, I was so frustrated, I was tempted to rip out all of the late-season plants and start all over again, but before I did that, I decided to see if I could tone down the ultraviolet by adding some other colors. I got some pale yellow and dark red dahlias from my neighbor Ross. I increased the number of warm pink dahlias by dividing my old ones. I pulled out all the pink and white cosmos as soon as I knew which was which and left only the maroon ones. Ron and Bobbie's friend, George McCue (the man whose farm I was visiting the day I fell in love with nature), had given me a small spirea (*Spiraea japonica* 'Goldflame') with light yellow leaves, which I planted next to the path leading to the arbor. Finally, I pulled out a clump of magenta-pink phlox and replaced it with a red rose bush.

I'd like to pause here to tell you a little more about this rose, because it really is one worth having. This is a new one that grows to about four feet. It's called Scarlet Meidiland, and it's from the French company, The House of Meilland, who brought you the famous hybrid tea Peace, among others. I bought it at a large local nursery near here last August. I always shop at nurseries in late July and August, rather than in May or June, and you know why. In the half-price section, this rose was blooming away in its pot, and it was the only red one left. (It's just as well, because then I might have been tempted to buy more.)

Actually, the Meidiland rose came in three colors, pink, red, and white. The pink and white ones didn't appeal to me; I was up to here with pink and white. But the red seemed perfect. This one is a strong true red, like the lipstick Red Tartan by Elizabeth Arden, instead of that dark pinky magenta color that rose catalogs fraudulently describe as "red."

It blooms continuously, it really does. It produces new buds even as the old flowers are dying off. Best of all, I have yet to see any pests or diseases on it. As good as this rose is, it has one disadvantage, as far as I'm concerned. The red rose starts to bloom in June, just at a time when my pastels are at their best. I don't want so much red right in the front of the path at that time. So what do I do? I just cut off all the flowers and bring them in the house and put them in a vase! That's a little trick I made up myself. I use it whenever I have made a planting mistake and have flowers blooming in the wrong place, either because of their color, or because they are too tall and are blocking something else. I can move the plant later when I get around to it, and if I forget, I just cut the flowers again the following year.

Now, in the dog days of August, the side garden is no longer pure pastel as it is in May, but at least I can stand looking at it. Along with the raw pink phlox, the magenta obedient plant, and the dusty rose-pink cone-flowers, I have lots of sweet pink dahlias, deep red and pale yellow dahlias, white cleomes, maroon cosmos, and a blood red rose. The pale yellow and deep red warm up the magenta-pink without fighting with it. If by chance my hybrid tea diva, Helen Traubel, decides to make her apricot appearance, I cut off the flowers and use them for table decorations. Helen's orangey color clashes in the pink, red, and pale yellow garden, but she looks and smells wonderful in the dining room.

(Incidentally, I have discovered that large bouquets of unwanted, clashing flowers make lovely hostess gifts when you're invited to a dinner party, and it's a lot cheaper than a bottle of wine. Just another economy-minded tip from me to you.)

I can just see you sitting there with this book in your hands, scratching your head in wonder and amazement, asking yourself, "How did she know what colors to choose to offset all those magenta flowers? Boy, am I impressed!" Okay, maybe you're not actually scratching your head and exclaiming in wonder. You may actually be thinking that I have made some ugly choices and, as a result, you've lost your confidence in me as a reliable guide. Be that as it may, I'm going to tell you how I chose those colors, anyway.

I didn't choose pale yellow, dark red, and maroon by reading Gertrude Jekyll, although she has a lot to say about it. I chose those colors by personal observation, using a method described by Vita Sackville-West, who wrote extensively about gardening in the 1930s and '40s. Like Miss Jekyll, she was a rich English gardener with a deep sensitivity to color. (Unlike Miss Jekyll, however, she had a very interesting sex life, which I would love to tell you about but space does not permit. Suffice it to say that gardening was not her only hobby.) She and her husband, Harold Nicolson, created the gardens at Sissinghurst, a restored castle whose old moats and walls were made into a series of garden "rooms," each with a different color scheme. Ironically, the most famous of the rooms was the White Garden, which must have seemed to Vita like a vacation from all that inspired color coordinating she'd been doing. All of the plants in it had white flowers or gray leaves in subtle and beautiful combinations, and it was a tour de force of flower gardening. I shouldn't use the past tense to describe this garden, because even though the Nicolsons are gone, Sissinghurst has been maintained just as they left it and is still one of the great tourist attractions of England, at least for garden-lovers like me. Theater-lovers go to the West End.

When Vita—everyone who is anyone in the glamorous world of horticulture calls her Vita—when Vita wanted to move a plant to improve her garden design, she would first pick a flower and carry it around her various garden rooms, placing it next to other plants, looking for the most pleasing combination of both color and form.

I have used this technique myself, and it works. I walk around the garden, flower in hand, and go from plant to plant, holding it up against flowers that are blooming at the same time in another part of the garden. If I'm not sure whether I like the combination, I wedge the flower in between the leaves of the plant I want to combine it with and step back to get a better look. If I like it, I make a mental note to move that flowering plant in the fall. This method is the horticultural equivalent of taking paint chips home from the hardware store. You get to see what the color will look like in situ.

Another advantage is that I am absolutely sure that everything I'm looking at blooms at the same time. This is a lot simpler than trying to coordinate bloom times while juggling catalog descriptions in the middle of winter.

I confess this trick only works if you already have a garden with a fair amount of flowers in it. But then again, if you only have three plants, mixing and matching their flowers is not that much of a problem, anyway.

The most foolproof way to plan a harmonious flower border is to pick your favorite color and get all the plants you can find in that shade. You don't want flowers of all one color, however. A one-color flower border is as dull as a date with a monk who has taken a vow of silence. For the sake of interest, you have to add a few plants that have flowers in complementary or contrasting colors.

I did this with a client last summer. He wanted perennial flower borders to line the path between his deck and his pond, a distance of about thirty feet. Okay. The first thing I asked him before choosing any plants at all was, "What's your favorite color?"

He said, "Well, I love purple flowers and hot pink flowers." Purple and hot pink—magenta! Ha! Ha! Ha! Ha! Ha! Magenta! I pointed to the magenta phlox.

"You mean that color?"

"Yes, yes," he nodded enthusiastically. "Isn't it fabulous?" He wanted magenta flowers! He *liked* magenta flowers! God bless him! This was wonderful! For the first time in my life, I had the opportunity to deliberately make a magenta garden! I had the chance to correct some of the mistakes I had made in my own garden when dealing with this difficult color, and to do it right from scratch. And since the area was only going to be used in June, July, and August, when the weather is hot enough to make the pond inviting, I didn't have to include any spring or fall flowers. This garden would peak in August, just when all those (previously irritating) magenta perennials were at their height! Oh, joy! This garden would be a celebration of magenta, an ode to magenta, a paean to purply pink!

So, after measuring the area, I sat down with pencil and graph paper to design the magenta garden.

I selected a dominant magenta plant for each month—hot pink peonies

for June, magenta phlox for July, *Physostegia* for August—just to make sure there would be a sequence of bloom. There would be more of these plants than anything else. Then I added a few more magenta plants, just because I liked them. I added cranesbill (*Geranium sanguineum*) to spill over the path at intervals, gay-feather (*Liatris spicata*) for its interesting plume shape, and two hundred bright pink Asiatic lilies, just to impress the client in that first June, when everything else would still look puny. If this sounds like some kind of calculating, callous ploy to fool the client, remember that perennials are a disappointment the first year, and the last thing I wanted to do was disappoint a paying customer.

Now came the fun part, finding colors that flattered magenta. My object was to soften the yowling pink with grays, soft blues, and pale yellows. I also had a lot of space to fill, two thirty-foot borders six feet wide. To give mass to everything, I chose two small shrubs to be repeated at intervals along the borders. One was Russian sage (*Perovskia atriplicifolia*), with gray leaves and soft blue flowers, which resembles a large, airy lavender plant and blooms fairly continuously from July onward. The other one was *Potentilla* 'Katherine Dykes', which has very pale yellow flowers on a fat four-foot bush. Along the edges of the path, I interspersed lady's mantle (*Alchemilla mollis*) with the cranesbill. Lady's mantle has light green interesting leaves and chartreuse flowers in June and July. I also used lots of silver-leaved lamb's-ears (*Stachys lanata*) along the edges and blue-leaved rue (*Ruta graveolens*) wherever I found a couple of feet of space. I included lots of white Shasta daisies (*Chrysanthemum maximum*) with yellow centers and two or three bright, buttercup yellow marguerites (*Anthemis*), for contrast. Just for fun, I added three hundred allium bulbs to be planted in drifts between the perennials, in shades of mauve, lavender, purple, and yellow. This would be some terrific flower border, especially if you like magenta, and maybe even if you don't.

I drew the map as neatly as I could, and I listed the plants and their catalog prices on a separate sheet of paper. The total came to well over a thousand dollars. When the client saw the tally, he began to fan himself with the map. He got out his checkbook, paid me for the work I had done so far, and I've never heard from him again. I should have known that anybody whose favorite color was magenta would also be cheap.

Say your favorite color is blue. Blue is a much more upscale plant color than magenta, anyway. In December, sit down with the catalogs and order every plant described as having blue flowers, like irises, Japanese fan columbines (*Aquilegia flabellata*), forget-me-nots (*Myosotis sylvatica*), delphiniums, balloon flowers (*Platycodon grandiflorus*), anchusas, perennial cranesbill (*Geranium* x 'Johnson's Blue'), New England asters, and whatever else is available in light blue, dark blue, wedgewood blue, lavender blue, dilly, dilly, et cetera. Order a couple of shrubs with blue flowers, like *Caryopteris* and Russian sage. These small shrubs look great in a flower border, and they even bloom in August, a frustrating month for blue flower lovers. Go to the nursery and look for plants with blue or bluish gray leaves. If it's blue, you want it.

An all-blue garden is not only boring but is also completely invisible from ten feet away. So, if you haven't blown your budget by now, begin to add a few flowers in colors opposite to blue on the color wheel. These will make all the difference between a washed-out, blah flower border and one that is drop-dead gorgeous.

Now you go back and look at the time of bloom of each of the blue-flowering plants you have. Find a contrasting plant to go with each season. The most dramatic example of what I mean is a group of blue delphiniums. Seven-foot spires of blue the color of the design on Blue Willow pottery are pretty fantastic-looking, but seven-foot spires of Blue Willow–blue delphiniums with yellow or orange Asiatic lilies in front of them are almost supernaturally gorgeous.

Gertrude Jekyll describes walking past a cottage garden and seeing blue delphiniums blooming next to orange tiger lilies, and she considered it one of the most beautiful combinations she had ever seen. The reason is no secret. Contrasting color makes blue look more blue. You may have already noticed that a lot of plants that the catalogs describe as blue are actually lavender-blue or bluish purple. Yellow will make the blue look truer. Conversely, if your main color were yellow or orange, some blue flowers here and there would calm down the yellows and make the bright colors clearer and more defined, if not refined.

Monochromatic flower gardens were a popular fad at the turn of the twentieth century. Here is Miss Jekyll's reply to the idea of using nothing but blue in a "blue" garden:

> It is a curious thing that people will sometimes spoil some garden project for the sake of a word. . . .

(Doesn't she write beautifully? You can almost hear her English accent. And she never even *heard* of a word processor.)

162

For instance, a blue garden, for beauty's sake, may be hungering for a group of white Lilies, or for something of palest lemon yellow, but it is not allowed to have it because it is called the blue garden, and there must be no flowers in it but blue flowers. I can see no sense in this; it seems to me like fetters foolishly self-imposed. Surely the business of the blue garden is to be beautiful as well as to be blue.

(She doesn't mince words, that Gertrude.)

My own idea is that it should be beautiful first and then just as blue as may be consistent with its best possible beauty. Moreover, any experienced colourist knows that the blues will be more telling—more purely blue—by the juxtaposition of rightly placed complementary colour.*

Well, I can't beat that, except to mention that, in England, "colour" means color and is pronounced "colah," and when Miss Jekyll talks about a "colourist," she is not talking about a hairdresser.

To sum up this chapter, I'd like to give you a few rules for a well-colored flower border. Rules like these were made to be broken, but it gives one a sense of security to have them as guidelines when in doubt. In general terms, when choosing a color scheme for the garden, warm colors—shades of red, yellow, and orange—look best with cool-color accents, and cool colors, like blues and violets and purples, look best with warm-color accents. (The proportion of main color to accent color should be about three to one.) It is also helpful to vary the intensity, texture, and shape of the main-color flowers to avoid monotony, a lesson I learned from my Pink Nightmare and put to good use when designing the magenta-lover's garden.

That's really all you need to know about color. If you already have flowers of various colors all growing together in no particular combination, it might be fun to start moving them around and make small areas where one main color predominates. I can't tell you what the psychological effect of a refined color scheme has on the psyche, but I can tell you

*Gertrude Jekyll, *The Gardener's Essential Gertrude Jekyll* (Godine Country Classics, Boston, 1986).

that it looks much better. If you have a group of warm reds in one part of the garden, a group of yellow and whites in another, and some pinks in another, each group planted with a bit of contrasting color, it will seem obvious and contrived to you, but I have noticed that most visitors are not consciously aware of it. It just looks much better than average, but they don't know why. And we don't have to tell them, either.

GASOLINE GARDENS

Every Saturday morning, the voice of the power lawn mower is heard across the land. Varoom, varoom in Fort Lauderdale, Florida. Varoom, varoom in Sacramento, California. Varoom, varoom in Fairbanks, Alaska; Bangor, Maine; Honolulu, Hawaii; and every hamlet, village, and town in the nation! Varoom, varoom . . . I hear America "gardening"!

The more I have studied gardening, the more I have learned about nature and ecology, the more I have come to realize that the modern suburban yard is a wasteful, unnatural, greed-inspired disgrace to our country. Pretty strong words. You've probably never heard a nice suburban lawn called a disgrace before, but I think it is, and I'll tell you just why I think so.

A lawn is, ecologically speaking, a desert. No flowers bloom, no food is produced, no birds sing. Grass manufactures only a fraction of the oxygen that trees growing in the same spot would produce. Most American lawns are maintained by gasoline-powered lawn mowers. One lawn doesn't use that much gasoline, even though the average lawn mower gets less than two miles per gallon, but multiply it by millions of yards all over the country and you get the idea. And I won't even mention the air and noise pollution, as well as the vast amounts of chemicals, fertilizers, and pesticides that are used to keep the grass perfect. Okay, I mentioned it.

Recently, while reading a magazine survey in the dentist's office, I learned that forty-four percent of Americans said that their main hobby was gardening. Astounding. Forty-four percent? Look around the countryside. Where are the gardens? I suspect that what the respondents meant by gardening was mowing the lawn every Saturday. No wonder so many people I talk to say that they hate gardening! And this is not always right after my lecture, either.

What a thankless task it is to maintain a lawn! You've got to water it, feed it, and lime it so it will grow so well you have to cut it down the next week. That's what the garden writer Rosalind Creasy says, and she's right.

Last year, I attended a presentation given by Rosalind Creasy at the New York Horticultural Society. She lives in a suburban California town and had turned her front lawn into one of the most beautiful flower and vegetable gardens I've ever seen. It was inspirational.

165

All right, we all want some space that is cleared for walking or sitting or just as negative space between stands of shrubs and trees. That's landscaping; that looks good. But the current practice of having endless lawn in place of everything else in the landscape is a recent innovation. It's amazing how quickly it has become a convention.

The first time people began to use lawn to make landscapes was in the eighteenth century. Wealthy landowners in England had a lawn for the same reason people buy fancy cars and Rolex watches today—to show off. In those days, having a lawn meant that you could afford a large staff of servants to hand-scythe the grass. Even then, the lawn was an expanse between groups of shrubs and trees. It was never the only feature in the landscape. Middle-class townspeople and rural cottagers usually had flowers and vegetables around the house, hardly any grass at all.

The situation changed about 150 years ago, when a cloth manufacturer invented the lawn mower. I'm sure he thought of it one day while watching the nap being cut by a rotary machine. The blade cut the pile evenly, so, the manufacturer thought, why won't this work on grass? Hallelujah! The lawn mower! The early version was so heavy that it took two strong men to pull it, but as we know, the design has been "improved" since then.

But human nature is a funny thing. The lawn-mowing machine made lines as it went over the grass. We think that the lines look neat. But to the upper classes, who were accustomed to seeing hand-cut grass, the lines meant that the lawn had been mowed by a couple of guys and a machine, thereby eliminating the lawn's usefulness as status symbol. So they would send the gardener back over the grass with a broom and make him sweep it to eradicate the lines!

By the 1950s, everyone who had a house had a hand-powered lawn mower and had neatly cut grass between the shrubs and trees in the yard. But there is a limit to how much mowing one person can do on a Saturday morning using human power. Until the power mower came into general use, it was rare to see the large expanses of grass that now surround suburban homes.

You can see how little grass was used by observing some of the older suburbs developed before World War II. For the most part, the streets are tree-lined and the front yards are extensively planted with rhododendrons or other shrubs. The whole feeling tends to be leafy and cool, very welcome in the summer, and sunny in the winter because the tree leaves are gone. This type of planting makes a lot of sense when you remember that these houses were built before the advent of the home air conditioner. A couple of shade trees planted on the south side of a house will keep it ten to twenty degrees cooler in the summer. This commonsense planting is just another bit of useful folk knowledge that we seem to have forgotten as our world has become more and more obsessed with conquering nature through technology. It really astounds me to see houses all shut up in the summer, air conditioners on full blast, baking out in the middle of the lawn like cars in a parking lot.

Actually, it was the developers of huge suburban tracts who made lawns the landscaping of choice. They would buy up a forest or a farm, bulldoze everything in sight, and build anywhere from fifty to several hundred houses as cheaply as possible. Often they would sell off the topsoil to make even more profit off the land. Then, in order to make the houses saleable, they had to add some greenery to hide the desert they had made, so they planted some evergreens in front of the gray cement foundation and then exploited some immigrants, who would work cheaply, to seed or sod over the rest.

This pattern has been repeated millions of times all over America. I would venture to say that since the 1950s, this has become the most uniform-looking country of its size in the world, as I have observed in my travels. This is a huge, magnificent continent. We have mountains, seacoasts, northern plains, and subtropical river deltas. But everywhere you go—everywhere, even in the desert city of Phoenix, Arizona—there they are, those same accursed suburban lawns, maintained by millions of gallons of water, petrochemical fertilizers, and gasoline. It's strange and frightening, like being followed by someone and seeing him over and over again, thousands of miles apart.

The wasteful shame of it all is that there are hundreds of desert plants that would beautifully landscape the yards in places like Phoenix with no special effort at all, but few, if any, are used. Instead, everybody has to have that same obnoxious, superfluous, redundant, death-enhancing desert on a desert, postage-stamp lawn.

Let's keep some grass for the spaces that we want clear or open, but use the land as it was meant to be used—not just mow it because we don't know what else to do with it. If you never use one side of your yard, plant trees there and some ground cover underneath. You don't have to mow all the way out to the street. Plant some evergreens and shrubs near the road to shut out the street noise and smog. Trees and shrubs clean the air by filtering out pollutants. If you have a big backyard and the children are grown, why not turn it into a bird sanctuary? The Audubon Society will be happy to tell you what to plant to attract birds. There is so much we can do to enhance our land, from growing vegetables and flowers to installing natural plantings that require no power machines, no petrochemicals, and about one tenth the effort on our parts, that it's a wasteful, greed-inspired disgrace that we don't use them.

I think the overuse of lawns in the suburban landscape all over the country is just another example of bad taste, the attempt to look like what you're not, like an elderly woman who dresses like a teenager, or a wealthy politician who wears a $100 work shirt just to prove he's one of the guys, or a ranch house with classical columns in an attempt to look like Tara. And worst of all, much worse than indiscretions in attire or ridiculous architecture, is an entire continent trying to look like an eighteenth-century English landscape painting, only with millions of little houses, driveways, parking lots, and shopping malls all over it.

What about an American landscape of the late twentieth and early twenty-first century? What's wrong with that? One that recognizes the fact that all those little houses are, in fact, cottages that would look a lot better if they had suitable gardens and trees around them?

I have a fantasy, a vision of the countryside to which trees and birds have returned to live among the houses of the people, where the Developer's Nightmare has been replaced in each part of the nation with plants that belong there. I can imagine a time when we will make the most of what we have, instead of always wanting something else. I'm not suggesting that we use only native plants or trees, although there are some purists who have done that. I'm only saying that we should use more plants that do well in the places where they are grown. I have a dream that one day I will be able to travel across the country and be fascinated. Every yard will be different, every region will have its own unique character and beauty, like every face of every person, and every garden will be like no other place in the world.

WHAT AUGUST DOLDRUMS?

It's usually about this time of the year that the garden and the gardener have just about had it. It's hot. It's humid. Who wants to go out and plant and dig and all that strenuous stuff? For those of us without air conditioners, August is the month to leave home and go traveling, preferably to someplace cool, like Lapland. Since I can't afford to travel anywhere that far, even in the winter, I just content myself with a cold shower and a hot novel followed by a trip to Napland.

By five o'clock in the afternoon it is cooler. Shadows are beginning to lengthen, but there are still several hours of daylight left. Now is the time to go out and see how the little darlings are doing. I'm not referring to my son, who has gone to visit a friend with a pool, but the little darlings in the garden. The plants in the front are in the shadow of the house in the afternoon, but the ones in the side garden have been baking out in the sun, and they do suffer. I put my straw hat on my head, spread number 30 sun block on my arms, and last of all, slip my trusty pruners in my pocket.

Here's what I don't do: I don't go around the garden and stare at the weeds in dismay, think what a mess it is and start pulling at random. That way lies heat exhaustion, frustration, and madness. What I do is to place a pair of hedge shears, a few stakes, a ball of string, and some twiggy branches into the wheelbarrow. I take the wheelbarrow over to one corner of the messiest border and work my way down the border in four-foot intervals. I start by weeding the area. When the weeds are out, I take out the pruners (without which I do not leave home) and cut off everything that's dead, or spent, or is blocking something else. Nothing makes a plant look better than having all its old dead flowers, stems, and leaves chopped off. Some perennials, like peonies, need only their spent flowers cut, but others, like the veronicas and Shasta daisies, should be chopped down entirely after they've finished blooming. The way to tell is to look at it. If any portion of the plant is leggy, brown, or yellow, cut it off. Don't bother cutting each separate stalk with the pruners, however. That takes too long. Use the hedge shears and cut off a lot of leaves at once. With only one or two chops of the hedge shears, it's done, with an efficiency that Monsieur Guillotine would have admired.

I throw all the weeds and clippings into the wheelbarrow, then I take a good look at what's left. If there are plants that have flopped over, I stake them, using the string and the plant stakes I've brought with me. Today, the lilies are filling the late afternoon with their incomparable scent. I insert the stake about four inches from the stem and tie the string with a figure-eight loop, leaving a couple of inches of play between the stem and the stake. If I have to stake a plant that has many weak stems, it would be slow torture to try to tie each one individually, so I use pea sticks.

Pea sticks are twiggy dead branches off nearby trees and shrubs. They are certainly cheap; in fact they're free. The branch end goes into the ground next to the plant, and the twigs support the floppy stems. It takes anywhere from five to fifteen minutes to do a four-foot area. Most of the time is spent staking.

At the end of a hot muggy day, the plants are beginning to recover. If there is a water shortage, and there often has been in the past few years, it pays to exercise both self-discipline and your arms by getting out the big watering can instead of the hose. Young plants and shrubs should get a good drink of water around their roots. Half a can for each perennial and two cans for each shrub is not too much. Don't waste water and risk fungus infection by watering the leaves, especially if you do it in the evening. It's impossible to get around to all the plants in a garden every day, but soaking a few plants a day encourages self-discipline in the plants, as well as the gardener. Frequent superficial watering has the same effect on a plant as frequent superficial praise has on children. It encourages a plant to make shallow roots that dry out quickly, leaving the little fellow helpless and always greedy for more. Deep watering at intervals causes roots to go more deeply into the ground, making both plants and people better able to survive stress.

The biggest favor we can do for our plants during hot weather is to keep their roots cool. (Air-conditioning is out of the question; I don't have it for myself.) I use mulch. Mulch is anything you place around the roots of the plant to shade the roots and retain moisture. When placed between plants, some mulches also inhibit weeds.

My favorite mulch has always been a thick layer of partially rotted debris from the compost pile behind the garage. The best part about this mulch is that it's free, but it does contain lots of weed seeds and it breaks down too quickly to be of much use by August.

Nature did me a big favor this year, however. A wind storm split an enormous tree in the backyard of the house next door and when my neighbor had it cut down, one of the by-products of the demolition was a large pile of wood chips. He said I could have as much as I liked. (I want it all.) When the sun starts baking the garden this year, I'll be able to shade the roots of my plants with fancy wood chips. I won't really use it all over the place, because (a) that would be excessively greedy and strain our friendship and (b) too much in the way of wood chips makes the garden resemble the landscaping in front of McDonald's—shrubs and flowers that look like they are adrift in a sea of weathered composition board.

Because of my "Magnificent Seven" plus six, which include black-eyed susans, false dragonheads, Oriental lilies, and phlox, as well as heleniums, dahlias, and the self-sown annuals that are really beginning to hit their stride about now, the August garden looks pretty good. There are even a few shrubs that are at their blooming best, like the rose-of-Sharon, Russian sage, potentilla, peegee hydrangea, and the lovely butterfly bush (*Buddleia davidii*). I have two butterfly bushes, a blue one in the side garden behind one of the Helen Traubel roses and a lilac-pink variety next to the Paul Neyron rose in the border along the porch rail. Since the roses usually take August off, the flowers of the butterfly bushes are very welcome in those spots. They are supposed to die back to the ground in this climate every winter, but in the past few relatively warm ones, they have made it through to become substantial additions to the side garden. Having said that, I'll probably lose the tops of both of them next January. (It doesn't matter, the top of the *Buddleia* will come back to its full height anyhow.)

After straightening out a section of the front border, and schlepping water around for an hour or so, there is one other thing to do—move the irises and daylilies. Unlike most perennials, which I divide and replant in spring and fall, some of the fleshy-rooted perennials are happy to be moved in late summer. I love this because it gives me something more interesting to do than weeding and staking. Irises can be moved right after they bloom, but in June and July I'm too ecstatic and busy to do the job. And since the daylilies have just finished flowering in August, I do them both at the same time.

The wonderful thing about dividing perennials is that you always wind up with more than you need. This is especially true of irises. I've been known to put a box of them out on the sidewalk with a sign: "Irises, assorted colors, take some or all." I could sell them for a buck apiece, but then that would mean I would have to stand next to them all afternoon to collect the money, and worse, get into long conversations with the prospective buyers and probably wind up giving them a garden tour for their lousy buck. It's too hot, forget it. I am comforted with the knowledge that somewhere in town my leftover irises will be blooming in coming years.

Irises, especially the fancy hybrid ones that I grow, must be lifted and divided every four or five years because they use up the nutrients in the soil around them. (The smaller old-fashioned flags seem much better adapted to a policy of laissez-faire.) I don't lift and divide all of my irises every four or five years, of course; I just do a few of those that have not bloomed as vigorously as I would like the previous spring.

I gently dig around the clump with a spade or a spading fork and lift the whole thing out of the ground and dump it on the path. It has a tendency to lose all the dirt from around the rather feeble roots and to fall apart into separate pieces. That's fine with me and the irises, because the plant is actually resting in August and couldn't care less if I used the tubers as juggling pins. I add about three inches of compost to the area, which for a large clump is about three feet square. Then I pick out the largest, plumpest, healthiest tubers from the pile, cut off the leaves halfway down (the plant is resting, remember), and set the plants on top of the soil, about six inches apart. Iris tubers should never be buried, only the roots, which are located directly under the leaves. To make this clearer, imagine that the iris is a dog, the leaves are the head, and the roots are the front paws. You only want to bury its front paws. If you bury the tuber, the plant will have to work its way up over time, or the tuber will get a slimy rot that makes it resemble a slug a lot more than it does a puppy. I water it all in and I'm done.

It's perfectly okay to cut the leaves of the daylily halfway down when you're dividing it, as well. Like the iris, the daylily has storage sacs that allow it to be treated pretty roughly at planting time. Unlike the iris, however, it is not absolutely necessary to divide it at intervals. I do it because I want more daylilies in interesting colors. There was, for example, a particularly pretty pale yellow (almost white) one in the side garden, a mature specimen, one of the survivors of the One Hundred Bargain Daylilies Fiasco, and last summer I decided I wanted to make two drifts out of it. Like irises, daylilies have many divisions, and if I wanted to, I could have made a separate plant out of each fan of leaves as long as they were attached to a cluster of roots. I wanted the new clumps to be large enough to bloom the following year, however, so I decided to cut the plant into six pieces, so there would be three plants to a drift.

I dug around the clump, using a spade as a lever to lift the whole thing a little at a time. After going all the way around, I threw away the shovel, got down on my knees, flung my arms around the leaves, and wrestled with it, grunting and cursing, determined to pull it to and fro until it let go or I did. A moment later, the daylily and I were rolling together on the grass like Burt Lancaster and Deborah Kerr in *From Here to Eternity* without the beach.

Brushing earth from my clothes, I stood up at last. Now I was ready to divide it. Innocently, I attempted to pull it apart with my hands. It laughed at me. I went into the kitchen and brought out a small paring knife. It took five minutes to cut out one section. Finally, I went into the shed and got out the ax. With two chops, it was in quarters. Now that the sections were smaller, I decided to use a more delicate approach. I arranged the section so that the point of my spade was between the fans of the leaves. Then I jumped up as high as I could and wham! It broke apart under my weight. (A sequoia would break apart under my weight.) I ended up with eight smaller daylily clumps, which I planted in two groups of three and five in the side borders. This July, the drifts of pale yellow daylily flowers looked so refined and tasteful next to the hot pink phlox, no one would ever guess that both the daylilies and the nice garden lady who tended them had the souls of Attila the Hun.

Sometime in August, the fall bulb catalogs arrive. When that happens, I put aside my afternoon novel and use that time to give them a good look. I must say my reaction to them is ambivalent. The flowers—lilies, tulips, daffodils, and hyacinths—are beautiful, but it's too hot to start planning a new season. Thinking about spring in August is like planning a new family at the age of sixty. The children are grown and out of the house and this is no time to start thinking about babies. Nevertheless, I go through the catalogs, knowing that next May I'll be glad I did.

Rather than tediously describe the proper way to order spring bulbs, I thought it would be helpful to show you my mental processes and share my innermost thoughts as I look through the Dutch Gardens bulb catalog:

Well, those two-tone pink tulips on the cover look awfully pretty. Let's take a look inside the catalog. Oooooh. These tulips are gorgeous. Let's just mix and match a few. I like to plant tulips in the front borders to bloom with the Henry lilac, so I look for tulips whose colors will complement the lilac-pink. The black tulip Queen of the Night goes beautifully with the lilac, and my old planting is beginning to play out. There are fewer flowers each year, so I'll order more of them. Where is Queen of the Night? It's not listed anymore! How annoying. There is another one called Black Diamond. Okay, I'll get twenty-five of those.

Let's see, the price is five for $2.25. Twenty-five will cost $11.25. That's not bad. Eleven dollars and twenty-five cents is the price of dinner for two at McDonald's. I can afford that.

Okay, but black tulips, like all purple or blue flowers, look dull, if not invisible, all by themselves. They need a pale or bright color planted next to them to set them off. What else will set off the black tulips but not clash with the lilac? Mmmmm. These white lily-flowered tulips are tasteful. Maybe too tasteful. Ah, here's a new introduction, called Yellow Present. It's a very pale yellow, the color of a baby blanket you give to a pregnant woman when you don't know what sex the baby will be. I want at least ten of those to plant behind the black tulips. Ten for $4.25.

Okay, $11.25 plus $4.25 equals $15.50. Not bad. Fifteen dollars and fifty cents is the price of dinner for two at the local diner. I can afford that.

Since I'm not going to plant the tulips directly in front of the lilac, but in the flower border opposite it, I want to add one more color to the tulip display, just to keep everything in balance. Here's one called Magier. It's white edged with the same color as the lilacs. *Very* nice. Thirty of these will balance out the lilac nicely, and repeating the color in a different form will add what's known as "visual interest." I love visual interest. I met my husband through the use of visual interest. I wore tight pants. Thirty Magier will come to $13.50.

Well, well, well. We're up to $29 here. Dinner for two at the local trattoria. I can afford that. I make Italian food at home.

I must have tulips for the side garden off the porch. Anything will go with the white lilacs along the side of the property. Rembrandt tulips, yes. I love them. They're striped and mottled like those in seventeenth-century Dutch paintings. Ironically, Dutch Gardens doesn't carry them. For those, I go to the Van Engelen catalog. Van Engelen sells tulips by the hundred, and Rembrandt tulips cost only $35 a hundred. A hundred striped tulips will be just about right in the side garden, planted in groups of twelve or twenty here and there in the flower borders. Okay, 35 plus 29 is $64. Dinner for two at Louie's Lobster House. Lobster has mercury in it, anyway.

This Van Engelen catalog is so cheap I'll get 200 species crocus. They bloom in early March when nothing else does—only $10.50 a hundred! And of course, I must have a hundred more daffodils. Flower Record—$42.50. I've always wanted drumstick alliums! They look like maroon lollipops on long sticks. Charming. A hundred for $10.50. Irresistible.

Now I'm up to $127. That's okay. I've never had dinner at the Russian Tea Room next to Carnegie Hall, and now I won't have to!

Now I'm finished. That's enough bulbs for one year, even for me. I close the catalog. But wait. What's this on the back page? Lilies! I can't live without lilies, especially wholesale lilies. What the heck, I'll order a hundred dollars worth. Boy, they'll be gorgeous! I can picture them all in my mind's eye: blood red Asiatic lilies in June, pink and white trumpet lilies in July, and Oriental lilies in August. This is heaven. This is gardening. This is dinner for two at Maxim's in Paris.

But that's all right, I can afford it. Think of all the money I've saved by not eating out!

SEPTEMBER

Digging is hard work!

Double Digging and How to Avoid It

Contrary to common practice, I prefer to do my digging in the fall. Because I took possession of my house in August, I first started to dig in September and October, and I have kept up with the habit ever since. I like it. Fall digging saves hours of time in the spring for shopping at the nurseries, planting the seeds and perennials bought in the catalogs, and just tiptoeing through the tulips. But whether you choose to do your digging in spring or fall, there are several effective methods of going about it.

Digging is hard work, but there are a few things you can do to make it easier on yourself. First of all, never use a shovel. A shovel is for moving masses of heavy material, like gravel. Workmen use shovels to move sand when they're making cement. Farmers use shovels when they're cleaning out the barn. Presidential candidates use shovels when they're making campaign promises. Shovels are for shoveling, not digging.

For digging, use a spade. The handle is shorter than a shovel's and the business end is flat rather than curved. It cuts the earth; you can step on it; it's light. I use a small rounded spade for moving plants around, but for serious digging, a straight edge is the best.

Before you dig out an area, water it a day or two beforehand. This softens the earth without leaving it so wet that it's like making mud pies. If I've forgotten to water the area beforehand, which is a frequent occurrence, impulsive creature that I am, I water it a little just before I start to dig. If you have heavy clay soil, like I do, digging in dry earth is like breaking rocks on the chain gang. So, to avoid mud pies and rocks, dig when the earth is damp.

There is an art to digging, an easy, graceful way that resembles dancing. That's the way I dig. I never bend over, for that way lies the chiropractor's office. I put the spade straight up and down on the sod and jump on it. Then I jump off and pull the handle toward me without using my back muscles once. Then I continue cutting around the hole I'm digging as if I were making a slice in a giant wedding cake. (Orson Welles's wedding. His third marriage.)

I cut the area into smaller sections and then lift the sections out and put them behind me and slightly to my left. It is very important to put the weight behind you because it forces you to use your arm muscles. When you put the weight in front of you, you are using your back muscles. If you've ever tried to lift a weight that is out in front of you, you know how easy it is to pull something, and if you have tried to do this recently, you may be reading this in traction. When you are placing the sod section in a wheelbarrow, try to arrange it so that the barrow is beside you on your left, if you're right-handed, and vice versa if you're a lefty.

Now I'm going to tell you the correct way, the English way, the kosher way to dig a flower bed, and that is by double digging. Double digging means digging a border to a depth of two spades deep instead of one spade deep. That's about eighteen inches to two feet. The purpose of this is to establish a deep root run filled with fabulous soil for perennial plants. Once you dig a border this way, you never have to dig it again. Thank God.

The first thing I do when starting a new border is to mark off the area where I want to put the flower bed, using string and some sticks in the ground. Then I start at one end with a two-by-four-foot rectangle. That will be my first hole.

I dig out the topsoil, grass, weeds, and all and save it on an old blanket next to the hole. Then I dig the subsoil out and dump it. The subsoil is where the earth changes color. It's usually not as dark and rich-looking as the topsoil. In my neighborhood, it is a sickly yellow color and is as dense as old Cheddar cheese. It comes out in big lumps. I get rid of the subsoil and use it to fill in low spots in the yard. Here's a tip: if the lumps are allowed to harden for a day or two, they make wonderful cannonballs. Unfortunately, there are very few castles around at which to lob them.

When the spade is so far down you can't reach the handle, the hole is deep enough. No, no, I'm just kidding. Actually, when the blade is below the level of the surrounding ground, the first hole is dug, and you can stop.

I place a layer of stones or gravel on the bottom of the hole for drainage and then anything organic on top of the stones. I mean anything. Gertrude Jekyll used a dead rabbit. She got one of the gardeners to shoot one. But I put in leaves, shredded newspaper, old socks, or last night's chicken bones. Then I move over to the next adjoining two-by-four-foot area and throw some of the top layer of sod from that area into the first hole to cover the garbage.

Now I make garden lasagna. I put in a layer of compost (or composted manure will do) over the sod, followed by a layer of topsoil dug from the second hole. I keep making layers until I get to just over the top of the first hole. Voilà! I've made garden lasagna! *Sono buoni!*

By the time I've used the topsoil from the second hole, the second hole is half-dug. I finish digging the second hole, place a layer of stones on the bottom, then some garbage, and use the sod from the third section to cover it. I make the garden lasagna using the topsoil from the third hole, et cetera, all the way down the line. When I get to the last section, I use the topsoil from the first section, you remember, the earth that's been sitting on a blanket for six weeks, getting moldy waiting for me to finish double digging.

You might try having a double-digging party and get some suckers . . . uh, friends, in to help you. But if you are doing this by yourself, you should do this slowly. It should take weeks to double-dig a flower border properly. Rushing will only make you miserable. Trust me, I've rushed and paid the price in Ben-Gay. But if you dig well, you'll never have to dig again, and if you dig poorly, you never will dig again.

When I started digging my flower beds, I figured mine would have the same square footage as Gertrude Jekyll's perennial border, 120 feet long by 20 feet deep. After fifteen minutes of double digging, I thought it would be just as nice if it were fifty feet long and ten feet deep. After an hour, ten feet long and six feet deep sounded attractive. After two hours, I decided to do a four-by-four-foot patch. Who can afford to fill a 120-foot border, anyway? After two hours and five minutes of double digging, I went in and had a beer.

I have described the process of double digging in my lectures, and I've gotten a lot of flak about it, especially from elderly people. They seem to feel that it's too much work. Some complain that they have heart conditions, or arthritis, and double digging would cost them a great deal of pain and possibly their lives. I listen sympathetically, and then I tell them: "You namby-pamby bunch of sissies. Don't give me that old heart condition excuse. Get out there and sweat, you bunch of lazy bums. What's a little excruciating pain compared to the joy of a well-dug perennial border? And if you drop dead while digging, think of the money your family will save in cemetery expenses. They could just cover you over with topsoil from the adjoining two-by-four-foot section. Don't be so selfish."

After being slapped around several times by irate eighty-year-old gardening-club ladies, it occurred to me that I ought to investigate other methods of soil preparation, ones that are less labor-intensive than the method described above. The object is to have soft, friable earth that is full of organic material.

So here they are, three ways to avoid double digging:

1. *Raise the bed.* Instead of digging down into the earth, use bricks, stones, or wooden planks to form what amounts to a very large flower pot. All you have to do is wedge some planks into the ground or pile up the bricks to a height of about six inches. Loosen the earth underneath, and get someone else to dump compost and topsoil into the area. Then you're ready to go ahead and plant. My next-door neighbor Ross, who has a heart condition, has done this to grow both flowers and vegetables and it seems to work just fine. Raising the bed is also an excellent way to garden under trees, because the tree roots won't compete with the flowers, at least for a few years. Trying to dig through a network of roots is a nightmare anyway. The only one to be careful about here is the tree. The raised bed should be several feet away from the trunk or the tree may smother and die!

2. *The old newspaper trick.* This works splendidly when you want to clear a very large area, like a meadow or a very large flower border. You just lay old newspapers over the ground, in layers about three or four sheets thick. To hide the newspapers and to keep them from blowing away, cover them with a couple of inches of grass clippings, discarded weeds, leaves, mulch, or any other organic material that's handy. It's also helpful to lay down tree branches or stones every few feet, just to keep it all in place. You leave all this on the ground for a whole season. By the following spring, all the grass and weeds underneath the newspaper will have died and turned into compost. Some of the newspaper will have turned into compost, as well, along with the leaves and grass clippings on top.

After removing the branches, go ahead and plant. As you dig each planting hole, make it a little deeper than normal and put the compost from the top of the soil in the bottom of the hole. When all the plants are in place, add more mulch between them. After a few years of planting and mulching, the earth will be as rich and soft as Rockefeller's baby.

3. *The big hole.* This is a variation of the Old Newspaper Trick. This requires you to dig up all the weeds on the flower-bed site, throw down mulch, and plant. The trick here is to make each planting hole deeper and wider than normal. Before setting in the plant, you add compost or rotted manure mixed with peat moss to each hole. This method saves digging out the entire flower bed at once and provides plenty of nourishment for each individual plant. If you think about it, this is the same method we

all use when we're planting a shrub or tree. You don't dig up the front yard to plant one cherry tree, you just dig an extra big hole for it.

This method was told to me by Jim Miles, who plants acres of flowers and trees for clients. He laughed scornfully when I asked him if he had double-dug all his flower borders. "Do you think I'm crazy?" He guffawed. "Nobody but an idiot would double-dig."

Call me idiot.

How I Plant Bulbs

I learned a lot about gardening by reading, but my education really began the first time I put a spade into the dirt. As a result, I've discovered quite a few techniques on my own that I've never seen in books. Take bulb planting, for example. The books I read gave very specific instructions on how the ground should be prepared:

> . . . the ground should be dug deeply, putting in a generous quantity of old manure or compost, well down, so that the bulbs when planted will not be in direct contact with it. A dressing of 3 oz. of bone meal to the square yard, mixed with the upper soil, will be of benefit; and so will a sprinkling of hydrated lime if the soil is markedly acid.*

The article contains a bulb-planting chart which indicates that tulip bulbs should be planted three to four inches deep (that is, measured from the top of the bulb; five to six inches when measured from the bottom of the bulb) and eight to nine inches apart. Very neat.

Instructions for planting tulips in the *The New York Times Garden Book*, edited by Joan Lee Faust (New York: Alfred A. Knopf, 1962), are no less rigid. Planting instructions feature a black-and-white photo of a pair of anonymous hands, one holding a trowel and the other placing a tulip bulb next to a tape measure and string. The caption reads: ''When planting tulips in rows, a ruler and string lines are helpful to keep bulbs even.'' I have no doubt that a ruler and string will sure as shooting keep bulbs even. When planted with this much attention to uniformity, the tulips will look as correct as West Point cadets on parade.

When I plant tulips, I ignore all of the above instructions. Not because they're wrong. (Mr. Everett, who, incidentally, died recently in his nineties, and Ms. Faust, who was alive and kicking at the time of this writing, are two of the most famous names in American horticulture.) I do it because I have worked out my own way of planting tulips, an idiosyncratic method that works best for me. I don't want my tulips to look as if they are on their way overseas to defend democracy. I want the tulips to look natural, as if they just happened to be growing among the other

*T. H. Everett, *Illustrated Encyclopedia of Gardening* (The Greystone Press, New York, 1960).

plants. So, instead of arranging the bulbs in neat rows eight or nine inches apart, the way it's done in parks, public squares, and in front of factories and military bases all over the world, I plant tulips in drifts around the perennials in the flower borders.

I dig a narrow trench no wider than my spade in long curving lines between the plants that are already there. Placing the bulbs between the perennials has another advantage, as well. In May, when the tulips are blooming, the daylilies, phlox, and the other perennials are small, but by the time the tulips are finished and the leaves are ripening, the other plants have grown big enough to cover the browning tulip foliage nicely.

I make the curving trench about ten inches deep, put a couple of inches of compost on the bottom, and place the tulip bulbs in irregular intervals on top of that. Then I cover them and throw some bulb food (a delicious combination of bonemeal and dehydrated sewage sludge from Holland) over the soil, as if I were sprinkling pepper over eggs. And that's it. If I forget to throw the bulb food at planting time, I do it later when I remember, even while the flowers are blooming the following spring. With my method, there is no need to elaborately prepare the earth in a special tulip bed, since the soil in the flower bed is presumably already in great condition.

I plant them deeper than the recommended six inches from the bottom of the bulb because (a) I don't carry a ruler out in the garden with me, I carry a shovel; and (b) I've noticed that when you plant tulips deeper, they are more likely to come back every year instead of splitting into lots of little bulblets and producing nothing but leaves. I'm sure we've all had this experience.

After a couple of years, there are usually only three things left to do with old tulip bulbs: (1) dig up the split bulbs and replant them, (2) dig them up and throw them out, or (3) ignore them. I usually ignore them.

The trick of planting tulips eight inches deep instead of six is not in most instruction books, but personal experience has taught me that it works, believe me. My tulips bloom for four or five years, instead of one or two.

I plant daffodils the same way I plant tulips, in long curving trenches. The S-shape is perfect for naturalizing daffodils under the lilacs, since the whole idea of naturalizing is to make the plants look as if they had grown there without human intervention. Good naturalizing requires a lot of human intervention, of course, but nobody is supposed to know that. The elongated S-shape gives my daffodils that devil-may-care randomness for which Mother Nature is so famous. You may recall that this S-shape is the same one that I use in flower arranging, William Hogarth's "line of beauty," the most pleasing form to the human eye. (At least to Hogarth's eye. It probably reminded him of his wife.) Who knows if he was right or not, but since reading that, I always try to use this shape when I plant anything in drifts, and it always looks great.

I lift the sod, or the weeds, or whatever is growing there, away from the trench and dig the trench out. I then add compost to the bottom, set in the daffodil bulbs, and replace the sod. The bulb food gets sprinkled over the surface of the soil, and I'm done. This is a great way to plant twenty or twenty-five daffodils in one shot, since each trench is five or six feet long and four or five inches wide.

I plant daffodil bulbs about eight inches deep. As I mentioned before, I don't use a ruler. As a married woman, I know perfectly well what six or eight inches looks like, so it's easy to make a good estimate. This mental measurement makes planting time much more interesting than it might be otherwise.

I set the bulbs in the trench at irregular intervals. Some of them are two inches apart, and some are as much as six or eight inches apart. It is not necessary to make any sort of exact measurement of the distance, but I do it mentally, while humming "Light My Fire."

"What about that bulb-planting tool I see advertised in some of the garden accessory catalogs?" you may ask. We've all seen it. It looks like a tin can with the lids removed, attached to a metal pole with a crossbar on top. You step on it and remove a plug of earth, drop in the bulb, replace the plug, and stomp on it. I bought one when I first started gardening. I planted a hundred daffodils with that torture device. A couple of times I hit a rock and the crossbar turned around and walloped me in the solar plexus. Planting one hundred bulbs that way, one plug at a time, was as tedious as tweezing hairs. I know a couple of people who swear by this bulb planter and say it's great, but I suspect these people are obsessive-compulsives who also like to tweeze hairs.

Walter devised a method for naturalizing small bulbs that I thought was a stroke of genius.

In our efforts to eliminate as much lawn mowing as possible, we decided to let the grass in the backyard between the vegetable garden and the run-down grape arbor grow into a meadow. To beautify this area, and to get a little more color in the yard in early spring, I ordered six hundred early spring bulbs: a hundred dainty blue *Iris reticulata*, a hundred species crocus in mixed colors, a hundred *Fritillaria Meleagris*, also known as the checkered guinea-hen flower, a hundred pale blue star-shaped *Chionodoxa*, a hundred yellow miniature *Narcissus* called Tete a Tete, fifty species tulips, mixed, and fifty normal-sized *Narcissus*, Barrett Browning, which is white with a geranium red cup.

No way was I going to use one of those dinky bulb planters to get six hundred bulbs the size of marbles into the ground. I'd be fuming around that patch of grass until Christmas. Instead, Walter decided to dig up long sections of the sod, about two feet wide by ten feet long. As he dug under it, I rolled it up the way you'd roll up a red carpet after a visiting dignitary has passed by. I dug out another couple of inches and applied an inch of compost. I then mixed up the bulbs in a paper bag and randomly placed them on the ground. We then unrolled the grass "carpet," stomped on it, and threw some bulb food over it all. We continued in this manner until all the bulbs in the bag were used up. The whole process took about two hours instead of two months, and this spring we had a flower show that lasted from March until May. I can't tell you what a thrill it was. Walter Greenthumbs is a genius.

I just spoke to Jim Miles, and to my disappointment, he told me that rolling up the sod and planting the bulbs under it is standard landscaping practice! In other words, Walter had reinvented the wheel, horticulturally speaking. So what? Is the guy who reinvents the wheel any less intelligent than the person who invented it in the first place? I don't think so. More ignorant, perhaps, but no less brilliant.

So here are my favorite bulb-planting tricks: Plant tulips around and among perennials in the flower borders to give them a natural, nonmilitary appearance and so that the emerging perennials will hide the tulip foliage as it ripens. Remember, the only way to make tulips truly "perennial" is to dig them up in the fall, divide the split bulbs, and replant them. Most any tulip will lose its vigor after a few years in the same spot, but they will last longer if planted a little deeper than normal.

When planting daffodils en masse, use Hogarth's "line of beauty" wherever possible. And last but not least, roll up the grass like a carpet when naturalizing bulbs in grass. It will save hours.

Now, I don't want to seem too preachy and strict about these rules. But I had to learn these bulb-planting tricks by trial and error and bitter experience. No one handed me a book like this one on a silver platter, kid. I had to earn my information the hard way. I had to pull myself up by my own muddy bootstraps and hang on by my green thumbs. Yeah, and if you think that last metaphor was painful, imagine how my stomach felt when I got hit by that bulb planter. I'm sure that you will make quite a few mistakes and discover your own personal methods. That is as it should be. All I have to say to you is: "Good luck. You're going out there a reader and coming back—a gardener."

OCTOBER

There they stay all winter, cool and snug in their peat moss.

FALL GARDENING

I do more work in the fall than I do in the spring. I set in bulbs, dig up the dahlias and the cannas and store them in bags in the basement, divide and replant overgrown clumps of perennials, move this year's failures, and cut down the stalks of the rest. I harvest vegetables, turn over earth, bring in the houseplants, paint the fence, send my son back to school, get a haircut, have a yearly checkup with the doctor and dentist, buy clothes, clean house, cook meals, do dishes, swab decks, tote dat barge and lift dat bale. By October, I long for winter, when I can sit in an easy chair with relatively little to do but dream about next year's garden.

I do a lot of planting in the fall because that is the time when all the nurseries have sales, and I can purchase some of the more expensive items that I've put off buying in the spring. For instance, last fall, I bought a few shrubs that I've always wanted: a peegee hydrangea (*Hydrangea paniculata* 'Grandiflora'; p.g., get it?) and three hollies.

The peegee hydrangea is a handsome shrub that was very popular in the nineteenth century and was often used for public plantings, in churchyards and courthouse squares, and is familiar to anyone who frequents old cemeteries or who has to appear in court. It has long, fat panicles of white flowers that age to a tasteful mauve during August and September. The flowers look marvelous in a vase in the winter, because they keep their color and form even when dried. I planted the hydrangea on my side of the fence that separates the driveway area from the parking lot next door.

I planted the three hollies in the front border. One of them is called Blue Prince and two are Blue Princesses. A holly bush is either male or female, so you need at least one male if you want the females to have berries.

The reason I bought the hollies is that *there were no evergreens along the foundation in the front of my house!* (This is so unusual in the United States that it deserves to be italicized.) As a result, my front garden lacked what horticulturalists call "winter interest." Everything in the garden was brown and bleak until spring.

I wanted to have some evergreens in the front garden, but I didn't want the usual suspects, such as yew, juniper, and arborvitae, and I certainly didn't want to put them along the foundation. Foundation evergreens are so hackneyed and overdone and have been planted in front of so many ugly houses, they not only fail to provide winter interest to anyone except the deer, they are stupefyingly boring at all times of the year.

So, to avoid this cliché, I planted the hollies in the flower borders that flank the path leading to the front door. One Blue Princess is in the left border, next to but about six feet in front of the Henry lilac that looks like Scarlett O'Hara's dress, and the other two, the Prince and his number-two wife, are in the larger right border. In their first year, they are not much bigger than large perennials, but I know that they will grow much larger and will have to be pruned as time goes on. I want to keep them about five feet high and six to eight feet wide. Their eventual height and mass will change the character of that front border, but that's okay. I can always move the perennials around. And in the summer, the dark, forest green leaves of the hollies will be a perfect foil for the rather loud red, gold, orange, purple, and white color scheme of the flowering plants.

I must say, planting the hollies in the front border gave me instant gratification. For someone like me, who grows mostly perennials, instant gratification is a rare experience. I had the immediate pleasure of seeing the Blue Prince looking handsome and green and the Blue Princesses all dolled up in their red berries that very next Christmas. "Instant" is not exactly the perfect description of the pleasure I had. I planted them in October, and I actually had to wait two months until Christmas.

I'd like to take a paragraph or two to say a few words about instant gratification as it pertains to gardening. It doesn't exist. Don't get me wrong, there are miles of gratification to be had from gardening. I should know. Gosh, it's one of the chief joys of my life. But instant, it's not. Shrubs and perennials take their own sweet time to reach their full growth and beauty. And trees—well, you can just forget it. The only instant plants that I know of are those annuals that you buy in the nursery in the spring. You can just take them home, plant them in front of the evergreen foundation shrubs, and whoop-de-doo, you have instant color! No wonder annuals are so popular; a lot of people buy nothing else. We're an instant kind of culture. We drink instant coffee, eat instant soup, and dream of becoming instant winners. There are even magazine articles with titles like "Instant Orgasms," for heaven's sake. (I read it. It didn't work.) Since we don't want to wait for food, money, or sex, why would we want to wait a *whole year* for some posy to bloom?

I've often heard it said that gardening teaches you patience. That's true. You have to learn to be patient or go mad. But I think it is more accurate to say that gardening teaches you that the process is more important than the result. The result of your efforts might be a beautiful yard that is the envy of the neighborhood, but if that is the only reason you do it, you might as well park a couple of Cadillacs on the front lawn and impress the hoi polloi that way.

The best part about gardening in the fall is that it is cool enough to dig without risking heat prostration, for the gardener as well as the plant. Neither one will perspire as heavily in the cool weather. When moved in October, the plant gets a couple of months to establish its root system before the ground freezes, at least in my climate. The gardener gets a good long rest, also. By spring, perennials planted in the fall have a good head start, because their roots have had a chance to establish themselves.

A lot of people are nervous about planting perennials in the fall because they're afraid that the frost will come and kill them. The plants, I mean. I felt that way the first year I had my garden. I had purchased a dozen Round Table delphiniums for a dollar. It was October, and the guy who owned the nursery was going to throw them out the next day since it was a small place and he didn't have the space to hold them over for another year. I was doubtful that they would survive, but for a buck, I figured what the heck. I planted them carefully with plenty of compost, mulched them well, and watered them in. I neatly inserted labels next to each one, so I would remember which color was which. I gave them every chance.

A week later, a frost came and killed them, dead.

Okay, *c'est la vie*. That winter, I bit the bullet and spent the money to order delphiniums from a catalog to replace the failed experimental ones, and when they arrived the next spring, I decided to plant them in the same spot as the dead ones, since I had already prepared the soil so beautifully there. I brought the seedlings out to the side border, and lo and behold, there were the dead delphiniums, resurrected and more robust than ever, like Lazarus, only better—like Lazarus with a beauty make-over. The "born-again" delphiniums were much larger and huskier than the puny seedlings I had in my hand. I planted the babies elsewhere, and that summer, those dollar delphiniums had many seven-foot, drop-dead blue spires.

The moral of this story is: Don't ever be afraid to plant late, especially if you can buy cheap.

I have been known to buy seeds in the fall. I admit this is really the height of parsimony, because even by my standards, seeds are hardly what you'd call expensive, even at retail. But in the fall they're really cheap: ten cents a packet, five cents a packet, sometimes free. You can't beat that.

I confine myself to hardy annuals. Hardy annual seeds will live over the winter and germinate in the spring, so I plant these right away. Perennial seeds can also be planted in the fall. Many of them, like columbines and poppies, not only tolerate, but actually prefer, to be frozen before germinating.

The sun is not so strong in the fall. This means that I can stay out in the sun longer to get everything done. Unlike mad dogs and Englishmen, I don't go out in the noonday sun. As I mentioned in the August chapter, I garden in the morning or in the late afternoon during the summer, confining myself as much as possible to those areas that are in shade. I wear a straw hat and sun block on my arms.

I have always disliked being out in the sun. I was never a beach person, even before the depletion of the ozone layer made sunbathing about as safe as skydiving. When I was a teenager in the 1960s, it was stylish to wear white lipstick and have a dark suntan, but I always came back to school in September with the same sallow pallor as I had when I left in June. Without a suntan, the white lipstick I wore made me look green; I must have appeared to be a real dork. (I was a real dork and suffered years of social ostracism.) It wasn't easy being green. In a way, you might say that I knew what it was like to be discriminated against on the basis of color. Perhaps the sallowness of my complexion gave me the deep affinity for plants that I feel today, not to mention my nom de guerre, Mrs. Greenthumbs. But that is a topic for my psychotherapist to address, and like so many other fascinating subjects, outside the immediate sphere of this book.

When preparing the garden for winter, I leave the stalks that look good standing and cut down the messy-looking ones and place them on the ground around the plants. I prefer to leave plant material on top of the soil in the winter, rather than leaving the garden denuded, if only because I would feel sorry for anyone who has to go through the winter naked. As I mentioned in the chapter on spring cleaning, the only leaves that I remove from the garden are those that might harbor disease.

The way to tell if a particular plant harbors diseases, incidentally, is by a scientific method known as Empirical Observation. In other words, look at it. If the leaves have dots and blemishes all over them and the plant looks like it's dying, it has a disease, but if it looks healthy, leave it alone.

In my garden, the leaves of peonies, irises, and hollyhocks all get taken away in the garbage. I don't even put them in the compost heap. The leaves of these plants tend to get rust and fungi that can live over in the soil from year to year, and the best defense is good hygiene; if the disease is not present in the soil, it is not likely to launch an effective attack on the plants.

Cutting down plants used to be a real pain in the neck for me. I would cut each stem and leaf individually with a pocket pruner, the same one I used to cut flowers. I can't tell you how boring that was. Then one day, while I was trimming back the *Kerria japonica* next to the arbor with a hedge trimmer, a large tool that resembles a giant pair of scissors, I got a great idea. It occurred to me that if the hedge trimmer worked on the soft woody stems of the shrub, it would work beautifully on the stems of perennials, as well. Now I can cut down a big clump of peonies in two or three cuts, instead of forty-nine little ones. *Thwok, thwok, thwok,* and it's down! Books never tell you these things.

As I put the garden to bed in the fall, I like to give it a thorough weeding as I go along. It's easy to see the weeds when the plants are cut down, and getting rid of them now gives me, and the flower beds, a good head start in the spring. I like to think I'm pretty good at keeping the garden weeded all year, but it's amazing how much winds up in the wheelbarrow, and then into the compost heap, to become next year's humus.

Now is the perfect time to move and divide old perennials. As we look over the flower beds in the fall, it's easy to recall the successes and disasters of the previous season, because they're sitting out there staring at you. Remember the orange poppy that looked so hideous next to the red rose last June? One of them has *got* to be moved. The hosta has completely overgrown the Japanese painted fern and should be divided. Those lilies that are beginning to get puny-looking should be taken up and replanted in fresh soil. What about that idea of an all-yellow flower border along the fence next to the vegetable garden? Now is the time to take up the yellow-flowering perennials, divide, and replant them there.

Taking up and dividing plants is very easy, at least on paper. As I mentioned before, all you have to do is dig around the clump, lift it out of the soil entirely, then divide it into smaller sections by pulling it apart or cutting it with a knife or, in really hard cases, a saw. Then you replant the pieces just as you would new plants. It sounds so simple, but it is an awesome procedure, especially for a beginner.

I used to be very nervous about dividing plants. I was afraid that any sort of root disturbance would kill them, and I would lose the whole thing. The thought of mutilating one of my babies in this way horrified me. I would sooner have done kidney surgery on my son. So, for years, the only way I would divide a perennial was by digging out a small piece off the side of a large clump and replanting that, leaving the greater part intact—more like foot surgery. This method worked very well, and I recommend it to all beginners, as well as to the faint of heart. Plenty of good gardeners are shy in this way, believe me. To this day, my friend Bobbie would rather buy three new plants than dig up and divide one that she already has.

I learned courage from my neighbor Ross, a man with both a green thumb and medals for valor during World War II. He has the right stuff. When he moved next door about four years ago and wanted to bring his old garden with him, he didn't spend hours putting plants in pots the way I would have done; he just dug them all up, wrapped them in wet newspapers, and transported them in cardboard boxes. He then divided the clumps and planted them, taking his own sweet time about it, too. Some of those plants waited hours, or even days, before they were put in the ground! I was horrified but too polite to say so. He'd line up the divisions on the lawn in front of the flower bed and leave them there with their guts hanging out until he was ready to plant them. His lawn looked like the battlefield after Dunkirk.

Needless to say, they all lived.

Now I have no compunctions about moving and dividing anything. The wet newspaper trick works very well when taking a plant any distance greater than across the yard. I have even divided shrubs by taking up the whole thing, sawing it apart, and planting both halves. If the shrubs look a little piqued after such major surgery, I cut back the stems to restore the balance between the reduced root system and the leaves. I divide siberian irises with an ax. Just call me *Doctor* Greenthumbs.

Putting My Tender Bulbs to Bed

Somewhere between late October and early November, the frost arrives and it's time for my last chore of the season, digging up the dahlias. Dahlias are a pain in the neck. They have to be dug up every fall, stored in the basement, and replanted every spring. But I don't care because I love them, especially the big ones. Dinner plate dahlias, those with flowers from eight to ten inches across, were extremely popular in the late nineteenth and early twentieth centuries but have since gone out of fashion among sophisticated modern gardeners. Jim Miles, the professional, laughs out loud when he sees them in my garden. George McCue is openly contemptuous of them, calling them "flowers for a horse's funeral." Others have been known to sneer and roll their eyes, or politely ignore them. But I don't care, because I love the large, vulgar guys. Their outrageous size is perfect for my storybook garden. When the dahlias are planted next to Southern Belle hibiscus, a ten-inch tropical-looking flower on a four-foot plant, everything is so out of normal scale, you might really think that you have suddenly turned into a bunny in a waistcoat at a tea party with Alice. And three enormous dahlias in a vase make a bouquet.

I think that a lot of gardeners dislike dinner plate dahlias for the same reason that I love them. Their muscular growth and admittedly ridiculous size are all out of proportion to the tasteful and more refined blossoms of a modern "low-maintenance" perennial flower border.

Actually, dahlias come in many shapes and sizes. The smaller ones must be very popular, because I see them on sale along with the annuals at the local nurseries every spring. Most of them resemble daisies, but there are also other shapes, like pom-poms, as well as cactus dahlias with spiky double flowers.

The small ones are okay, and they do come in all the wonderful dahlia colors, and that's about every color of the rainbow except blue. Really, every color of the rainbow except blue. Sometimes you read that claim in catalogs about other plants, like irises and daylilies, but it isn't true. As we know, daylilies, for example, come in every color of the rainbow only if the rainbow is seen through orange-colored glasses. With dahlias, the claim is true, however, and the colors are clear and sparkling, never muddy. This makes them very useful, since they'll go with any color scheme. I use dark, blood red and gold ones in the front borders and pink, lavender, pale yellow, and white ones in the side borders off the porch.

Since the big dahlias require the extra effort of being staked, dug up, and stored every year, they seem to be a bit more trouble than most gardeners think they're worth. And there is another reason for their unpopularity, as well. To make it through the winter without shriveling up, the tubers must be stored in fairly low temperatures, but above freezing. Years ago, during the Dahlia Decades before World War II, people generally kept them in the unfinished, unheated basements of old houses, but most new homes have no place to put them. Modern basements are often heated and are even used as rec rooms, decorated with knotty pine paneling. Nowadays, there is no room for the dahlias; their place has been usurped by a wet bar and a BarcaLounger.

My old house has an unheated basement. During the winter, the temperature ranges from about thirty-five to sixty degrees, depending on the outside weather, so it's a perfect place to store tubers. If you are not so fortunate, an old refrigerator, the vestibule by the backdoor, or any location where they will be cold and dark but not frozen will do.

I plant the tubers outdoors during lilac time in early May, and the plants get bushy all summer and start to bloom in August, when most of the showy perennials of early and midsummer look like hell. What troopers they are.

The dahlia plants are four feet tall and have fresh-looking, green leaves that remind me of tomato plants. And, like tomatoes, they must be staked. I've found that the best stakes for dahlias are old wooden broomsticks. Old mop handles are even better, because they are longer when the mop has been removed. Painted a dark green, they're practically invisible in the garden. Unfortunately, they are hard to come by, especially when you need a lot of them. Whenever I see one sticking out of a trash bin I grab it and take it home, and I feel as if I've found a treasure.

Failure to stake a dahlia plant firmly is an invitation to disaster, because their stems are as hollow and brittle as former first lady Nancy Reagan. When the dahlia is big enough to flop over, I insert a stake or two next to the plant, but not so close that the stake will impale the tuber. After all, I want to support a plant, not kill a vampire. Some books tell you to insert the stake at planting time, but that means looking at a naked pole for half the summer, and that seems a bit vulgar to me, so I prefer to wait until it is absolutely necessary. I tie each hefty stem to the stake individually, using string that I've saved from bakery boxes and Chinese laundry packages. (I'm *really* cheap.) If the string is too thin, I double it. Brown twine is better, because it is less likely to bruise or damage the stem, and the soft earth color is much harder to see. The trouble with brown twine is that you have to buy it. Some old-fashioned gardeners use torn strips of old sheeting or rags or even old nylon stockings to avoid bruising the stem. Cheap, it is, but beautiful, it isn't. Don't do it.

I use plenty of string (I can afford to) and tie loosely, so that there is room for the stem to move. I don't want the stem to look as though it is lashed to the stake like Joan of Arc at her execution. We've all seen plants tied up in this way, and it looks terrible. Maybe not as terrible as tying it with an old stocking, but ugly, nevertheless. The whole idea of staking any plant is to make it look as if it just happened to be growing perfectly without visible means of support, not as if it were being sent to an auto-da-fé by the Grand Inquisitor.

But it's almost November and time to get to work. At the earliest opportunity after the first frost, I pick a sunny day to dig up the dahlias. Sometimes it's cold, but I can't be too choosy about the weather this late in the season, so I do it anyway. After cutting off the slimy frost-blackened leaves down to a four-inch stem, I'm ready to dig up the dahlia tubers. Some experts say to use a garden fork to avoid damaging them, but in my experience, I've found that I was just as likely to spear a tuber with a fork as I was to slice one with a spade, so I use a spade. To be on the safe side, I assume that the clump of tubers will extend about a foot around the stem. I dig around the clump slowly at first, and then with more confidence once I've found it. Then I lift it out and heave it onto the lawn. If it has been a good growing year, what started out as a clump with one or two tubers at the beginning of the season will have increased to a cluster of tubers by fall, and it's pretty heavy. I put all the clumps of the same variety in a pile and try to keep all the piles separate from each other. Once the plants are cut down and out of the ground, all the clumps look like yams and it's impossible to tell one from the other. I note the color of each variety on a separate piece of paper and stick it under the appropriate pile. If I don't do this, by lunchtime I'll have forgotten which was which, and next year, I'll have surprise dahlias growing in all the wrong places.

I hose down the clumps to clean the dirt off and leave them out to dry in the sun. Cold and wet, I go inside and have a hot cup of coffee.

Intermission.

Later, I come back out again with a bale of peat moss (shredded newspaper will do as well) and a collection of plastic bags from the supermarket. I mark the outside of each bag with the color of the dahlia, pack them two or three clumps to a bag, and cover them with the peat moss. When I'm all done, I take them down into the cellar and hang the bags by their handles from nails that Walter has driven into the old wooden beams. There they stay all winter, cool and snug in their peat moss until next year, and I go upstairs to get warm and snug in my bed until suppertime.

In May, I reverse the procedure. When the dahlia clumps are removed from the bags, they have pink buds or even pale green shoots already emerging from the base of the old stems. Each of these buds is a potential new plant. If I want to increase the number of dahlias I'll be growing that year, I simply cut the stem so that I have at least one or two pink buds attached to the tubers. A lot of people think that the tuber itself is the new plant, but it won't be anything but compost unless there is a bud attached to it. The tuber is only a storage sack, the dahlia's version of a lunchbox.

Until they're planted, I keep the clumps in the plastic bags. I can't tell you how easy it is to get them mixed up if they're scattered all over the place. I take the wheelbarrow and fill it with compost, then mix the compost with a little peat moss from the bag. Then I add the mixture to each planting hole as I go along.

All the dahlias don't have to be planted in one day; it can be done over the course of a couple of weeks, although if it's a glorious day in May, the job is a pleasure. In fact, it can even be done a few days earlier, before all danger of frost is passed, because it's the tops of the dahlias that are in danger of being killed by a light frost, not the tubers. And the tops won't be making their appearance for another two weeks after planting. Once they are in the ground, the tubers are protected from everything except a deep freeze. The ground freezing solid in May is an act of God so unlikely that I don't even worry about it. Of course I realize that having said that, we'll probably get a mini–Ice Age next year.

You can see that growing dahlias in the North is a bit of trouble. It's a lot of trouble, actually. But then, so is everything else in life, except for watching television.

COMPOST AND LIFE IN GENERAL

Before we leave the garden for the winter, I have to talk about compost, because I love it. Compost is the greatest thing to have in your garden. It's a mixture of decaying substances and earth. Because it has trace minerals, bacteria, and elements essential to make life, it is the most perfect growing medium for plants. To gardeners, compost is the sweet mystery of life.

Let me explain. In the beginning, the earth was made of rock and sea. The first most primitive forms of life came out of the sea, grew on the rock, and died. Their remains combined with the rock to make enough soil for moss to grow. The moss died and mixed with gravel on the rock, and the next larger plant grew and died. Pretty soon, a tree grew in the fissure of the rock. The tree died and pretty soon—a hundred million years or so later—there was a forest and birds were singing, just like Jeanette MacDonald and Nelson Eddy, "Ah, sweet mystery of life at last I've found you! Ah, at last I know the secret of it all!"

Compost. You've got to have it. And it's easy to make.

I have a compost heap. I started it as soon as Walter and I began clearing out the yard. Behind the garage, where I don't have to look at it, I throw weeds, leaves, coffee grounds, eggshells, leftover minestrone soup, broccoli stems, banana peels, and those funny green things you find in the back of the refrigerator that look like they were once either lemons or cheese.

Every time I add a few inches of organic material to the pile, I throw a few spadefuls of earth on top. The earth is full of bacteria. Not the bad bacteria that gives you acne, but the kind of bacteria that works on all this assorted effluvia and turns it into something that any gardener would kill for—compost, gardener's gold.

I don't put meat in the compost pile at all. Meat and bones would smell bad. A healthy compost pile should never stink at all. If it does, it means the pile needs more soil or air between the layers. It isn't absolutely necessary to turn the pile over, although if you have the energy and a pitchfork, it does make the varied junk break down into compost faster.

If you don't have room or an out-of-the-way spot for a whole heap, you can buy a compost bin. There are plain wire ones that look neat. Or you can buy a status composter. It can be found in many glossy garden accessory catalogs, and it is called the "Cadillac of Composters." It's made of brown plastic with a woodlike finish, which looks pretty realistic—from a quarter of a mile away. The price is around a hundred bucks. Why does it cost a hundred bucks? Because that's what they can get for it, that's why. There is also a compost drum made in Germany, another item calculated to separate you from a large sum of money. It's very German. You have to turn the drum every day, or else! And it's just a little less attractive than a Grecian urn—it looks like a large green hazardous waste container on metal legs.

Compost is really wonderful and fascinating to make, the plants will love it, and it teaches you something about life.

In nature, nothing is ever lost, only changed. Science calls this the Law of Conservation of Matter and Energy. It is the basis of Einstein's theory of relativity, several major world religions, and the making of split pea soup.

Some people say we are born, we live, and then we die. That attitude is very straightforward, very simple, and very realistic, but I don't think it's altogether true. The larger picture is that we are a part of the cycle of life. We are as much a part of the cycle of life as a drop of water is a part of the ocean. The truth is, we are born of our mother who is herself alive, we live by consuming the plants and animals of the living earth, and after less than a century, whether we like it or not, kicking and screaming or singing a hymn, we go back to the earth to make more life. We think that our lives interrupt the cycle, but they do not. As I write this, I know that we are all a part of the whole living creation, not separate from it. As the mythologist Joseph Campbell said, "Our eyes are the eyes of the Earth, our voices are the voices of the Earth. What else?"

A few years back scientists at NASA sent a probe to Mars. They were looking for signs of life. Martians, plants, bacteria—even a mold or something. And when it was found that there was no life, none whatsoever, I cried. I cried for loneliness. Our little blue-green heaven is the only living place in this solar system. No wonder real-estate prices started to boom right after that mission.

But what a privilege to be alive on this planet, to be a part of this rare and precious sea of life! And how delightful to be human for a while and to be able to know it! Ah, sweet mystery of life, at last I've found you!

NOVEMBER

He ate everything in sight, even one of those berries hanging from the chandelier.

Holiday Decorations

 I used to be very impressed by the beautiful pictures of holiday decorations in magazines. We've all seen them—country-house rooms festooned with three-dimensional della robbia wreaths, graceful swags, and evergreen garlands casually draped around the balustrades of winding staircases. I was especially enchanted by the decorations that used "natural" materials, such as nuts, gumdrops, popcorn, cranberries, fruit, and red peppers. How clever to decorate with food; and how artistic! Not at all like the Christmas decorations that I was used to seeing in the days of my youth in Brooklyn—a few pathetic sprigs of holly surrounding red candles, sleazy flashing colored lights, discount outlet ornaments, plastic mistletoe, and plaster of paris Santas with flaking paint on top of the television set. In my neighborhood, holidays were viewed as an opportunity to have a big meal with the family, not as a vehicle for personal artistic expression.

Now that I had my own house and a more sophisticated world view, I was determined to be tasteful and cultured in my approach to the holiday season. I would use nothing plastic or artificial in my holiday decor. Not only would "natural" decorations proclaim my commitment to the environment (since all the decorations would be one hundred percent recyclable into the compost heap), as well as my antagonism toward the commercialization of the holidays and the overuse of technology in everyday life, they would look swell in my Victorian Gothic cottage.

With wreaths on the doors and swags over the mantelpiece, the place would look positively Dickensian, like the setting for *A Christmas Carol*, after Scrooge became generous.

The first year that I tried to make della robbia wreaths, swags, and garlands, I realized it was a mistake. First of all, the cost of the thirty-five pounds of fruit was not inconsiderable. Lunch for one at Lutece, at least. Another problem was time. If you've ever tried to wire apples and pears onto evergreen branches, you know it takes several hours to do even one lousy wreath, much less a whole garland the length of the staircase. By the end of two fourteen-hour days, I wound up with two wreaths, twenty-five feet of naked, shedding evergreen garland, ten packages of assorted nuts in their shells, a shopping bag full of pine cones, three apple pies, and twenty pounds of rotten fruit.

My main difficulty was lack of hand-eye coordination. I found it very hard to get the wire through the fruit. Following the instructions in *Ladies Circle Magazine*, I used a knitting needle to make the holes. But I found it almost impossible to control the knitting needle once it was inside the fruit, and this resulted in sending projectiles of apple and orange out onto the kitchen walls, appliances, and floor. After spending hours affixing the fruit to the wreaths, it took another hour to clean up the slimy mess.

I might as well admit that I had another difficulty: no talent. Believe me, I'm not being overly modest here. There are some things I can do very well, such as gardening and making jokes, but figuring out where to put the apple so that it looks artistic next to the pine cone is not one of them. Even my best efforts in this regard were not great. Out of desperation, I tried copying a della robbia wreath from the magazine exactly, but it still fell short of the glistening living sculpture of the photograph. For one thing, my fruit started to rot prematurely, due to the holes gouged through their middles. It's hard to rot and glisten at the same time, especially for fruit.

Now, every time I look at those perfect photos in the magazines, I smell a rat. I suspect that the magazine photographer takes the picture only moments after the garlands are completed, and then only after his assistants have sprayed everything with glycerine.

By the time the holiday guests arrived, a week after the decorations were in place, I was exhausted and cranky, the fruit was moldy, and my house smelled like a cider factory.

The following year, it was my turn to do Thanksgiving dinner for the family. A word of advice here: When given a choice, always opt to have Thanksgiving rather than Christmas dinner at your house. It's the same turkey dinner, but you'll save a fortune on decorations. Since the big bash was occurring on Thanksgiving instead of at Christmastime, I could dispense with the holly and the red candles and the wreaths and the fresh-fruit-as-decoration thing, and confine myself to an autumnal theme, which is much cheaper. If you are willing to forgo the gourds and Indian corn, Thanksgiving decorations are simple and understated, consisting mainly of dead plant life. There are autumn leaves, red rose hips, dried seed pods, and brown grasses. They grow in empty lots all over the place, to be had for the few minutes' effort of going out and cutting them.

I really enjoyed decorating the house for Thanksgiving. I arranged autumn leaves across the mantelpiece in the living room and dried grasses, seed pods, and hydrangeas in vases around the house. The dried hydrangea flowers were from Bobbie's garden, and you know where I got the leaves and grasses. I was even able to procure a large stand of cattails from my next-door neighbor Ross. Since I had saved money on the decorations for the rest of the house, I decided I could afford to splurge on the one room where everyone would be spending the most time, namely, the dining room. After all, Thanksgiving is an eating holiday. Unlike Christmas, the guests don't all troop into the living room to open presents after dinner. At most, they sneak in there to find a comfy place to sleep.

In my area, where hard winter frost doesn't set in until December or January, lots of plants are still green in late November. The wild honeysuckle, which grows all over the run-down grape arbor in my backyard, still looks fresh and green at Thanksgiving time, even though it is no longer actively growing. Entwined with the honeysuckle is the deadly nightshade vine. Despite its unfortunate name, deadly nightshade is very attractive. Its poisonous berries are as red and shiny as Lucrezia Borgia's nail polish. I decided to use both vines to decorate the chandelier above the dining-room table, the honeysuckle for the greens and the deadly nightshade berries for a touch of red. The chandelier has five plain brass arms supporting light bulbs with little shades on them, and the arms made a perfect place from which to drape the vines. I also draped vines around the mirror over the mantelpiece, for opulence.

Not content with greenery and a few red berries, I went all out and bought several pounds of red grapes in bunches from the supermarket, which I hung from the chandelier and around the mirror, as well. As a centerpiece, I used burgundy red potted chrysanthemums, surrounded by more grapes and vines, and silver candlesticks with candles exactly the same color as the grapes. When the table was all set with my best dishes, a set of twenty-four in ivory with gold rims that I had bought at a house auction for thirty bucks, and my charmingly mismatched silver plate and stemware, it was beautiful enough to make Martha Stewart drop dead.

Having done all my decorating the night before, I had all of Thanksgiving day proper to cook. I made chestnut soup (Walter and Sam peeled the chestnuts). I made turkey with corn bread stuffing, mashed potatoes, turnips with nutmeg, braised Brussels sprouts, and sweet potatoes with real maple syrup. My new sister-in-law Lydia was bringing homemade pies for dessert, and her father Tom was bringing his own special cranberry sauce. I was expecting a total of twenty-four relatives, and they began arriving at twelve o'clock. They were supposed to arrive at two, but I've noticed that the family always tends to arrive early to "help out," as my mother calls it. ("Helping out" consists of sitting in the kitchen drinking coffee while Walter and I trip over their feet.) For some reason, the earliest arrivals come from farthest away—Long Island, that fish-shaped Isle of Suburbia east of New York City.

Aunt Jo and Uncle Ted had started out at five that morning to take the long drive up the Taconic Parkway. The ride should have taken no more than two and a half to three hours, but Uncle Ted is very cautious and never exceeds his own personal speed limit of forty miles an hour, established in 1936 when he first obtained his driver's license. He refuses to drive on highways and only travels on secondary roads. Since secondary roads often have only one lane in each direction, Uncle Ted is constantly being passed by other motorists, cursing and shaking their fists, as they risk a head-on collision in order to get by him.

When it is raining, Uncle Ted's speed decreases to an even safer twenty-five. This Thanksgiving Day, it was raining, thank heavens, or they would have found me in my bathrobe, dancing with the turkey. Their progress was further impeded because they had to pick up Walter's parents in Levittown, Long Island, and then my mother. None of them were ready when Uncle Ted and Aunt Jo arrived to pick them up, and that cost them another hour, according to Aunt Jo. That six-hour ride up the Taconic must have been like a road show version of *Long Day's Journey into Night*. But in spite of all the difficulties, they arrived early anyway.

By midafternoon, everyone was on hand. Aunt Harriet and Uncle Ed, their daughter, Cousin Laura, and her husband Fotie and their two children, Sonya and Alex, Bob and Lydia, Sam's cousins, Abe and Polly, Walter's sister Liz and her husband Fred, a seven-year-old boy I couldn't identify (probably a neighbor), Lydia's dad with the cranberry sauce, Aunt Ann and Uncle Fred, the aforementioned Aunt Jo and Uncle Ted, Walter's mom and dad, my mother and her gentleman friend Nat, and last but not least, my cousin Helen and her parents Uncle Charlie and Aunt Dotty, herself. It is well known in our family that Aunt Dotty has a mouth like a pit bull.

Aunt Dotty had never been to our house before, and she was not impressed by Victorian architecture. Before she even got into the front door, she suggested that we could improve the value of such an old place by installing aluminum siding and getting rid of all the gingerbread. She also suggested that we replace those old mullioned windows with new double-track aluminum storm and screens. If it hadn't been a holiday, and I hadn't known her, I would have assumed that she was a salesman for a home-improvement business.

She also had landscaping advice for me. "Why don't you get rid of that big bush?" she demanded, eyeballing the Henry lilac in the front yard malevolently as we attempted to drag her in out of the rain. "Prowlers lurk in bushes."

"Yes, but so do birds, Aunt Dotty."

"Yeah, but birds don't rob your house."

Cousin Helen followed Aunt Dotty in. She gave me a big wet kiss on the cheek, coughed in my face, and told me she had bronchitis. I know she expected sympathy, but I've known her since childhood, so all I said was, "Why don't you just kill yourself, Helen?"

Uncle Charlie was nowhere to be seen. Apparently, he had gotten lost on the way from the car and was wandering around the neighborhood, knocking on doors.

A half-hour later, Uncle Charlie appeared, and everyone was finally seated in the dining room. I lowered the lights and lit the candles. The dining room looked like a page from the November issue of *House Beautiful*. The older relatives pretended not to notice that there was food hanging over the dining-room table, except for Aunt Dotty, who mumbled something about hay fever allergies and broke off a honeysuckle stem near her head for fear it would mess up her carefully coiffed, helmetlike black wig. The younger cousins and the children liked it, although they would have preferred cookies.

Before the meal, my brother's new wife Lydia suggested a moment of silence. She and my brother had been attending Quaker meetings recently, and they were into silence. This seemed like a good idea, since the rest of the family consisted of the usual mixed bag of New Yorkers—Catholics, Jews, Lutherans, Orthodox Greeks, Zen Buddhists, atheists, and Presbyterians, very few of whom had much religious conviction in any case. So we had a moment of silence, broken only by Aunt Dotty, who continued her conversation with my mother about the dangers of having Thanksgiving dinner in a fire trap.

After dinner, as predicted, Uncle Charlie and some of the other guests went into the living room to sleep, while the ladies and some of the liberated men "helped" with the dishes. Aunt Harriet, Cousin Laura, and my brother Bob had an argument over who was actually going to wash. Fighting for martyrdom, they kept shoving each other away from the sink: "I'll do them! You dry!" "No, I'll wash, you dry," et cetera.

Between bites of leftover turkey, Aunt Dotty gave a course-by-course critique of the dinner to my mother, who was torn between politely agreeing with her and defending my culinary abilities. Eventually my mother left the room, saying that she needed to take off her cardigan. Without missing a beat, Aunt Dotty turned to me and launched into a critique of Uncle Charlie. Her tongue must have had a groove in it from playing that old record. I only half-listened. "Charlie is a slob . . . Charlie is a blah-blah-blah . . . Charlie eats like a pig . . . Blah-blah . . . He ate everything in sight today . . . Blah-blah . . . Even one of those berries that was hanging from the chandelier."

Instantly, she had my riveted attention.

". . . I never heard of food hanging from a chandelier before," she continued, not noticing my sudden interest.

"What berries, Aunt Dotty?" I asked with false cheer, hoping against hope that she meant one of the grapes. "One of the grapes?"

"No, no, one of the red ones. It fell in his soup and he ate it, the pig. Who hangs food from a chandelier, anyway?"

I dropped the aluminum foil with which I had been wrapping up the leftover turkey before Aunt Dotty could eat it all and ran out of the room.

I looked around for Lydia, who works as a volunteer on an ambulance squad and is familiar with emergency resuscitation procedures. She was off someplace, but I found Walter in the dining room and drew him to one side. "Walter, Uncle Charlie ate a deadly nightshade berry!"

We raced into the living room as fast as we could while still retaining a "gracious host and hostess" demeanor. My heart was pounding. What would Aunt Dotty say if I had murdered her husband? Plenty.

There was Uncle Charlie in an easy chair, his head back, eyes shut, a drop of spittle glistening from the corner of his open mouth.

Walter is great in an emergency. "Quick," he hissed into my ear, "what's the antidote to alkaloid poisoning?"

I tried to think of it, but then I remembered. "Walter, it wasn't an alkaloid, it was a berry."

"Yes, that's right," he responded patiently. He is always patient, even during a crisis. "But deadly nightshade is an alkaloid. It's related to the potato and the tomato, parts of which are also poisonous."

I had no time to listen to a lecture on botany, although under normal circumstances, I would have found it very interesting and said so, but perhaps not in those terms.

I grabbed Uncle Charlie and shook him hard. No response. Walter began pounding on his chest. Nothing. He was dead. And I had killed him. I had killed him as surely as if I'd slipped strychnine into his Miller Lite. Me and my stupid yuppie holiday decorations! Why couldn't I have bought some Indian corn and a crepe paper turkey like everybody else?

Fred, Uncle Fred, Uncle Ted, and Uncle Ed, who had also gone into the living room for a snooze, were alarmed. Fred and Uncle Fred thought Uncle Charlie had a heart attack, Uncle Ted thought that we had caught him stealing the silver, but Uncle Ed got it right.

"Alkaloid poisoning from one of the deadly nightshade berries, I bet," said Uncle Ed. He's on my side of the family.

"No! No!" I screamed, defensively. Visions of Uncle Charlie's autopsy danced in my head.

Suddenly, Walter, whose attempts at CPR bore a striking resemblance to assault and battery, reeled away from the body, as Uncle Charlie's fist connected with his jaw. In a moment, he and Uncle Charlie were on the floor, shouting, cursing, rolling around, and grappling with each other; Uncle Charlie punching, Walter trying to fend him off. Ted, Fred, Fred, and Ed grabbed Charlie by the arms to subdue him. All five of them lay on the floor, looking like a professional wrestling tag-team match, when Aunt Dotty entered the room.

Everybody froze.

I will leave this happy holiday scene in freeze-frame. It is imprinted on my memory as clearly as an old family photograph. I don't have to describe the subsequent events to you. You can imagine what Aunt Dotty said (demandingly), what I said (truthfully), what Uncle Charlie said (unprintably), what Aunt Dotty said (abusively), what Walter said (apologetically), what the rest of the family said (derisively) as they all rushed into the room, what Aunt Dotty said again (redundantly), and so forth.

While Lydia attended to Walter's and Cousin Helen's bloody noses (Helen's nose had begun to bleed in sympathy), Uncle Ed explained that while one deadly nightshade berry might kill a very small child, it would have little or no effect on a grown man, especially when mixed with a large turkey dinner, including three slices of pie. Deadly nightshade, or *Solanum Dulcamara*, is related to the potato and the tomato. "In fact," he continued, "it was once believed that raw tomatoes were poisonous and could only be safely eaten after being thoroughly cooked, hence, tomato sauce, and where would Italian cooking be without tomato sauce? Eh?"

Uncle Ed's discourse had a calming effect on the crowd. Bless him.

"Actually," he chuckled, "you could sooner have killed Uncle Charlie with a potato."

"You mean, by shoving a whole one down his throat?" my niece Polly asked, helpfully.

"No, by serving him a potato that has been left out in the sun and has turned green. It would be poisonous."

As the children and Uncle Charlie gathered around Uncle Ed to hear more exciting tales about deadly and disgusting plants, everyone else went back to what they were doing. The rest of the holiday afternoon flowed along and slipped around a bend of the great river we call Time.

In other words, by six o'clock, all the relatives were ready to hit the road. Actually, they started to leave by six, because it would take another hour before everybody got their coats and said good-bye to everybody else. Uncle Ted, Aunt Jo, and Walter's parents were going to stay the night because Ted didn't like to drive in the dark. They left at five the next morning to be home in time for lunch.

About six weeks after Thanksgiving, I received a letter from a lawyer. Aunt Dotty was suing me for criminal negligence! At that moment, with the letter in my hand, I swore I would never decorate with anything but crepe paper and plastic again.

Aunt Dotty eventually dropped the suit when she realized that she would actually have to pay the lawyer. But I am a changed woman. I no longer decorate the house for Thanksgiving, Christmas, Chanukah, Chinese New Year, or any other winter holiday. If I want a little natural-looking decoration, I buy a couple of winter bulbs, like amaryllis or paperwhite narcissus. Most years, the house looks more like Scrooge's apartment before he was visited by Marley's ghost.

DECEMBER

Be careful, my darling. The pot is full of dirt.

MAKING AMARYLLIS GROW

In early winter my thoughts turn to the houseplants that are now my only connection with the world of the green and growing, and in particular the lily-flowered Christmas amaryllis that I'm looking at right this minute.

Houseplants remind me of my college days. I started to grow them when Walter and I had an apartment in Carroll Gardens in Brooklyn, not far from Long Island University, where we went to college. This was in the late '60s and early '70s and growing plants indoors was all the rage.

Exposed brick walls were all the rage, also. Anyone with a little gumption and a crowbar removed the plaster from one wall of his or her apartment with all the enthusiasm of a Visigoth sacking Rome. If I had to give my personal image of that whole period, it would not be film clips of peace marches or bell-bottom trousers and long hair. No, it would be an exposed brick wall with an Art Nouveau poster and a dumb cane in front of it. This arrangement was repeated in every home, office, and restaurant in the United States from 1968 through the 1970s. Exposed brick walls, Art Nouveau posters, and houseplants were to the '70s what flowered chintz was to the '80s—the height of style, de rigueur, à la mode, the cat's meow.

Some friends of ours took the brick-wall idea to its natural conclusion and removed the plaster from all four walls of their studio. When they were finished, their apartment looked a lot like the inside of a warehouse, if the warehouse had been decorated with posters and dumb canes. If I had been their landlord, I would have sued them for vandalism. (This couple moved into a real warehouse in SoHo in 1986, which by then was called a co-op loft, and were thrilled to pay a quarter of a million dollars for it. It's a crazy world.)

Our first apartment occupied the top floor of an old, ungentrified brownstone off Henry Street, in what is now a very posh neighborhood but was then the turf of the Bello family, a name well known in the annals of organized crime and the files of the Federal Bureau of Investigation. Actually, I have changed the name of the mob here because I'm afraid of getting my typing fingers broken.

It was a real old-fashioned Brooklyn neighborhood, the kind with a bakery shop that smelled of fresh bread and a fish store with salt cod hanging in the window. They ran numbers in the local laundromat, and our grocer could point to a bullet hole in the wall of his shop, evidence of the night Vinny the Hat went after his brother-in-law with a forty-five because he had been "fooling around" with Vinny's wife. Fortunately for the brother-in-law, Vinny was a member of a family that was famous for its poor aim. In fact, my old neighborhood was the setting for the novel *The Gang That Couldn't Shoot Straight*, by Jimmy Breslin. The title of the book tells the story. The brother-in-law lived to fool around another day.

Living in a mob-controlled neighborhood sounds dangerous, but in fact it was very safe. The garbage was always picked up on time, policemen patrolled the streets with unusual vigor, and street crime was almost unheard of. This was partly a result of the fact that some of the residents were very active in city politics, although rarely as officeholders. They tended to work behind the scenes. The other reason was that no casual wrongdoer had any desire to victimize the elderly mother of an organized criminal with a personal army at his command. A mugging would be quickly and mercilessly avenged, without the obnoxious interference of courts and lawyers. As a result, I could walk the streets in security at any time of the day or night, with all the law and order enjoyed by persons living under a totalitarian regime.

Politically incorrect as it was, I loved the old neighborhood, with its colorful characters out of the pages of Damon Runyon and Jimmy Breslin. I didn't know then how soon it would be gone. There was the ninety-four-year-old lady down the block with dropsy, who sat on the stoop with her retarded son, who was in his seventies. What a lifetime of devotion she represented. There was the man next door who raised pigeons on the roof and the old man who grew tomatoes, eggplants, and even a fig tree in the postage-stamp yard behind his brownstone. To protect the top of the marginally hardy fig tree every winter, he would swathe it in black tar paper and cover the top with an empty gallon paint can, so it looked as if it was wearing a black raincoat and top hat. Fig Tree the Hat.

The neighborhood must have been changing, even in 1970, because we were able to rent an apartment there. Our landlady, Mrs. Romano, called us "the hippies upstairs," but she was good to us. I think she was just grateful to have tenants who paid the hundred dollars a month rent on time. Her husband, who rarely left their apartment, was a former longshoreman on disability. One day on the docks, someone he owed money to dropped a refrigerator on his head but missed and crushed his foot instead. In my neighborhood, if they had aimed for his foot, they would have hit him in the head.

Mrs. Romano was a five-foot-three, 110-pound bundle of energy, with graying hair and a wandering left eye, so that when she spoke to you, it looked as if she were examining the wall next to you at the same time.

It's possible that she was examining the wall, because she was very house proud and had obviously invested a good deal of her small income to beautify it. At least it was beautiful to her. She had covered the front of the brownstone with fake white granite, the kind that comes in sheets. She also had installed a large, green Fiberglas awning over the front door, which she kept clean by hosing it down with soap and water at weekly intervals. I've never seen anyone bother to clean a Fiberglas awning before or since. Most people let the rain do it for them, but Mrs. Romano was a conscientious homeowner; her pride of ownership even extended to the street in front of her building. After painting the brownstone stoop battleship gray, she kept going and painted the sidewalk. She even painted the trunk of the plane tree near the curb. I doubt that you've ever seen a tree whose trunk is painted battleship gray. All I can say about it in a positive way is that it's washable. I lived there for four years, and every spring she repainted it, and every week gave it a thorough scrubbing with a brush and soapy water. I'll tell you one thing, she never had any trouble with aphids.

Surprisingly, she let us do what we liked with our apartment. It had a tub in the kitchen and a kitchen sink in the bathroom. Needless to say, the first things Walter and I did when we got the place was to pull the plaster down from the chimney wall, put up a reproduction of an Art Nouveau poster, get a cable spool from a nearby construction site to use as a table, and put a dumb cane on it. The rest of our furniture consisted of objets trouvés from off the street and other interesting but unwanted furniture from our parents' homes. The bed was a mattress on the floor. *Very* fashionable.

The dumb cane grew, an accomplishment that fascinated me and moved me deeply. I began to collect houseplants at an alarming rate and soon had a jungle in the front, south-facing window of the apartment. I grew everything, from angel-wing begonias to avocado trees started from pits. These seemed very beautiful to me, and normal. Remember, at this time, I thought all plants grew in pots or had to be fussed over to survive.

I gained most of my houseplant information, not to mention inspiration, from garden expert Thalassa Cruso's public television series, "Making Things Grow." The program was all about the care and feeding of houseplants, as was the book that followed, a book I studied with all the care and avidity of a bible-college student reading Revelations. The title of Ms. Cruso's program was very apt. With houseplants, you have to *make* things grow; you can't just let them grow. Raising houseplants requires a commitment to watering, feeding, and grooming, because if you ignore a houseplant it will die. That is why my first trip to the open countryside was such an awesome experience. I simply couldn't believe that there could be millions of plants in the world that no one was taking care of!

This brings me to the subject of this chapter, the amaryllis. My first amaryllis was given to me by my mother. She had received one as a gift the previous Christmas and didn't know what to do with it. To her, plants of any kind were aliens, little green creatures that just stepped off a flying saucer from Mars. A city dweller to her fingertips, she eyed all nature, including tame, domestic animals like cats and poodles, with xenophobic suspicion. Her comment as she handed me the amaryllis was "Be careful, my darling. The pot is full of dirt."

The amaryllis was a large, healthy-looking specimen with long leaves that looked like old-fashioned razor strops and an enormous bulb that stuck halfway out of the plastic pot. The plastic pot was inside a cardboard box, decorated with a lurid picture of a huge red lilylike bloom. The picture on the box was the only flower in sight, however, since the original bloom had long since withered away.

I took it home and consulted my well-thumbed copy of *Making Things Grow.* Ms. Cruso's directions were concise and easy to understand, once you got used to her particular manner of expressing herself.

> . . . Put the bulb in a properly crocked clay pot which is only one size larger than the circumference of the bulb itself; they do not do well in large pots.*

I knew by then that when Thalassa Cruso talked about "properly crocked" clay pots, she was not referring to inebriated pottery but to the placement of stones or clay shards in the bottom for drainage. I transplanted the bulb as per directions in a clay pot that allowed only about an inch of soil around the bulb. It immediately looked much better, quite

*Thalassa Cruso, *Making Things Grow* (Alfred A. Knopf, New York, 1969, p. 95).

handsome actually, but then again, any container would look better than a cardboard box.

. . . grow on the leaves to full and lasting maturity in a sunny windowsill.*

She meant: Keep growing it as a houseplant while the leaves get bigger. I had a very sunny windowsill, but not much more space, so I had to evict an avocado plant and relocate it on the floor. I apologized to the avocado profusely. In those days, it was considered beneficial to plants if you talked to them. In my eagerness to do the right thing for my houseplants, I used to yak away at them for hours about world politics, social mores, college gossip, my personal problems, and anything else I could think of. I think I might have bored some of them to death. I'm much wiser now. I've since come to realize that talking to plants makes absolutely no difference to them, although I still find it therapeutic.

Even Ms. Cruso seemed unsure as to the best way to get the amaryllis to bloom a second year. She had her own method, but warned that it was not the conventional one.

. . . Mine do best if they are forced into dormancy by a complete withdrawal of water in June. I put the bulbs in their pots into the cellar where they remain totally dry but in a relatively cool place during the hot weather . . .**

I didn't have a cellar in my apartment, and I sure wasn't going to ask Mrs. Romano if I could use hers for fear I would go down there in September and discover that my bulbs had been painted. So I did what I often do when faced with an insoluble dilemma—I ignored the problem entirely. I simply treated the amaryllis as a leafy houseplant and let it do whatever it wanted to.

By the following autumn, the amaryllis went into a sort of dormancy all by itself. The leaves got brown, and taking the hint, I cut them off, took the pot out of the window, switched it with the avocado again, and ceased watering it altogether. By January, it began to show signs of life; little green tips were sprouting from the center of the bulb. I gave it some

*Ibid.
**Cruso, p. 95.

new soil on top of the pot, as was recommended by Thalassa Cruso, and began to feed, water, and schmooze with it, as usual.

That February, the bulb sent up huge red flowers that were much more sensational than their portrait on the original box. The picture couldn't show the height of the flowers, about two feet tall, and their delicacy and iridescence. And no picture could express the joy and triumph I felt about it. I was so gratified, I read to it from *Ulysses*. I had been very impressed with this book in English Lit., and I read it the part where Molly Bloom says yes, yes, yes. It was Walter's favorite passage, as well.

That was twenty years ago, and I have grown many amaryllis bulbs since. Of course, I've never actually bought one. All the amaryllis I've ever owned were either given to me as gifts before they bloomed for the first time or given to me as cast-offs once the party was over. But no matter, to me the challenge, and the fun, is still to get them to bloom that second time. Now that I have a cellar in my house, I can keep them cool from June until November, so they will bloom at Christmastime, like they're supposed to. And as Ms. Cruso herself admits, it doesn't always work. Sometimes the bulbs come up "blind," as she calls it. She means without flowers. But it does work some of the time, and the pleasure of seeing the large flowers is doubled. It is both a spectacular show and the happy result of personal effort. Best of all, the bloom reminds me of college days in Brooklyn, in that Old World neighborhood that has changed so much.

I went back to visit about a year ago and found that the neighborhood has become gentrified. The grocery store now sells running shoes, and the laundromat is a real-estate agency. The only numbers they run are the six-figure prices of the now-fashionable brownstones. The bakery with the fresh loaves of Italian bread is still there, but it has become a sort of historic landmark, instead of a real-life bakery. They still make bread there, but the place was used as a movie set for the film *Moonstruck* with Cher and Nicholas Cage, so now it is famous, and somehow unreal.

The building that we had lived in is still there, of course, but the fake stone has been removed and the new, but historically accurate, brownstone finish has been meticulously restored. No doubt Mrs. Romano sold the building for what must have seemed to her to be a fortune and moved out, like so many of her neighbors. I'm sure she's now living in New Jersey or, more likely, Florida, painting the palm trees battleship gray.

Garden Catalogs

December is the month when the plant catalogs start arriving. To me it is July in Christmas. Reading a good garden catalog is pure joy, like taking a garden tour, shopping for bargains, and attending a class in horticulture all at the same time. I even learned to speak Latin from reading garden catalogs. I had to. Some of the catalogs I received were strictly for dedicated plant buffs. They gave only the botanical names of the offerings and didn't even bother to translate or to include illustrations. So I determined to learn the botanical names of plants, because I knew that once I had mastered them, I would sound as if I really knew what I was talking about, and more important, I would be able to understand the lecturers at the Horticultural Society.

At first, botanical names all sounded to me like the names of opera singers. I could almost hear them being announced on the Texaco opera radio broadcasts:

"This afternoon, the role of Carmen will be played by mezzo-soprano Rosa Multiflora. The role of the toreador will be sung by that outstanding tenor, Hemerocallis Fulva."

Of course, *Hemerocallis fulva* is an orange daylily, the roadside kind.

Basically, there are four ways that plants get their botanical names. Many are named after the person who discovered them, only Latinized. For instance, the dahlia is named after the Swedish botanist Anders Dahl. He lived from 1751 to 1930. He was one of the oldest botanists in Europe.*

Plants also get their botanical names from the place where they were first discovered. *Iris siberica* is a perfect example. It is obviously from Siberia, probably exiled there by Stalin for political reasons.**

Much of the time, though, the botanical name is a description of some particular feature of a plant. For example, orchid comes from the Greek word *orchis*, which means testicle. This is a random example that I happened to think of by chance. However, I find it highly symbolic that the orchid has become the flower that boys give to their dates on prom night.

*Not true, but an amusing idea, isn't it?
**See asterisk above.

Usually, plants have two or more botanical names, the second one being a more specific description. Take our opera singer Rosa Multiflora, for example. Rosa is a rose, is a rose, and multiflora means many flowers. A *Rosa multiflora* is a rose with many flowers on each stem. If the same rose had many flowers on each stem and they were white, it would be called *Rosa multiflora alba.* And if there were different varieties of white roses with many flowers on each stem, each one would have the varietal name added, so it would be called *Rosa multiflora alba* "Snowflake". You'll notice, too, that the first name and the varietal names are capitalized, and the second and third ones are not. This is customary and not to be worried over. Actually, there's no reason why you can't name your own roses. I have a rose in my garden that has Japanese beetles all over it. I call it *Rosa swisscheesaflora* "Cassandra".

Sometimes the botanical name of a plant is the ancient one. The botanical name for daffodil is *Narcissus.* Daffodils were first noted in ancient Greece 2,500 years ago.

This plant was called *Narcissus* because it was believed to have narcotic properties. In fact, we get the word *narcotic* and the word *narcissus* from the same Greek root *narke,* meaning "to stupefy." All I can say is that I hope it was never used as a drug, because it is now well known that all parts of the narcissus are poisonous. (I don't want to offend anybody who is deeply into herbal medicine, but when I read about the herbal folk beliefs of the ancients, some of their so-called wisdom is so far from reality, I can only conclude that they were a bunch of superstitious, ignorant clods. No offense.)

The Greek myth about Narcissus is well known among people who know that kind of thing. Like so many folk myths, as well as folk medicine, it is charming and loopy.

Narcissus was a handsome young man who lived all alone in the forest near Athens. The fact that there are no longer any forests near Athens should give you some idea of how old this story is. It is also a cautionary example of what 2,500 years of human habitation can do to an ecosystem . . . but back to the charming part.

Narcissus was a youth of rare beauty, in other words, a hunk. It will help the story if you can visualize him looking like Tom Cruise, or perhaps if you are a bit older, Tyrone Power. As I say, he lived alone in the woods, probably naked, except for a quiver of arrows worn casually across his tanned, muscular back.

One day, a lovely nymph named Echo was romping through the woods. She saw Narcissus and instantly fell in love with him. Who wouldn't?

"Yoo-hoo! Yoo-hoo," she gaily laughed, tripping gracefully over her own feet. "I love you, I love you!" Or words to that effect. She began to follow him around, making a pest of herself.

Narcissus was a bore. He was conceited, self-involved, and dysfunctional. He was a narcissist. Whenever he saw Echo coming, he stomped off and ignored her completely. Maybe he figured he could do better. Maybe he was right, who knows?

After a while, Echo pined away, leaving only her voice, which could only repeat what was said to her, over and over again. Sad. And obnoxious.

The goddess of love, Aphrodite, was furious because Narcissus had spurned *amour*. After all, sexual love was her personal mission. She was fit to be tied, a situation that she ordinarily would have enjoyed. She caused Narcissus to fall in love with his own reflection in the lake, and while he was trying to kiss himself, he fell in and drowned and turned into a flower. So Greek.

It's easy to see that reading catalogs can lead you to acquire a great deal of information. Some of it is trivial, I admit, but most of it is a necessary part of a gardener's education.

That first year when I started my garden, I ordered every catalog listed in *Horticulture* magazine. Most of them were free, but some cost anywhere from a dollar to five dollars, and when you are ordering seventy-five catalogs, that can be quite a little investment. But I told myself that the money was refundable on the first order, and the catalogs were so informative, it was worth it. I neglected to tell myself that to get a refund on the first order from each of those companies, I would have to spend a fortune. How easily we make excuses for ourselves to get what we want.

To make life a bit easier (and less expensive) for you, my friend, here is a short list of some of my favorite catalogs, the ones from which I actually order plants and seeds. I have included only those companies that have proven reliable and/or relatively inexpensive. (Fear of libel laws prevents me from mentioning the ones that gypped me, although I'd love to.) This list is by no means exhaustive. There are hundreds of big and small nurseries and seed companies around the country, as good as the ones I'm touting. Catalogs that specialize are indispensable, especially if you live in a part of the country where, because of heat, cold, or dryness, you'll have to make up your own "Magnificent Seven." These nurseries are listed in a book called *Gardening by Mail: A Source Book*, by Barbara J. Barton (Houghton Mifflin, San Francisco, 1990). This directory of catalogs gets updated every few years, so if you buy the current edition, the nurseries listed are likely to be still in business. Anyway, here's my list.

Bluestone Perennials
7211 Middle Ridge Road
Madison, OH 44057

Free

For anyone who is serious about starting to make a flower garden, Bluestone Perennials of Madison, Ohio, is a must. I love this company. The catalog lists hundreds of perennials, but the most interesting thing about them is that they are sold in quantity—seven to nine dollars for six. I've ordered many cartons of plants from them over the years. When I began my garden, the perennials seedlings were three or four dollars a six-pack, but *tempus fugit* and so does inflation and now they cost a bit more. In those days, I could plant nice drifts of each variety very inexpensively instead of waiting for one plant to get big enough to divide. They had, and still have, an excellent selection: many different and unusual varieties of hollyhocks, yarrows, phlox, pinks, chrysanthemums, astilbes, asters, you name it. The only drawback is that the plants are small and take about a year before they are mature. I didn't mind that because even large pot-grown plants don't reach their full glory until the second year, anyway, and the extra season gives the seedlings a chance to establish themselves nicely in my garden.

The best buy of all is on the inside of the back page of the Bluestone catalog. For a very low price, they will send you a flower border in a kit, including the plants, the plans, soil preparation and planting instructions. There is a starter set for a sixteen-by-four-foot border and a complete perennial border thirty-two feet long by five feet wide. The larger one contains sixty plants in twenty-four varieties—a horticultural paint-by-number kit. Judging from the plant list and the layout, the perennial border looks easy to grow, well balanced as to time of bloom, and colorful. They also offer a shade border in a kit. At less than a dollar a plant, these kits are also a good way to increase your stock of perennials, even if you have your own ideas about where to place them.

Wayside Gardens
1 Garden Lane
Hodges, SC 29695-0001

Free

The prices in this catalog are tastefully upscale, but I don't want to get too nasty about them. Many of the plants offered are unusual and of excellent quality, and the cost is frequently justified. For example, Wayside lists a *Styrax japonica* named Carillon for sixty-eight dollars. Even I can understand paying that much for something as unusual as a weeping Japanese snowball tree, especially if I were a wealthy collector. My hackles rise, however, when they charge five bucks for a single columbine (*Aquilegia*)! Columbines reproduce like alley cats. Anyone who can grow one columbine can grow a hundred. All you need to do is plant a dollar packet of columbine seeds and you can have columbines for the rest of your life. If I could sell all my columbine seedlings for five smackaroos a pop, I could take a trip to Japan and get a weeping Japanese snowball tree wholesale, too.

Using the Wayside catalog, I discovered a marvelous way to plan a flower border. I cut out the pictures and arrange and rearrange them on the floor to get a good idea of form and color. The size of the flowers in the photographs are not all on the same scale, but you'd be amazed at how helpful pictures can be when you want to see whether a yellow daylily will look good next to a purple clematis, for example. (We know it does.) And since the Wayside catalog is informative and well written, you can jot down the height, month of bloom, and any other pertinent facts right on the photo, so you can also plan to have your combinations all bloom in the right place and at the same time.

White Flower Farm
Litchfield, CT 06759-0050

$5.00 for 3 issues a year

The White Flower Farm catalog is very classy, with beautifully reproduced photographs that illustrate the well-organized plant lists and descriptions written in a tasteful, elegant, understated prose style that makes me jealous. It is so well written and so artistically illustrated, it compares favorably with many gardening books I've read. In fact, I like it so much that I order something from them every year, just to keep the catalogs coming. And they do have quite a few items that are worth ordering. This year, I sent for a witch hazel (*Hamamelis* x *intermedia* 'Diane'), which cost $24.95—not outrageous. After all, a witch hazel is a shrub that will eventually reach twelve feet in height, so I figure the cost comes to about two dollars a foot. The wonderful thing about witch hazels is that they bloom in late winter or very early spring—March in my garden. Most varieties have sweet-smelling yellow flowers that look like the tufts on a chenille bedspread, but Diane is a hybrid with coppery red petals. The White Flower Farm catalog describes the petals as ribbonlike, but I already have a witch hazel, so I know it will look like chenille, no matter what hyperbolic euphemisms they use to describe it. But I forgive them. The coppery red of the witch hazel will look tastefully smashing against the backdrop of my brown house, especially since practically everything else except for the hollies will still be in shades of late winter beige, dun, and gray. Next fall, I will plant yellow species crocus and blue Siberian squill in little drifts around the witch hazel, and in a couple of years, that spot will look like an advertisement for the month of March. Note: Once you order from White Flower Farm, the subsequent catalogs are usually free.

Milaeger's Gardens
4838 Douglas Ave.
Racine, WI 53402-2498

Free

Truth in advertising is a refreshing experience anywhere, and catalogs are no exception. As we have seen in the chapter about ''The Magnificent Seven,'' a lot of catalogs lie like dogs, so it's a sheer pleasure to find one that tells the absolute truth for a change. That's why I like the Milaeger's Gardens catalog.

Milaeger's Gardens is run by the Milaeger family in Racine, Wisconsin. I know this because right inside the front cover, there is a photo of Joan and Dan Milaeger themselves, standing like figures in Grant Wood's *American Gothic* with a delphinium between them instead of a pitchfork. They inspire confidence, and it turns out that my confidence has not been misplaced. All the plant descriptions in their catalog are to the point with no gushing. Nothing sounds as if it were written by the plant's mother, if you know what I mean. If there is a problem with a plant, they will tell you. For example, one of their feature plants for 1991 is a miniature daylily called Eenie Fanfare. The color is described as a "showy red," but, say the Milaegers, "it will begin to fade by day's end." They go on to say that Eenie Fanfare is very popular anyway, and I believe them.

There are several other reasons why I have enjoyed reading this catalog so much over the years. First of all, it lists all the plants alphabetically by their botanical names. (Common names are noted, but not emphasized.) This has been a good way for me to learn the botanical names of many plants, because unlike some of the other catalogs that listed their plants by botanical names, Milaeger's is bountifully illustrated and I could easily match the name to the plant.

Reading this catalog has been an education in plant cultivation, as well. After each name is a code that gives the time of bloom, as well as the plant's eventual height and width. Cultural requirements are noted in the description, along with color and any peculiarities of growth or bloom; in other words, it tells you everything you've always wanted to know about a plant but were too knocked out by its beautiful flowers to remember to ask.

One of the joys of ordering by mail is the variety of plants that are available, and Milaeger's lists a lot of plants that are almost impossible to find elsewhere. It offers scores of native American perennial wildflowers along with garden plants. For example, it lists sixteen different varieties of bee balm (*Monarda*), instead of the usual two or three, and twenty varieties of sedum. And need I mention that Milaeger's is not expensive? The prices are about one third less than the fancy catalogs.

Dutch Gardens
P.O. Box 200
Adelphia, NJ 07710

Free

Dutch Gardens sends two catalogs a year, one in the winter that features dahlias, cannas, and other summer bulbs for spring planting, and one in the summer that features tulips, daffodils, hyacinths, and all the smaller bulbs for planting in the fall. Subtle it's not. The illustrations win the loud award, but it's reliable and cheap. How many people can make that claim?

Van Engelen Inc.
Stillbrook Farm
313 Maple St.
Litchfield, CT 06759

Free

I buy from the Van Engelen bulb catalog because the prices are one half to one third off retail, and the quality is excellent. Every year, I leave some money in my budget to order bulbs from them. Van Engelen is located in Litchfield, Connecticut, but it imports its bulbs directly from Holland. Some people I know have been scared off by the fact that you have to buy in quantity—lots of fifty or one hundred bulbs; this catalog is not for somebody who gardens in a window box. At first hearing, fifty or a hundred bulbs sounds like a lot, but when a hundred Rembrandt tulips are blooming in May, it doesn't seem like too much at all. And let's face it, twenty-five crocuses scattered in the lawn are nice, but five hundred is better.

Roses of Yesterday and Today
802 Brown's Valley Road
Watsonville, CA 95076

Free

Roses of Yesterday and Today of Watsonville, California, specializes in old roses, those that were in cultivation before 1900. Some are rare, and this catalog sells them as well as newer and better-known ones for a little over half the price of both the expensive catalogs and the large nurseries in my area.

Schreiner's Iris Gardens
3647 Quinaby Road, N.E.
Salem, OR 97303

$2.00

Some of the most interesting catalogs come from companies that specialize in just one plant. Schreiner's Gardens specializes in irises, only irises. Irises, irises, irises. It lists hundreds of hefty German irises, dwarf irises, intermediate irises, species and hybrids, and all of them are eye-poppingly illustrated in all the rainbow colors that the name iris so richly implies. Okay, almost. The reds are muddy. And like all monomaniacs, the Schreiners go too far. In their compulsion to achieve the largest, most colorful, most unusual irises possible, they have managed to come up with a few that resemble brown ruffled kitchen curtains. I give those the go-by, but there are so many others that are stunning. They have hundreds of irises on sale at half price every year, so the main problem for me is self-control. I don't have room for more irises! Enough! But boy, when they bloom in May, the thick, heavy substance of the irises contrasts with the dancing blossoms of the columbines (which have sown themselves around for free) and they look absolutely delicious together. After ordering, subsequent catalogs are free.

Gilbert H. Wild & Son
790 Joplin St.
Sarcoxie, MO 64862-0338

$3.00

This is an old company. The son must be 110 by now. It specializes in peonies and daylilies, mostly daylilies. Some of the daylilies they list are thirty-five bucks or more, but they have an amazingly large amount of cultivars at three dollars apiece and from time to time they send me a pamphlet listing the cheaper offerings at half price! Irresistible, and some of them aren't orange.

Their peony list contains most of the better known varieties, many of them at eight to ten dollars each (as of this year), which is not a bad buy when you consider that a peony plant can be divided endlessly and will outlive you.

Logee's Greenhouses
141 North St.
Danielson, CT 06239

$3.00

It's a houseplant catalog. (Yes, they exist.) Many of the plants that are so gorgeously displayed in the full-color photographs are strictly for people with greenhouses, but Logee's has plenty of plants that can be grown in anybody's house, even mine, like begonias. Begonias don't need wallpaper-peeling humidity and will do very well in a sunny window. I ordered five varieties at three bucks apiece that I could never have found in a florist's shop for twenty.

Thompson and Morgan, Inc.
P.O. Box 1308
Jackson, NJ 08527

Free

So far I've been talking about catalogs that send live plants through the mail, but I have a couple of favorite seed catalogs. The mother of all seed catalogs, the one to order if your ambition is to grow every plant on the planet, is Thompson and Morgan. Even if you only want to purchase some columbine seeds, for example (an excellent choice considering their ease of germination and the aforementioned expense of buying the plants individually), Thompson and Morgan lists eighteen different varieties in separate colors and species. You can choose between such diverse examples as *Aquilegia canadensis*, a small North American wildflower, or the showy *Aquilegia* hybrid Spring Song, which grows to three feet tall! Since the seeds are only a dollar or two per packet, you can order both! If you plant them both within a hundred feet of each other, don't be surprised if another variety shows up in the garden after a couple of years. Because columbines intermarry with the abandon of movie stars, they produce different forms and colors that are unique and fascinating. This catalog is another great Latin instructor.

Shepherd's Garden Seeds
30 Irene St.
Torrington, CT 06790

$1.00

This catalog features old-fashioned flowers and gourmet seeds for the vegetable garden. I buy foreign salad greens, herbs, and beans from them.

I know they're foreign because in parentheses next to the name of each variety is the word *French, Italian Heirloom, Japanese, British,* or *Dutch.* To its credit, Shepherd's has "combed the globe" for seeds that will do well without pesticides and artificial fertilizers. The seed packets are more expensive than the ones you get at the hardware store, but you won't find these vegetables there. It's not that I think food tastes better with names like Rouge d'Hiver and Gigante d'Italia. I *know* that they're just red-leaved lettuce and giant Italian parsley, for heaven's sake. I am not a pushover for the romance of faraway places with strange-sounding veggies. I learned my lesson with the cassoulet. But I must confess, as I stir-fry my "Haricots Verts" (green beans) with olive oil, fresh pepper, and garlic while listening to *La Bohème* on the radio, everything tastes a bit better with a little romance attached, and some white wine doesn't hurt, either.

GARDEN PHILOSOPHY

Here's what I think: Unlike almost any other human endeavor you can think of, including politics, law, manufacturing, engineering, competitive sports, art, war, construction, communications, housing, community relations, education, and Scrabble, gardening has an invincible ally, an eternal partner that makes it the easiest work in the world—the awesome power of nature itself, the will to live. Admittedly, sometimes our ally turns around and hits us on the head with a hurricane or an earthquake, but for the most part, everything we grow in our gardens wants to live, and all we have to do is provide benevolent conditions. We get into trouble when we fail to understand how to put ourselves in tune with nature. A garden is nature domesticated, but not tamed. A garden is nature reorganized, but not conquered. A garden is a way of living with nature, as we live with those we love.

My definition of a garden includes three simple elements that make a garden beautiful and pleasurable. Some of these elements have been mentioned before in relation to other chapters, but since we're getting near the end of the year, I thought it would be nice of me to repeat them more succinctly here. Here are the three elements that I think constitute a garden:

1. *A separate place.* In this hustle-bustle world, full of hustlers and bustlers, the garden is a place to get away from it all, a place to enjoy the beauties of nature and the wonder of life. You don't absolutely need a garden for this purpose if you happen to own a hundred acres of virgin forest or if, like Marlon Brando, you own an island in the South Seas. But most of us are lucky if we have a fifty-by-a-hundred-foot lot to call our own. We must make our own island of beauty, and we can, even though we might live in the Midwest and the nearest ocean is two thousand miles away.

2. *A place to sit.* A seat invites you to come in and sit down. Furniture does for a garden what it does for a room; it makes an empty space livable. A stone, cast-iron, or wooden bench under an arbor is a lovely thing, but a garden seat doesn't have to be a big deal. An antique Chinese Chippendale bench made of teak is gorgeous, but it certainly isn't essential to a

lovely garden or to a happy life. Garden furniture needs only to be service-able and relatively weatherproof. Rusticated chairs made of unfinished logs, Adirondack chairs, metal lawn chairs, or yes, even folding aluminum chaise longues, all make the difference between a space to look at and a place in which to dwell. Even a board placed across a couple of stones will serve as a bench if you're really cheap. It's also nice to have a little table near the seat, so you have a place to put the coffee cup.

A couple of years ago, Walter and I took the idea of furnishing the garden to new heights. We were throwing a Fourth of July bash for about thirty people, and we wanted to make places in the garden for the guests to eat comfortably once they had served themselves from the buffet table on the porch. We put whatever lawn furniture we had in various nooks and crannies in the back and side gardens, but we needed more.

Luckily, the weather promised to be divine, so that morning we decided to move some of the indoor furniture outside. I found a threadbare Orien-tal rug in the garage, and Walter and Sam unrolled it under the square grape arbor in the middle of the side garden. Straining and cursing, we managed to haul out the dining-room table and chairs, one of those heavy, dark wooden Jacobean reproduction ''suites'' from the 1920s.

Walter and Sam complained like heck, but they had to admit that it looked great. The effect of having indoor furniture outdoors was surreal. Inspired, I carried the idea even further. I covered the table with my best damask tablecloth (a yard-sale find) and decorated it with a pair of candela-brum, flowers, and fruit.

We considered attaching the dining-room chandelier to the beams of the arbor to hang over the table, but Walter moodily refused to detach and rewire a light fixture just for a party. He also nixed the idea of hauling out the living-room sofa and chairs. He's such a good sport about most things that I didn't have the heart to argue with him, at least not for more than an hour or so. But I think it would have been marvelous, like a scene out of a Fellini movie. And knowing our friends, it would have been entirely appropriate.

So the point of all this is, furniture makes a garden a comfortable place to live and is also an element of . . .

3. *Structure.* I define structure as anything in the yard that is man-made. All plantings, whether flowers, shrubs, or trees, look better in relation to an object or a structure of some kind. This structure can be

anything—a path, a doorway, a wall or fence, a tool shed or garden house, a pool, a statue or a column, a mailbox, a gazebo or arbor, a birdbath or, of course, a garden bench. A structure immediately draws the eye, just because it is man-made. Man-made objects usually have straight lines, or at least definite forms, unlike the many-patterned colors and curving lines of nature. This contrast between straight, solid forms and complicated patterns is always visually interesting and, as in the case of the dining-room "suite," sometimes downright fascinating.

When you don't know where to put a flower bed, look for an object in the landscape and plan the design so that the garden is between there and the place where you look at it the most, such as the backdoor of your house. For example, a path leading from the kitchen door to a garden bench is the first step to making a garden, even if it is surrounded by weeds. If you go ahead and enclose the area with a fence or a hedge and plant roses, flowers, or even vegetables along that path and around the bench, not only will you have created a beautiful garden, you will have made a new place to live.

If you don't have an object, add one. I once put an eight-foot wooden post with a birdhouse on top on one side of the garden just to add some height to a flower border.

I know that an eight-foot vertical pole with a birdhouse doesn't sound too exciting, but a garden structure doesn't have to be complicated to be effective. Vertical structures add enormous interest.

I read somewhere that flower gardens tend to be three feet tall, because that is the average height of most herbaceous plants. Adding an arch, a pergola, or even something as simple as a pole gives a whole new dimension to a flower border.

Strangely, I didn't figure out all this business about structure from books or from looking at magazines, as you might expect. The whole idea of the need for structure in a garden came to me in a flash of insight one day about five years ago, while I was visiting Ron and Bobbie at their farm in Pennsylvania on a Labor Day weekend.

My friend Richard took Bobbie and me to see a man who gardens on a very rocky hillside. The old dairy where Richard's friend lived was only half a mile from Ron and Bobbie's farm, but they had never met. The garden was a beautiful place. It lay on what had been a heavily rock-strewn slope between the house and the wall of the old cow barn higher up the hill. Instead of allowing himself to be defeated by all those rocks, Richard's friend had used them to make paths and serpentine steps leading up and down that hill, and each level was terraced with three-foot-high stone walls. None of these walls and paths had been made by a single machine; it had all been done by hand. In fact Richard had moved more than his share of rocks over the years, an act of devotion his friend felt he could never repay and didn't.

This garden was just loaded with structure. Richard's friend is a plant collector, and his collections of unusual shrubs, roses, and flowers were all spotlighted by the surrounding stone walls, and they in turn clothed the rocky walls and paths with great profusion. This was some garden.

But the nicest thing about it, the exclamation point to the whole picture, was an old porch post at the corner of one of the paths. The old porch post with its peeling white paint seemed somehow romantic. It reminded me of antique architecture, an old dairy farm equivalent of a doric column standing amid the ruins of the Parthenon. It was located about halfway up the hillside at the convergence of the central paths. Looked at from the house, it was slightly upstage left of the whole picture, so the post acted as a point of reference for everything else. I can't explain why, but this one vertical element made all the lovely and rare things he had planted make more sense.

It was then, suddenly, at that very instant that I realized in a blinding flash of illumination that the beauty of a garden had almost nothing to do with the individual plants—some of this guy's rare plants were gorgeous and some were positively weird—and everything to do with the space in which they were grown. The actual plants are the least important part of making a garden! I had always thought that you can have a beautiful garden only if you can afford to buy the most esoteric plants. This was not true! I now realized that a plant doesn't have to be unusual to be beautiful—familiar plants *are* beautiful, which is why they are so popular—it only has to be in the right place.

The realization hit me like a fist in the eye. It was a leap up onto another level of consciousness. I had been blind, but now I saw. How could I have been such a fool before?

I shouldn't have been so hard on myself. After all, buying plants is the first thing most people do when they start to garden, and sometimes that's the only thing they do. Practically everybody with a little land grows at least a few flowers and shrubs around the foundation of the house. This is loosely known as "landscaping the yard," but it is not a garden, as I would define the term. It is at best a collection of plants. Even my beloved gardening books often let me down in this regard. I can't tell you how many experts I have read that talk only about the plants themselves and never about how to make them all come together to create a real garden.

I began to look at the countryside differently from then on. I saw for the first time that most plantings in and around the lawns of suburban houses are not gardens at all, merely flower beds and shrubberies, more or less successfully realized, but connected to nothing.

Upon re-reading Gertrude Jekyll, I noticed that her fifteen-acre garden was in fact a series of smaller "rooms," broken up by various hedges and connected by paths leading from one environment to another. I saw that this was also true of the other great gardens that I admired, Vita Sackville-West's garden(s) at Sissinghurst and Monet's garden(s) at Giverny. Neither is *a* garden at all, but a series of gardens, laid out like rooms in a rambling house. Sure, Miss Jekyll, M. Monet, and Vita all knew a lot about plants, but they also knew where to put them.

The three elements of privacy, structure, and a place to sit seem to me to be the most important aspects of garden-making. Once you have created a separate place away from the rest of the world, a garden room, you needn't have any anxiety about what to plant. The plantings can be as esoteric or familiar as climate, preference, and pocketbook allow. Making the garden is the hard part. Choosing the plants themselves is the fun part.

Another quality that is even more important than the plants themselves is the way in which they are planted. There are four important things to remember when planting a cottage garden.

1. *Plant generously.* Use large masses of one variety of a plant, the way nature and famous landscape designers do, so your efforts won't look skimpy and pathetic. If, like me, you can't afford to buy more than one of anything, be prepared to divide it into several plants as soon as it grows big enough.

We know that shrubs can be divided, as well. I'm sure that the folks who planted my lilac hedge started out with one white lilac and kept replanting the suckers as they emerged around the mother lilac, until they had established an entire hedge, just like the young couple who took the divisions from mine. I admit, the poor woman's method takes longer, but it just goes to show that time really is money.

2. *Pack it, pack it, pack it.* This is the advice of Vita Sackville-West. Plant spring bulbs around later-blooming perennials and later-blooming vines over earlier-blooming shrubs. A favorite trick of mine is to throw some cleome seeds in a new flower bed after I've planted the young perennials. As we know, perennials are a disappointment the first year, so the annual cleomes will make sure I have some flowers right away. Then, when they reseed themselves the following year, I have the choice of pulling them out to make room for the perennials, or moving them around to fill in gaps.

Pack for continuous bloom. Take my aforementioned eight-foot post with the birdhouse on it, for example. My rusticated post illustrates how a simple structure can be the focal point of a planting scheme, and it also illustrates the benefits of packing. It is located in the side garden in the border behind the Henry lilac. I set it in next to the Harrison's Yellow rose. Around and underneath the vines and perennials in this area are hundreds of self-sown *Chionodoxa*, small, sky blue bulbs that bloom in April. Around and under some daylilies are hidden about twenty-five tulips, all of which bloom ahead of the rose in early May. Around the post I planted vines: *Clematis* x *Jackmanii*, perennial sweet pea (*Lathyrus latifolius*), and blue morning glory (*Ipomoea tricolor* 'Heavenly Blue'). I have trained the rose (really a rambler) onto the post by pruning and tying it. The rose blooms in May and has yellow flowers, the purple clematis comes in June, the pink perennial sweet pea blooms through July and early August, and the blue morning glories go until frost. That post is "packed." I have flowering vines on that old post for the duration of the growing season.

The post and its viny inhabitants perfectly illustrate how a structure, even of the simplest sort, can be a perfect starting point for a flower border. I have several different kinds of perennials planted in the bed near the post, and they all bloom in conjunction with the vines. When the yellow rose flowers in May, dark purple irises bloom in the border. In June and early July, the royal purple clematis is accompanied by pale yellow daylilies, lavender-blue peach-leaved bellflowers (*Campanula persicifolia*), and white feverfew (*Matricaria*). As the clematis goes out, the magenta-pink perennial sweet pea vine is nicely set off by red bee balm, both of which continue flowering throughout the month of July. They are later joined by white garden phlox, which looks terrifically tasteful with sky blue morning glories. In September, there are self-sown white nicotiana blossoms and blue asters. All these plants, which are in large clumps, occupy a border that is only about five feet deep and extends for six feet on either side of the post. So, by packing, there can be flowers in this spot from early spring until late fall, and that is the whole trick to having a wonderful cottage garden.

3. *If it grows well, grow a lot of it.* Why fight nature? The most successful gardens tend to have one or two main flowers for each month of the season, with a supporting cast of less prominent plants around them. Larger gardens might have more. When you find those plants that stand out from the chorus, use them lavishly. "The Magnificent Seven" are the ones that carry my garden through the year in flowery abundance, but if I lived in the Southwest, there would be quite a few changes in that list. For starters, the gardening season is not determined by temperature but by rainfall in that part of the country, so the seasons in the Southwest are not "summer" and "winter," but "wet" and "dry." "Spring" is when the rains come. You can still make a beautiful flower garden in Santa Fe, not with plants from England and New York State, but from places like Greece, Italy, Turkey, the south of France, Mexico, Australia, South Africa, and the beautiful American Southwest itself. The point is, whatever the local growing conditions, you'll save money, time, effort, backaches, and ulcers if you take maximum advantage of your successes and experiment with new varieties as they present themselves. (If you get ulcers from gardening, you're taking it much too seriously, anyway.)

I'm not advocating growing nothing but weeds here, although if the weeds are beautiful enough, I'll never tell.

4. *If you can't move it, use it.* Mature shrubs give substance and dignity to a garden the way no flower bed can, no matter how elaborate. If you've ever planted a baby shrub, hedge, or tree and waited for it to get to be eight feet tall, you know how much such a plant is worth. What a heartbreak it is to see a large plant bulldozed in the name of "re-landscaping." And what a pain to move it without a bulldozer! Try to incorporate mature specimens as part of the landscaping plan, rather than starting from scratch with something else. You *can* make them much more attractive, even if they were planted in seemingly impossible, awkward, or undesirable sites in the first place.

A typical example of a badly located shrub that we are all familiar with is the bush in the middle of the front lawn. Along with foundation plantings, this placement of a lone specimen was a common practice in the first half of this century when a lot a suburban developments were new. Now we, the current owners, are stuck with a large quince, weigela, or forsythia stuck out in the middle of the front lawn like a pimple on the landscape, halfway between the front walk and the driveway. A lot of people would simply rip it out, but not me. I would use that big shrub in one of three ways as the starting point of a design. If the shrub were closer to the front walk, I would make it the back row of a wide perennial and shrub border that flanked the walk and curved toward the house. If it were nearer the driveway, I would make a border flanking the driveway. If it were really dead center and surrounded by a vast expanse of boring lawn, I would plant a tree behind it and make an island bed by planting similar and contrasting shrubs to the right and left of it, with shorter varieties in front.

One of the most frequent comments that I get from nongardening visitors is: "Gee, your garden is lovely, but it's a lot of work, isn't it?" My answer is usually no, but I can see that they don't believe me. Their next response is: "Well, I guess it's not a lot of work if you love it." That's true. Making a garden is not a lot of work if you love it, but then again, nothing is a lot of work if you love it and anything is a lot of work if you don't love it. But the real truth is, it doesn't have to be a lot of work if you know how to do it efficiently. It only takes me about four hours per week to maintain each garden. Okay, that's a lie. The truth is, I have no idea how long it takes because I lose track of the time.

The efficient way to maintain a garden is to do it in sections on a rotating basis. Refer to the "What August Doldrums?" chapter for details on exactly what to do. By the time you get to the last section, the first section will need attention again. This might sound like a vicious cycle, but then again, all maintenance is repetitive, as any good housekeeper will tell you—at length. The difference between housekeeping and gardening is that when you dust, the furniture doesn't grow and the kitchen floor doesn't bloom. Gardening is much more satisfying in that respect.

The metaphor of garden maintenance and housework is not so far-fetched, since cleanliness is the goal in both efforts. As I tidy up the plants and cut out the dead leaves and stems, I'm removing anything that is diseased. The simple act of cutting out dead, fungusy, or virusy stems usually cures or at least controls these problems. If I notice any insect pests, I squish them between my fingers or ignore them. And when I have a really bad infestation of aphids on the roses, for example, I get an empty Windex bottle—the kind that makes a spritz—and fill it with water and a couple of tablespoons of dishwashing detergent, like Joy. I spray it on the aphids; it kills or reduces the population drastically and boy, do my roses shine! I can see my face in them!

Most plants get diseases only when they are under stress. There's a lesson for us all in that. In the floral kingdom, the cause is usually lack of sufficient water, light, or the wrong soil. So the first thing I do when a plant is sick is to consider what it is about the location that is making it miserable. If it is too dry, I give it water. If it is too wet, I move it to a drier spot and hope that it stops raining so much. If the soil is inadequate, I throw some compost around the roots. If there's too much sun and the leaves are burning or wilting, I move it to a shady spot. Lanky stems and sparse flowers mean too much shade. I move it. I move it, move it, move it to a place that it likes, even if it looked beautiful in my mind's eye when I first planted it.

That's all I do. Armed only with an understanding of what makes a particular plant happy, and innocent of pesticides, herbicides, and all that junk, I've managed to grow a great many plants in good health. I have gained this understanding more by observation of the plants themselves than by any esoteric study. Needless to say, I have been wrong once in a while and things have died despite my best efforts, but all in all, my philosophy has worked for me. And that's why I am a happy woman today.

INDEX

Thompson and Morgan, Inc., 95,
    230
Thoreau, Henry David, 139
Tiger lilies, 12, 162
Tobacco, flowering, 95–96
Trees, 20, 168
    fruit, 123
    placement of, 30
    planting, 86–90
    pruning, 57–61, 90
    raised beds under, 18
    shade, 166–67
    weed, 4–5, 25, 57
Trumpet vines, 49
Tuberoses, 151
Tubers, 19–20
Tulips, 7, 12, 16, 17, 66, 123, 155,
    173–74, 184–85, 187, 227, 237
    Rembrandt, 18, 174, 228
    White Triumphator, 18

Van Engelen, Inc., 174–75, 228
Vases, 106–8
Vegetable seeds, 230–31
Veronicas, 19, 169
Viburnum, 3, 150

Views:
    enhancing, 24–26
    obscuring, 23
Vines, 49, 207
    on fences, 46
    shade-tolerant, 150
Violas, 16, 64, 124
Virginia creeper, 150

Walled gardens, 39–41
Water features, 40
Watering, 170
    before digging, 179
    trees, 90
Waugh, Evelyn, 51
Wayside Gardens, 29, 225
Weeding, 79, 169
Weed trees, 4–5, 25, 57
White Flower Farm, 225
Winterthur catalog, 15–16
Wisteria, 21, 46, 115
Witch hazels, 226
Wordsworth, William, 82
Wreaths, 205–6

Yew hedges, 46